Prologue to Democracy

Prologue to Democracy
The Federalists in the South, 1789-1800

Lisle A. Rose

University of Kentucky Press, Lexington, 1968

COPYRIGHT © 1968 BY THE UNIVERSITY OF KENTUCKY PRESS
Printed in the U.S.A. Library of Congress Catalog Card No. 67-29342

for Maribeth

Acknowledgments

This study was begun at Berkeley in the autumn of 1963 as a doctoral dissertation under the direction of Charles Sellers. I am indebted to Professor Sellers and to Professor Paul Goodman of the University of California, Davis, for their many valuable comments and criticisms. Professor George C. Rogers of the University of South Carolina was generous enough to share his detailed knowledge of the South Carolina Federalists with me and also to indicate to me some invaluable manuscript sources which I might otherwise have overlooked. Mr. James Broussard of Duke University was also helpful in pointing out the value of various manuscript collections, as were the staffs of all of the libraries in which I worked. I also feel a profound sense of gratitude to the Frederick Jackson Turner prize committee for their comments.

Lastly, my wife, Maribeth, has contributed so much in the way of time, encouragement, good humor, and incisive editorial criticism to the project that a dedication seems scant recognition. Of course, I am solely responsible for the errors of fact and interpretation which remain.

The Woodrow Wilson Foundation was more than generous in underwriting much of my graduate education. In particular, the Foundation provided a travel and research grant for 1964-1965.

Quotations from the Adams Papers in this volume and in the doctoral dissertation from which it has emerged are from the microfilm edition, by permission of the Massachusetts Historical Society.

Contents

Acknowledgments / vii

Introduction / xi

I. The Founding of a Political Interest, 1789-1793 / 1

II. The Friends of Government, 1789-1794 / 48

III. Crises and Collapse, 1795-1796 / 85

IV. Reconstruction, 1797 / 139

V. At the Flood, 1798 / 167

VI. Defense and Diversion, 1799 / 205

VII. 'The Violent Spirit of Party': The Election of 1800 / 232

VIII. Southern Federalists and the Party System, 1789-1800 / 283

Appendix / 293

A Note on Sources / 304

Index / 309

Introduction

In the past fifty years historians have recognized increasingly that the formation of the first American party system at the close of the eighteenth century represented a major landmark in the expansion of political democracy in the United States.[1] Growing conflict between Federalists and Republicans for control of the national government precipitated intense partisan efforts to gain the active support and enduring loyalty of the electorate. From these early struggles modern party organizations and effective techniques of mass appeal slowly evolved. Such developments stimulated popular interest in government affairs and led to the political awakening of an appreciable portion of the formerly dormant electorate[2] with a corresponding erosion of traditional elitist patterns of political behavior and practice. The nationwide political party thus became the vessel of democracy, the agency

[1] See, for example, Charles A. Beard, *Economic Origins of Jeffersonian Democracy* (New York: The Macmillan Co., 1915), 465–67; Noble E. Cunningham, *The Jeffersonian Republicans: The Formation of Party Organization, 1789–1801* (Chapel Hill: University of North Carolina Press, 1957), vii, 259; William Nisbet Chambers, *Political Parties in a New Nation: The American Experience, 1776–1809* (New York: Oxford University Press, 1963), 4–208 *passim;* Richard P. McCormick, *The Second American Party System* (Chapel Hill: University of North Carolina Press, 1966), 19–31.

[2] J. R. Pole, "The Suffrage in New Jersey, 1790–1807," *New Jersey Historical Society Proceedings,* LXXI (January, 1953), 38–45; "Suffrage and Representation in Massachusetts, A Statistical Note," *William and Mary Quarterly,* Series 3, XIV (October, 1957), 560–92, XV (July, 1958), 412–16; "Election Statistics in Pennsylvania, 1790–1840," *Pennsylvania Magazine of History and Biography,* LXXXII (January, 1958), 217–19; "Representation in Virginia from the Revolution to Reform," *Journal of Southern History,* XXIV (February, 1958), 31–34; "Election Statistics in North Carolina to 1861," *ibid.* (May, 1958), 227–28.

through which the governed finally removed the traditional deferential barriers separating them from their government and their governors.

Until quite recently the Federalists usually have been dealt with rather harshly. Students of this period have regarded them primarily as a negative reference group. Focusing upon the social status, partisan rhetoric, and unsavory activities of some party members near the end of the 1790's, several generations of scholars have dismissed the Federalists as hopeless reactionaries in a great age of liberal political change.[3] Historians have demonstrated that after 1790 in several key states those men who supported the Federalist cause represented the older, entrenched, ruling elites, and that individuals within these classes quite naturally exalted

[3] Sixty years ago John Spencer Bassett put the Federalist achievements and failures into a rigid perspective which subsequent scholarship has not changed materially. "The downfall of Federalism [in 1800] came because the party had outlived its usefulness. Its function of giving strength to the Union in the early days of 'the experiment' had been performed. It was the party of the superior classes, of men who were supposed not to be influenced by passions and who had strong purposes and conservative instincts. It had solved the problems of the effective organization of a new government; but other questions were now at hand concerning internal affairs. Should the people be trusted with a large share of government? The Federalists recoiled at the prejudice and violence of the masses, declaring that incompetence could not be trusted. They sought to restrain the violent; they expressed open contempt; and they developed a party selfishness which they wished others to believe was patriotism. They fell into factions and dreamed mad dreams of expansion till at last they gave the masterly leader of men who opposed them an opportunity to organize a majority of the people against their supremacy. So much did they bring into contempt the idea of government by the superior classes, that no capable politician since 1800 has dared to place his cause on any other ground than the will of the people." *The Federalist System, 1789–1801* (New York: Harper & Brothers, 1906), 295–96. Recently David Hackett Fischer, in an impressive study of Federalism in the Jeffersonian era, has reemphasized the elitist proclivities of the "Federalists of the Old School" in such forceful terms as to leave the inescapable impression that they were incapable of contributing anything significant to the American democratic tradition. *The Revolution of American Conservatism: The Federalist Party in the Era of Jeffersonian Democracy* (New York: Harper & Row, 1965), 1–28, 228–410 *passim.*

Introduction / xiii

the ideal of exclusivist governance and condemned democratic aspirations.⁴ When partisan rhetoric and social status were viewed in conjunction with the reactionary practices of the high Federalist faction in 1799 and 1800, the unpleasant stereotype of the party was complete: Federalists on both the state and the national levels were members of a loose, unstable coalition of self-seeking notables, wholly ignorant of the meaning and uses of modern party practice and ultimately unable, through weakness and incompetence, to retain either their rule or the supremacy of their values. According to this view, the election of 1800 inevitably constituted a revolution in practice and ideals, if not in policy and measures.

In the case of southern Federalists, neglect has been added to stigma. The early—and undeniably correct—impression of contemporaries that Federalism was given a far more hospitable reception in New England than in the South⁵ has doomed the southern wing of that party to suffer a decided

---

⁴ Fischer, *The Revolution of American Conservatism;* Charles S. Sydnor, *American Revolutionaries in the Making: Political Practices in Washington's Virginia* (New York: Collier Books, 1962). Sydnor's book was first published as *Gentlemen Freeholders* (Chapel Hill: University of North Carolina Press, 1952). Paul Goodman, *The Democratic Republicans of Massachusetts: Politics in a Young Republic* (Cambridge: Harvard University Press, 1964).

⁵ Tobias Lear to George Washington, August 5, 1792, Edmund Randolph to Washington, June, 1793, George Washington Papers, Library of Congress, Vols. 255, 261. Subsequent scholars quickly seized upon this impression and concluded that early party divisions were wholly sectional in nature. In their view, the central struggle of the 1790's was between "Federalist" Massachusetts and "Republican" Virginia for control of the Union, and this seemed to preclude the need to examine in detail Federalist strength and activity below the Potomac. James Schouler, *History of the United States of America under the Constitution* (7 vols.; New York: Dodd, Mead & Co., 1880–1899), I, 181; Bassett, *Federalist System*, 161; Beard, *Jeffersonian Democracy*, 126, 151, 229, 242, 373ff., 397–98ff. In recent years scholars have begun to suggest the extent of Federalist strength in the South in the later 1790's, but they have not stated their findings explicitly. See, for example, Stephen G. Kurtz, *The Presidency of John Adams: The Collapse of Federalism, 1795–1800* (New York: A. S. Barnes & Company, Inc., 1961; first published, University of Pennsylvania Press, 1957), 379–83.

eclipse of scholarly attention. Aside from a few thin monographs and one excellent study of a leading South Carolina Federalist, which often goes well beyond its immediate topic, little has been written on the subject.[6]

The following account is meant to suggest that from the perspective of southern Federalism a modest reassessment of the growth of the first American party system during the 1790's along lines already suggested by William Nisbet Chambers is in order.[7] I do not mean to resurrect the southern Federalists as forgotten democrats; they expressed consistent hostility to the notion of broad popular participation in the political decision-making process. Although, as I hope to demonstrate in the following pages, southern Federalists took their elitist and antidemocratic ideals almost wholly from their own experience and never attempted to systematize or rigidly fix them within the framework of a personal social philosophy, they nonetheless shared with northern Federalists an uneasy assumption that, as one of them put it,

---

[6] Ulrich B. Phillips, "The South Carolina Federalists," *American Historical Review*, XIV (1908–1909), 529–43, 731–43; Henry M. Wagstaff, "Federalism in North Carolina," *James Sprunt Historical Studies*, Vol. IX, No. 2 (Chapel Hill: University of North Carolina Publications, 1910), 5–44; Gilbert L. Lycan, "Alexander Hamilton and the North Carolina Federalists," *North Carolina Historical Review*, XXV (July, 1948), 442–65; George C. Rogers, Jr., *William Loughton Smith of Charleston; Evolution of a Federalist, 1758–1812* (Columbia, S.C.: University of South Carolina Press, 1962). One recent and valuable study of a leading North Carolina Federalist, William Barry Grove, and the forces which shaped his political commitment is Leonard L. Richards, "John Adams and the Moderate Federalists; The Cape Fear Valley as a Test Case," *North Carolina Historical Review*, XLIII (Winter, 1966), 14–30. Two monographs dealing with tangential subjects also contain some useful material on the evolution of southern Federalism: Delbert H. Gilpatrick, *Jeffersonian Democracy in North Carolina* (New York: Columbia University Press, 1931); John Harold Wolfe, *Jeffersonian Democracy in South Carolina*, The James Sprunt Studies in History and Political Science, Vol. XXIV, No. 1 (Chapel Hill: University of North Carolina Press, 1940). Marvin R. Zahniser, *Charles Cotesworth Pinckney: Founding Father* (Chapel Hill: University of North Carolina Press, 1967), appeared too late for inclusion in this study.

[7] Chambers, *Political Parties in a New Nation*, 1–169 *passim*, especially, 34–52.

Introduction / xv

"the immediate passions of the people" had to be checked to avoid the imminent disintegration of the social and political fabric.[8]

Recent scholarship, however, suggests that the Federalists of the 1790's in both the northern and the southern states often were no more conservative than their Republican opponents. Norman K. Risjord's study of the southern Republicans during and after 1798, for example, indicates that traditional eighteenth-century elitist values permeated "Jeffersonian democracy" almost from its inception until well into the 1820's. The conflict between Federalism and Jefferson Republicanism, as these "Old Republicans" viewed it, did not involve artistocracy and democracy. Rather, it was a contest between competing aristocratic views of the good society, or proper social organization, and of public policy. Federalist programs were opposed by many Republican leaders in the South, Risjord maintains, because such programs were designed to create a centralized, neomercantilist society and a commercial ruling interest—both of which would eclipse the old values of the decentralized eighteenth-century southern political society, traditionally dominated by the landed-gentleman interest.[9]

On the level of practical party politics, the findings of Noble Cunningham and Stephen G. Kurtz demonstrate that as late as 1796 initiative within the Republican party with respect to the conduct of the presidential campaign still lay with a handful of leaders and party managers in Congress. Party development still was "rudimentary in many respects, especially on the popular level." Except in Pennsylvania, managers of both parties in 1796 apparently concentrated

[8] James Iredell, "Marcus" Papers, January, 1788, in Griffith J. McRee, ed., *Life and Correspondence of James Iredell* (2 vols.; New York: Peter Smith, 1947), I, 186.
[9] Norman K. Risjord, *The Old Republicans: Southern Conservatism in the Age of Jefferson* (New York: Columbia University Press, 1965), 2–11.

the bulk of their energies on winning over the traditional ruling elites in those states where the outcome was doubtful rather than on popular party propaganda campaigns. Not until the eve of the presidential election of 1800 did Republicans begin to construct grassroots party organizations on state and local levels throughout the country to advance their cause.[10]

There is, then, impressive evidence to indicate that at least on state and local levels the growth of democratic practices and institutions in America during the last decade of the eighteenth century was in many ways an incidental byproduct of the ultimate displacement of one set of elitist-minded political interest groups by another newer set successfully seeking "an equal access to power."[11] Thus, to make a more balanced assessment of the origins of the first American party system—and of the measure of political democracy that system helped create—it is as necessary to study the activities and the responses of those whose power was challenged as of those who mounted the challenge.

While the Republicans organized slowly and haltingly in the 1790's and did not begin to build grassroots support much before the end of the decade, many outspoken partisans of the federal administration, despite strong elitist habits and attitudes, were at an early date implicitly pressed to influence public opinion by those they served. They were to act as a "mass of influence" in favor of national policy within their local areas, with the responsibility of curbing, if not suppressing, any massive demonstrations of popular antipathy to the "necessary" measures of government. Thus, these elitist-minded friends of government, in many cases directed by leading members of the national administration, were often the first to reach the grassroots. In so doing they

[10] Cunningham, *The Jeffersonian Republicans*, 89–115, 144–74; Kurtz, *Presidency of John Adams*, 145–208.
[11] Goodman, *The Democratic Republicans of Massachusetts*, 202.

Introduction / xvii

frequently found themselves caught in a paradox. Determined to curb popular political "passions," they encouraged an expansion of popular political participation. The Federalists' activities inevitably produced a gradual political awakening among the people and the erosion of the tradition of elitist rule which they so ardently wished to uphold.

Southern Federalists never unified themselves into a single party[12] and never formed a set of recognizable state parties in the modern sense. In the 1790's they never created general state caucuses, state central steering committees, county and local committees, and all the other machinery of party. Not until the election of 1800 did most Federalists make sustained, intensive efforts to organize and to develop effective techniques of mass appeal. But the friends of government did develop at an early date recognizably partisan interest groups —or "masses of influence"—everywhere in the South. Under the pressure of a steadily rising and attractive, if not always well-organized, opposition the friends of government subsequently expanded the membership of their interest groups in both breadth and depth. Through the activities of their partisan groups southern Federalists helped to establish an atmosphere of definable and respectable political contention and ultimately sought popular support. In this way they, only slightly less than their Republican opponents, nurtured the seed of a slowly ripening democratic temperament in the American South during the 1790's.

[12] For example, prior to Adams' presidency there seems to have been but one instance in the South when it was suggested that supporters of the administration in several states should retain close and consistent contact to coordinate policy. In January, 1795, Henry Lee urged James Iredell, who had remained in close touch with the political affairs of North Carolina, to participate in a regular exchange of "sentiments & information on public matters." But the extant correspondence of both men indicates that Lee's suggestion was never pursued. Interstate contacts between friends of government in the South remained superficial and trivial to the end of Washington's administration. Lee to Iredell, from Richmond, January 21, 1795, in McRee, ed., *Iredell*, II, 435–37.

I. *The Founding of a Political Interest, 1789-1793*

Those who ascended to national power in 1789 had no thought of creating a national party system. A few of them, however, had definite ideas about the value, place, and purpose of certain kinds of partisan interest groups within a republic. The "long shaping of the Federalist formation"[1] may be traced to the musings of Alexander Hamilton nearly a decade before the inception of national government. In 1782 the young New Yorker already was arguing the necessity of surrounding any future central government worthy of the name with rings of loyal factions in the countryside. "The reason of allowing Congress to appoint its own officers of the Customs, Collectors of the taxes and military officers of every rank," he wrote prophetically in *Continentalist VI*:

is to create in the interior of each State, a mass of influence in favor of the Federal Government. The great danger has been shown to be, that it will not have power enough to defend itself, and preserve the Union; not that it will ever become formidable to the general liberty; a mere regard to the interests of the Confederacy will never be a principle sufficiently active to crush the ambition and intrigues of different members. Force cannot effect it. . . . The application of force is always disagreeable, the issue uncertain. It will be wise to obviate the necessity of it, by interesting such a number of individuals in each State, in support of the Federal Government, as will be counterpoised to the ambition of others, and will make it difficult to unite the people in opposition to the first and necessary measures of the Union.[2]

The future Secretary of the Treasury never made a clearer statement than this of the underlying goals of the economic program which he unfolded during 1790 and 1791. In later years, of course, he spoke out against "parties" and "factions" in bitter language. But clearly what he deplored was not their existence or their form but the spirit which created and sustained them. "Much has been said about factions," Hamilton said to the New York ratifying convention in 1788. "As far as my observation has extended, factions in [the Continental] Congress have arisen from attachment to state prejudices. We are attempting by this Constitution to abolish factions and to unite all parties for the general welfare."[3]

Hamilton's eagerness to establish partisan political interests in every region of the country reflected his keen and uneasy awareness of the momentous changes that were sweeping through American political life in the late eighteenth century. Carl Becker's conclusion that the American Revolution represented not only a struggle for home rule but also a conflict over who should rule at home has been rejected implicitly by most modern historians as too extreme a view. It now seems clear that the winning of independence was not accompanied by a major shift in political power from the hands of traditionally dominant elites in each colony and state to the people. There can be no doubt, however, that the generation of the Revolution in America witnessed the breakup of the historically static relationship between governors and governed, and that few men, both conservative and progressive alike, were insensible to the change. Through mob action ultimately beyond the control of the governing classes, through petition and remonstrance, and through

[1] William Nisbet Chambers, *Political Parties in a New Nation; The American Experience, 1776–1809* (New York: Oxford University Press, 1963), 43.
[2] Quoted in John C. Hamilton, ed., *The Works of Alexander Hamilton* (7 vols.; New York: John F. Trow, Printer, 1851), II, 200–201.
[3] Quoted in Richard B. Morris, *Alexander Hamilton and the Founding of the Nation* (New York: The Dial Press, 1957), 140.

popular movements of an often violent nature, such as Shays' Rebellion in Massachusetts and Commodore Gillon's uprising in South Carolina, the great majority of the American people between 1763 and 1789 showed a growing awareness of their right to political participation in the new nation. Often their actions profoundly alarmed those accustomed to the exercise of political power and the orderly conduct of public business.[4] Few American political leaders, after Shays' uprising, for example, could share Jefferson's calm and kindly support of popular rebellion in a republic.[5] Madison

[4] The growth and expression of popular political agitation in America in the quarter-century after the Stamp Act crisis may be traced in Allan Nevins, *The American States During and After the Revolution, 1775–1789* (New York: The Macmillan Company, 1927), 395–403; Samuel Eliot Morison, ed., *The American Revolution, 1764–1788; Sources and Documents* (2d ed.; London: Oxford University Press, 1929), 9–13, 83–96, 146–48, 208–18; Herbert M. Morais, "The Sons of Liberty in New York," in Richard B. Morris, ed., *The Era of the American Revolution* (New York: Columbia University Press, 1939), 269–89; John C. Miller, *Origins of the American Revolution* (Boston: Little, Brown and Company, 1943), 129–30, 142–46, 211–12, 295–311, 320–21, 497–505; Edmund S. and Helen Morgan, *The Stamp Act Crisis* (New York: Collier Books, 1963; first published, University of North Carolina Press, 1959), 157–262 *passim;* Marion Lena Starkey, *A Little Rebellion* (New York: Alfred A. Knopf, 1955); Lawrence Henry Gipson, *The British Empire Before the American Revolution* (12 vols.; New York: Alfred A. Knopf, 1958–1965), XI, 137–38, 142–43, 185, 273, 275–85, 498–575 *passim* and XII, 86–89, 94–95, 148, 157–58, 168–238 *passim*. Richard Maxwell Brown, in *The South Carolina Regulators* (Cambridge: Harvard University Press, 1963), views that movement as, among other things, giving the underrepresented backcountrymen "a means by which to express their growing sense of worth and power, of pride and vigor" (p. 140).

As early as March, 1793, a Boston Federalist reported that there was a "great bluster here about *liberty* and *equality*" and noted with contempt "how far our tradesmen are advanced in this science." Jeremy Belknap to Ebenezer Hazard, March 23, 1793, "The Jeremy Belknap Papers," *Massachusetts Historical Society Collections,* Series 5, III (1877), 326.

[5] "I hold it that a little rebellion now and then is a good thing," Jefferson wrote, "and as necessary in the political world as storms in the physical. Unsuccessful rebellions indeed generally establish the encroachments on the rights of the people which have produced them. An observation of this truth should render honest republican governors so mild in their punishment of rebellions, as not to discourage them too much." Jefferson to Madison, from Paris, January 30, 1787, in Paul Leicester Ford, ed., *The Writings of Thomas Jefferson* (10 vols.; New York: G. P. Putnam's Sons, 1892–1899), IV, 362–63.

viewed the revolt in Massachusetts with horror, as did Henry Lee, who nonetheless noted the mildness of the movement during most of its existence.[6] George Washington best expressed the reaction of the majority of the American ruling gentry to Shays' outburst. In December, 1786, he wrote to an acquaintance in Massachusetts, "I feel, my dear Genl. Knox, infinitely more than I can express to you, for the disorders which have arisen in these States. Good God! who besides a tory could have foreseen, or a Briton predicted them!" Somewhat earlier the general had demanded querulously of another colleague whether "the wise and good" would not bestir themselves and "strive hard" to avert the evil of recurrent civil insurrection.[7]

The often crudely expressed democratic aspirations of a large segment of the American people at this period seemed to be in total conflict with the values of those who considered themselves suited by status, tradition, and temperament to mold the destiny of the young nation. Hamilton's plea for the establishment throughout the country of partisan interests that would rationally defend the central government and its policies represented an intelligent response to a potentially dangerous political impasse. The subsequent implementation of his plan reflects the basic civility of late eighteenth-century politics while demonstrating that the first outlines of a partisan national political system in America were drawn by those who supported national policies, rather than by those who opposed them.

Hamilton's desire to establish loose but effective partisan interests had other momentous consequences for the future

[6] Adrienne Koch, *Jefferson and Madison: The Great Collaboration* (New York: Oxford University Press, 1964; first published, 1950), 45; Henry Lee to Washington, September, October 11, 1786, Washington Papers, Vol. 236.
[7] Washington to Madison, November 5, 1786, to Henry Knox, December 26, 1786, in John C. Fitzpatrick, ed., *The Writings of George Washington* (39 vols.; Washington, D.C.: U.S. Government Printing Office, 1931–1944), XXIX, 52, 122.

political development of the United States. First, it meant that the Republican faction, which eventually came to oppose the policies of the federal government, would itself have to organize on a nationwide basis, and in disciplined fashion, to translate protest into meaningful political action. Second, it meant the end of any threat that a new nation of such political diversity as the United States might fall prey to a locally oriented multiparty system which would eventually lead to a political and administrative paralysis and the stagnation of government. Third, it almost guaranteed the emergence of a two-party system, given the necessity for those charged with the administration of the new government to set a definite, and thus inevitably controversial, public policy.

Yet the outlook was dim for the emergence of such partisan political interests in any of the states south of the Potomac. Between 1787 and 1791 the southern states constituted a particular challenge to the proponents of a central government. Nowhere else in America were fears so pervasively and so deeply expressed—even, on occasion, by supporters of the Constitution—that the creation of a federal union offered unparalleled opportunities for the exercise of personal and sectional tyranny.

Even the writings of Washington and Madison before and after the Philadelphia Convention revealed fears of dominance of the American political and economic system by northern interests and the northern states. The general and his political lieutenant for years had wanted to clear the Potomac River for navigation above Alexandria to bind the vast, politically unstable western territories more closely to the eastern seaboard and to strengthen the political economy of Virginia.[8] Washington's interest in the matter had strong

[8] Washington to Jefferson, from Mount Vernon, March 29, 1784, Washington to George Plater, October 25, 1784, *ibid.*, XXVII, 373–74, 482–84; Washington to Madison, December 28, 1784, Madison to Washington, from Richmond, January 1, 1785, Washington Papers, Vol. 231.

sectional overtones. During the early stages of the Potomac River venture he revealed he was concerned that Virginia not be slighted in the race to carve out an American empire in the West. He confided his fears most clearly in a letter to Jefferson in March, 1784, saying "that not a moment ought to be lost in recommencing this business; for I *know* the Yorkers will delay no time to remove every obstacle in the way of the other communication."[9]

Washington's sense of rivalry with northern interests in opening up the vast western country paled in comparison with Madison's later grim determination to secure the site of the permanent national capital for the Potomac area. The proper location for the national capital had been debated in Congress as early as 1784, but it seems to have been assumed at that time that ultimately it would be somewhere on the Delaware or the Susquehanna rivers or in areas to the north.[10] In the closing days of the first session of Congress in 1789, however, Madison abandoned his lofty nationalism to fight to secure the capital for Virginia. The issue was not resolved that year, nor in the brief interregnum between Congressional sessions; but Madison kept a wary eye on the constant politicking that went on. His correspondence on the residence question prior to 1790 bristled with such words as "threatened," "distrust," and "animosity," and the issue seems to have also deeply disturbed many of his colleagues.[11]

In the Constitutional Convention itself, strong expressions of sectional mistrust were heard occasionally in closed-door debate. Cotesworth Pinckney of South Carolina expressed unhappiness over the sectional imbalance inherent under the

[9] March 29, 1784, Fitzpatrick, ed., *Washington*, XXVII, 375.

[10] R. H. Lee to Washington, December 26, 1784, Washington Papers, Vol. 231.

[11] Madison to Edmund Pendleton, from New York, September 14, 1789, James Madison Papers, Library of Congress, Vol. 12; Richard Bland Lee to anonymous, from New York, September 12, 1789, Richard Bland Lee Papers, Library of Congress.

new system; William R. Davie of North Carolina and Pinckney's colleague, Pierce Butler, deplored the prevalence of abolitionist sentiment in parts of the North, as openly admitted at the time by Gouverneur Morris. Such uneasiness naturally led to the belief that there were, as Charles Pinckney put it, "two great divisions of Northern and Southern Interests" in the new nation.[12]

Certainly the struggle over ratification of the Constitution revealed that the majority of southerners shared many of the fears of consolidated government and sectional tyranny frequently expressed by their political leaders. In only one southern state—Virginia—could the friends of the Constitution claim to have won an open, though narrow, victory in 1788.[13] In South Carolina the seemingly impressive margin by which the Constitution was ratified actually masked widespread Antifederalist sentiment, for the backcountry dele-

[12] Max Farrand, ed., *Records of the Federal Convention of 1787* (3 vols.; New Haven: Yale University Press, 1911), I, 567, 605, II, 221–23, 450–51. In the New York ratifying convention of 1788 Hamilton too spoke of the existence of several conflicting sectional interests within the American Confederacy. "There are," he said, "navigating and non-navigating States. The Northern are properly the navigating States; the Southern appear to possess neither the means nor the spirit of navigation. This difference in situation naturally produces a dissimilarity of interests and views respecting foreign commerce." Morris, *Hamilton*, 139–40.

[13] The majority of citizens and politicians even in Virginia doubtless were Antifederal, indicating that the Federalists' considerable efforts in the ratifying convention probably tipped the scales in their favor. As soon as Madison left the state, Patrick Henry and his allies quickly retrieved the initiative in the legislative session of 1788. The Antifederalists called for a new convention, deprived Madison of a United States senatorship, and almost gerrymandered him out of a House seat as well. The Federalist forces, left in charge of Richard Bland Lee, were young, inexperienced, and powerless to turn Henry aside. Richard Bland Lee to Madison, from Richmond, October 29, November 25, December 12, 1788, R. B. Lee Papers; William Wirt Henry, *Patrick Henry: Life, Correspondence and Speeches* (2 vols.; New York: Charles Scribner's Sons, 1891), I, 423–33; Madison to Edmund Randolph, from Alexandria, March 1, 1789, Miles King to Madison, from Hampton, Virginia, March 3, 1789, Madison Papers, Vol. 11. See also Jackson Turner Main's brief essay in *The Antifederalists, Critics of the Constitution, 1781–1788* (Chapel Hill: University of North Carolina Press, 1961), Appendix B, 285–86.

gates voted overwhelmingly against ratification, and they represented a majority of the free population in the state. Only the grim determination of the older—and staunchly pro-Constitution—society along the coast and in the city of Charleston not to part with its dominant and grossly disproportionate representation in the legislature and in the conventions insured South Carolina's ratification.[14]

So strong was initial mistrust of the Constitution in North Carolina that by a lopsided majority the convention of 1788 determined to defer consideration of ratification for a year. Only the inconveniences of independence finally compelled the state to submit to pressure and join the Union.[15]

Even weak and remote Georgia, which desperately needed any assistance a strong central government might give, was invaded by Antifederalist agitation for a few months. Opposition to the Constitution was led by a Judge Bryon, who kept the state in political turmoil while playing on the uneasiness of at least some leaders over the prospect of joining in union with an abolitionist-minded North.[16]

As the First Congress began its deliberations, sectional animosities still were evident. South Carolina's Senator Ralph Izard did not hide his contempt for Vice President John Adams, and the fiery William Maclay claimed that "Lee and Izard, hot as the burning sands of Carolina hate [Pennsyl-

[14] William A. Schaper, "Sectionalism and Representation in South Carolina," *Annual Report of the American Historical Association for the Year 1900* (2 vols.; Washington, D.C.: U.S. Government Printing Office, 1901), I, 376–80; Charles Gregg Singer, *South Carolina in the Confederation* (Philadelphia, 1941), 165–66.

[15] Albert Ray Newsome, "North Carolina's Ratification of the Federal Constitution," *North Carolina Historical Review*, XVII (October, 1940), 287–301; Archibald O. Maclaine to James Iredell, September 13, 1788, in Griffith J. McRee, ed., *Iredell*, II, 240.

[16] John Hannum to Anthony Wayne, from the Turkshead, Georgia, November 1, 1787, Anthony Wayne Papers, Clements Library, Ann Arbor, Mich.; Lachlan McIntosh to Jonathan Wereat, from Skidoway Island, December 17, 1787, in Lilla M. Hawes, ed., "The Papers of Lachlan McIntosh, 1774–1799," *Georgia Historical Quarterly*, XL (June, 1956), 159.

vania]" as a result of the Quaker memorials calling for the abolition of slavery.¹⁷ However, it was Izard's son-in-law and colleague in the House, William Loughton Smith, who at this time most forcefully enunciated southern fears, not only of the North itself, but also of strong central government in general. As early as August, 1789, he feared for the future of the new Union, seeing the clarification of the presidential power of removability as a monarchist plot whose center was in Massachusetts and whose leader was John Adams. Smith feared that Adams would succeed Washington in the presidency and that that office would be closed forevermore to southerners. The man from Braintree would choose a cabinet of lackeys, Smith continued, and all "the great Officers of govt. will be his dependents." From there "every engine would be set to work," every strategem employed, to secure the perpetual reelection of Adams to the presidency and to subvert the other branches of government—beginning with the Senate—to his will. Eventually the Constitution would be wholly subverted; the republic would become a mockery.¹⁸ Smith's remarks reveal that he feared more than mere sectional dominance; he feared political subversion and subsequent tyranny which seemed to be symbolized in the person of the Vice President. It soon became clear that his fears were shared by many southerners, to the consistent detriment of the emerging administration interests there.

During the first Congressional session, however, it appeared that these fears might dissolve. Many southern representatives were impressed with the atmosphere of sincere compromise and cooperation which soon prevailed, and were

---

¹⁷ Izard apparently coined the popular description of John Adams as "his rotundity" after suffering through Adams' futile campaign to impose titles on leading figures of the government. *Journal of William Maclay* (New York: Albert and Charles Boni, 1927), 19, 29, 118, 217.

¹⁸ Smith to Edward Rutledge, from New York, August 9, 1789, Smith-Rutledge Correspondence, South Carolina Historical Society, Charleston, S.C.

optimistic that such an atmosphere ultimately might dissipate existing sectional prejudices.[19] When Alexander Hamilton submitted his successive plans for the redemption of the national credit, the chartering of a national bank, and the levying of an excise tax, however, sectional animosities were rekindled in all but one of the southern Congressional delegations and in all but one of the southern states.

Virginia led the way. Richmond financiers and Amherst County yeomen, former friends of the Constitution as well as its opponents, men from the northern counties as well as those from south of the James—all joined to oppose Hamilton's funding and assumption schemes. As early as May, 1790, David Stuart warned Richard Bland Lee that the Antifederalist spirit that almost had destroyed Madison's political career had not been so long interred that it could not be revived if a suitable issue were found. Even earlier that year Stuart had written a long, melancholy letter to Washington, the tone of which was captured in a few lines:

A spirit of jealousy which may become dangerous to the Union toward the Eastern states seems to be growing fast among us—It is represented that the Northern phalanx is so firmly united as to bear down all opposition, while Virginia is unsupported even by those whose interests are similar with hers. It is the language of all I have seen or therein mentioned.

Stuart, a closer observer of public opinion than most Virginians at this time, also noted that the recent abolition

[19] See *Annals of Congress: The Debates and Procedures in the Congress of the United States* (Washington, D.C.: Gales & Seaton, 1834), I, 108, 115–18, 202–18, 330, 379, 394–99, 441–43, 743, 803ff.; Richard Bland Lee to Leven Powell, from New York, April 30, 1789, in William E. Dodd, ed., "Correspondence of Leven Powell," *The John P. Branch Historical Papers of Randolph-Macon College* (Richmond: Everett Wadding Co., 1901), I, 221; James Jackson to Anthony Wayne, from New York, May 10, 1789, Wayne Papers; William Loughton Smith to Gabriel Manigault, from New York, June 7, 1789, in Ulrich B. Phillips, ed., "South Carolina Federalist Correspondence," *American Historical Review*, XIV (July, 1909), 776–77.

petitions to Congress from the Pennsylvania Quakers had intensified fear and hatred of the North below the Potomac. At one point "many who wished slaves" had circulated a report at Pittsylvania in southwestern Virginia that Congress was about to enact an emancipation law, and the credulous yeoman slaveholders had sold many of their hands "for the merest trifle."[20]

Stuart was not alone in warning of widespread public bitterness. Edward Carrington informed Madison that he viewed assumption as "iniquitous" unless "each state was considered a creditor for so much of its debts as it had already redeemed." Henry Lee predicted Virginia's ruin as a result of Hamilton's policy, and on two separate occasions during that spring Edmund Randolph suggested there was a universal opposition to the assumption plan.[21]

The almost immediate and ubiquitous presence of northern speculators increased the irritation of the Virginians. Even members of the Richmond financial community, who might have been expected to unite with northern financiers to make a killing, were enraged at the speculators' presence, and with good reason. As one Richmond observer noted, echoing Madison with presumable unintention, Virginia was specie poor;[22] and in the course of frantically buying up all available securities—which were a means of commercial transaction—northern speculators were making her poorer, since cash payments were made to parsimonious war veterans and widows, thus keeping money out of circulation.

[20] Stuart to Lee, from Abingdon, May 23, 1790, R. B. Lee Papers; Stuart to Washington, from Abingdon, March 15, June 2, 1790, Washington Papers, Vol. 246.

[21] Carrington to Madison, from Richmond, March 27, 1790; Lee to Madison, from Lee Hall, March 13, 1790; Randolph to Madison, from Williamsburg, March 10, May 20, 1790, in Madison Papers, Vols. 12, 13.

[22] George Nicholson to Thomas Blount, March 22, 1790, in Alice Barnwell Keith, ed., *The John Gray Blount Papers* (2 vols.; Raleigh: State Department of Archives and History, 1952), II, 31.

The climax of this abrupt and universal opposition to the policies of the federal government was almost predictable. In December, 1790, Patrick Henry emerged from retirement to lead the General Assembly in passing a set of resolutions bitterly condemning funding and assumption.[23]

This was not the end of Virginia's opposition to national policy. The excise, levied in part to pay off the national debt incurred by funding and assumption, aroused great anger in Virginia. In January, 1791, Edward Stephens, writing from Culpeper County, stated that "Congress is much abused here about the Excise plan." Jefferson reported in the following June that Henry Lee had informed him that open resistance to the excise in "the upper country of Virginia" was "possible." As late as September, 1792, Randolph said there was talk of disfranchising the excise officers in the state by legislative decree.[24]

The national bank plan met criticism, too, although it did not command the universal condemnation of the funding and assumption schemes or the excise. Carrington seemed to reflect popular opposition when he hinted that such an institution would menace the existence of private banks and would be a further means of taking already scarce specie out of circulation altogether.[25]

The same general pattern of opposition to Hamilton's system prevailed in North Carolina. Some former friends of the Constitution, it is true, praised Hamilton's boldness and imagination. Archibald Maclaine spoke out unequivocally for assumption upon its passage into law; he told James

---

[23] *State Gazette of North Carolina,* November 26, 1790.
[24] Stephens to Madison, January 21, 1791; Jefferson to Madison, from Philadelphia, June 21, 1791, Madison Papers, Vols. 13, 14; Edward Carrington to Alexander Campbell, January 25, 1792, Campbell-Preston Papers, Library of Congress, Vol. 2; Edmund Randolph to Washington, from Philadelphia, September 10, 1792, Washington Papers, Vol. 256.
[25] To Madison, from Powhatan, February 2, 1791, Madison Papers, Vol. 13.

Iredell that had it not taken place, "we could have been in a tottering condition—the Union must have been endangered as some of the States never could have discharged the load." The printer Abraham Hodge republished some proassumption essays and on one occasion editorially derided Madison's conduct.[26]

However, William R. Davie, who had so recently signed the Constitution, expressed relief upon hearing that the assumption bill had been recommitted. The Halifax lawyer explained that he was "tremblingly alive to every thing that threatens the prosperity of [the federal] Government" and that Hamilton's solutions to the financial crisis "were rather unfitted for its infant resources."[27] When the public credit legislation became law, Davie and Thomas Pleasants, who were convinced—rightly, as historians have recently proved—that the debts of most southern states were in the hands of northerners, proposed that the state undertake its own funding scheme "to avoid the evils of assumption," among other considerations.[28] Nothing came of the plan, but Davie had revealed clearly disapproval of Hamilton's public stewardship. The influential Blount family, who also had supported the Constitution, liked assumption no better. At first, Benjamin Hawkins, then a close friend of the family, seemed excited over the plan and sought to impart his excitement to the brothers. Soon afterward Hugh Williamson urged John

[26] Maclaine to Iredell, from New Inlet, N.C., August 21, 1790, James Iredell Papers, Duke University Library, Durham, N.C.; *State Gazette of North Carolina*, May 8, July 9, 1790.
[27] Davie to Iredell, April 20, 1790, Iredell Papers.
[28] Pleasants to Madison, from Raleigh, July 20, 1790, Madison Papers, Vol. 13; Davie to John Haywood, from Halifax, January 15, 1791, Ernest Haywood Collection, Southern Historical Collection, University of North Carolina, Chapel Hill, N.C. A recent study of the effects of funding and assumption on southern finances is: Whitney K. Bates, "Northern Speculators and Southern State Debts: 1790," *William and Mary Quarterly*, Series 3, XIX (January, 1962), 30–48.

Gray Blount to begin speculating in Continental and North Carolina securities.²⁹

Enthusiasm quickly waned, however. Abishai Thomas, the family's business agent in New York, predicted unhappy results "if any Steps are taken according to the proposed Plan." In North Carolina itself the northern speculators already were ahead of the Blount family and in April were at work at the Hillsboro Court and elsewhere. Apparently, William Blount came away empty-handed and decidedly chagrined.³⁰ By June, Thomas in New York was reporting that the assumption plan as it affected North Carolina "was a wicked thing & the more I think of it, the more I Dislike it."³¹

The following November the General Assembly, led by Governor Alexander Martin, decided that it, too, had no use for Hamilton, Congress, or the Report on the Public Credit. No resolutions were passed as in Virginia, but the state's two United States Senators, who had voted against funding and assumption, were censured publicly by the turbulent and suspicious legislature. "It seems," wrote one disgusted observer in Fayetteville, "they have not regularly corresponded with our Executive; and this alone, as far as I am able to learn, is the cause of the acrimony and malevolence shown them."³² Given the agitated state of public opinion in North Carolina and its recent conversion from Antifederalism, the

²⁹ Benjamin Hawkins to John Gray Blount, February 8, 1790; Hugh Williamson to John Gray Blount, February 24, 1790, in Keith, ed., *John Gray Blount*, II, 12, 21.

³⁰ Abishai Thomas to John Gray Blount, February 8, 1790, *ibid.*, 14; John Haywood to Iredell, from Hillsboro, April 10, 1790, Iredell Papers; William Blount to John Steele, from Greensville, April 18, 1790, in Henry M. Wagstaff, ed., *The Papers of John Steele* (2 vols.; Raleigh: North Carolina Historical Commission Publications, 1924), I, 57.

³¹ Thomas Blount to John Gray Blount, June 1, 1790, in Keith, ed., *John Gray Blount*, II, 60–61.

³² *Virginia Gazette and General Advertiser*, January 12, 19, 1791.

refusal of the two men to correspond with the Assembly during a time when national legislation inimical to many in North Carolina became law seemed sinister to those far from the scene of action.

The excise also agitated North Carolinians. In November, 1791, Davie tried unsuccessfully to get the Treasury Department to accept excise payments in North Carolina paper. Obviously, the tax had a cruel effect on a state that was specie poor yet burdened with a flood of nearly worthless paper currency. In this situation a national bank was seen by some as an added burden, since it would "help to make our bad Paper Money worse."[33]

The excise was the prime factor in unifying opposition to Hamilton in South Carolina's backcountry.[34] Georgians by 1791 and 1792 were unhappy with the federal government's quasi-benevolent policy toward the Creek Indians after the Treaty of New York. In its ramifications this treaty denied to Georgia certain lands west of her borders which the state claimed by prior treaty. A further result of this treaty was the national government's assumption of complete responsibility for the strict regulation of relations between whites and Indians on the Georgia frontier, including those of merchants and traders. To underscore the federal government's determination, three companies of dragoons had been sent by Washington, unsolicited, to the Georgia frontier. Georgians were incensed, and in many ways their estrangement from

[33] Davie to Hamilton, from Halifax, November 17, 1791, William R. Davie Papers, Southern Historical Collection, University of North Carolina, Chapel Hill, N.C.; Hugh Williamson to John Gray Blount, from Philadelphia, December 31, 1790, in Keith, ed., *John Gray Blount*, II, 160. Anti-excise essays appeared in Virginia and North Carolina newspapers as late as 1793. *Virginia Herald and Fredericksburg Advertiser*, August 23, 1792; *Fayetteville Gazette*, October 30, 1792; January 2, 1793.
[34] Hamilton to Cotesworth Pinckney, from Philadelphia, August 3, 1791, Charles Cotesworth Pinckney Papers, South Caroliniana Library, Columbia, S.C.; *Virginia Gazette and General Advertiser*, July 13, 1791.

the national administration threatened to become the most thorough and complete in the South after 1790.[35]

There had been, of course, powerful countervailing forces at work in each southern state that inclined some political leaders to support the creation of a sovereign and effective national government at the Philadelphia Convention and, subsequently, to support the adoption of the Constitution.[36] Georgia, notwithstanding the existence of an Antifederalist faction, had favored the Constitution almost unanimously from the beginning. Her frontier condition and the insatiable desire of her citizens to encroach upon Indian lands west of their settlements had left her exposed to the threat of harassment and even invasion by the Creek nation, whose chiefs often had the support of the Spaniards in East Florida and New Orleans.[37]

[35] Hugh Williamson to John Gray Blount, August 15, 1790, in Keith, ed., *John Gray Blount*, II, 94–95; Personal Memo, July 29, 1791, Thomas Jefferson Papers, Library of Congress, Vol. 58; *Georgia Gazette*, May 20, June 17, December 16, 1790, November 24, 1791. The mixed reactions of a progovernment Savannah merchant to the treaty and his comments on the intense popular opposition it aroused may be seen in Joseph Clay to William Few, from Savannah, November 5, 1790, in "Letters of Joseph Clay, Merchant of Savannah, Georgia, 1776–1793," *Georgia Historical Society Collections*, VIII (1913), 237–40.

[36] At Philadelphia the southern states *en bloc*, along with Pennsylvania, Connecticut, and Massachusetts, formed the most consistent force agitating for a strong and sovereign national government. For example, the southerners voted to establish a supreme national government with three coordinated but distinct branches: to give to that government all powers which the individual states were not competent to exercise, to strike down the New Jersey plan and any attempts to continue the institutions of the Confederation within the new government structure, to create a single executive exercising power for one long term, to strengthen and expand the federal judiciary, and, most surprising of all, to consider seriously the adoption of an assumption of state debts. Southern delegates also pressed for the provision that a bare majority of seven or eight states be sufficient to adopt the Constitution, which explains their vote against the nine-state provision. Farrand, ed., *Records of the Federal Convention*, I, 40, 53–54, 88, 97, 104, 121, 336–45; II, 327ff., 428, 437–38, 460, 477.

[37] Georgia's constant harassment by elements of the Creek nation in the years preceding the formation of the federal government may be traced in contemporary correspondence and newspapers. William Few to John Hous-

The Founding of a Political Interest, 1789-1793

The lowcountry oligarchy in South Carolina had staunchly defended the national government throughout the Confederation era.[38] Moreover, as a result of the efforts of its delegates at the Philadelphia Convention, South Carolina had also come to expect a generous assumption of its state's debts by the new federal government. Indeed, such a large grant of funds was to be given to the state by the national government that it seemed South Carolinians could expect an end to local taxation for several decades.[39] In addition, the establishment of a national government with sole power over the currency and over the making of treaties had promised to resolve South Carolina's tangled financial situation and to help reopen the state's formerly lucrative trade with the British West Indies, which had been barred formally since the Revolution.[40]

Two powerful political factions in North Carolina also had

---

ton, from Augusta, May 16, 1783, "Letters of Members of the Federal Convention," Dreer Collection, Historical Society of Pennsylvania, Philadelphia; Benjamin Fishbourne to Anthony Wayne, October, 1786, Wayne Papers; *Georgia Gazette*, June 11, 1789. Periodic Creek and Cherokee uprisings also threatened the western frontier of both Carolinas during the 1780's. But Georgia settlers, as well as the settlers in the Tennessee country, constantly suffered Indian warfare until 1800 and beyond. South Carolinians appreciated this fact; see Thomas Pinckney to the Governor of Georgia, from Charleston, November 7, 1788, Pinckney Family Papers, Library of Congress, Box 14. Even as the Georgia legislature began debate on the Constitution, Washington told Henry Knox that "in the situation Georgia is, nothing but insanity, or a desire of becoming the Allies of the Spaniards or Savages, can disincline them to a Governmt. which holds out the prospect of relief from its present distresses." January 10, 1786, Fitzpatrick, ed., *Washington*, XXIX, 377.

[38] Jefferson to Madison, from Annapolis, May 8, 1784, quoted in Koch, *Jefferson and Madison*, 11.

[39] Farrand, ed., *Records of the Federal Convention*, II, 327. Forrest McDonald has cogently discussed the importance of the assumption issue in inducing South Carolina to support the Constitution. *We the People: The Economic Origins of the Constitution* (Chicago: University of Chicago Press, 1958), 205–206.

[40] George C. Rogers, Jr., *William Loughton Smith of Charleston; Evolution of a Federalist, 1758–1812* (Columbia, S.C.: University of South Carolina Press, 1962), 135–36.

anticipated immediate benefit from the establishment of a national union. The first was a group of lawyers, headed by Archibald Maclaine, Samuel Johnston, James Iredell, and William R. Davie, who resided in the crude little commercial villages which dotted the eastern and west-central portions of the state. They had been led to expect that their potentially lucrative business as representatives of British and loyalist creditors, thwarted so far by the enactment of state confiscation laws in violation of solemn treaty obligation, would be unshackled by the creation of a national government possessed of sufficient power and authority to coerce the individual states.[41] The second faction, headed by William, Thomas, and John Gray Blount, represented the dominant native merchant and speculative interests in the state. As merchants, these men wanted all restrictions on trade with the British West Indies lifted, a goal beyond the power of the individual states or the Continental Congress. As speculators, the interests of the three brothers in western North Carolina and the Tennessee country had been threatened by a Cherokee uprising in late 1788, which the state government—standing alone—had been unable to handle.[42]

Virginia, of course, had supplied much of the original leadership in the movement for a greatly strengthened national government. Frustrating experiences with the Maryland and Virginia legislatures over the launching of the Potomac River project had led Madison and Washington to conclude that the individual sovereign states, burdened with an excessive indebtedness, an exhaustion of credit, and

[41] Sir N. Dinkenfield to James Iredell, from Sulham, England, August 24, 1787, Iredell Papers; McRee, ed., *Iredell*, II, 37–38n; James Hogg to Iredell, January 19, 1786; Iredell to William Hooper, January 29, 1786, *ibid.*, 132, 134.

[42] Charles Christopher Crittenden, *The Commerce of North Carolina, 1763–1789* (New Haven: Yale University Press, 1936), 168; Hugh Williamson to John Gray and Thomas Blount, from Annapolis, February 16, 1784, in Keith, ed., *John Gray Blount*, I, 150; Samuel Johnston to James Iredell, November 8, 1788, in McRee, ed., *Iredell*, II, 245.

The Founding of a Political Interest, 1789-1793 / 19

frequent political impotence caused by the selfishness of competing local interests within their boundaries, were barriers to large-scale political and economic expansion westward. As a result of their efforts in the Virginia and Maryland legislatures on behalf of the Potomac project, Madison and Washington had acquired an appreciation of the need for a stronger national government which could regulate interstate commerce. As early as 1785, therefore, Madison had used the problems encountered in starting the Potomac project as an excuse to call the first interstate conference to meet at Mount Vernon and deal with commercial regulation and related matters,[43] opening the way for subsequent meetings at Annapolis and Philadelphia which led to the dramatic change in the political structure of the nation.

Whether the loyalty of these influential southern interests could be retained or regained after 1790 ultimately depended upon the actions of key administration officials. From the beginning Washington, and especially Hamilton, sought in a variety of ways to establish interests in the southern states favorable to the leaders and policies of the national administration. In time both men came to rely heavily on members of the Society of the Cincinnati, an organization of veteran officers of the Continental Army, many of whom had served directly under Washington and who knew Hamilton personally. Throughout the early 1790's, Society members from both the northern and southern states were enlisted in the service of the administration; they held positions ranging from the highest cabinet posts[44] down to the more obscure—

[43] Irving Brant, *James Madison, the Nationalist, 1780–1787* (Indianapolis: The Bobbs-Merrill Co., 1948), 375–81.

[44] During Washington's term in office, for example, no less than five cabinet officials—Hamilton, Knox, Randolph, Pickering, and McHenry—held membership in the Society. Edgar Erskine Hume, "Light Horse Harry and his Fellow Members of the Cincinnati," *William and Mary Quarterly*, Series 2, XV (July, 1935), 277. Of these five all but Randolph, who was disgraced in the Fauchet affair, became staunch Federalist partisans.

though modestly remunerative—collectorships in the Treasury Department. Washington relied particularly upon these and other veterans of the Revolution. The President summed up his patronage policy in a letter written in November, 1791:

It is perhaps a fact too well known to make it necessary to mention it here, that numerous applications are made for every office created under this government, and it always happens where an office is desirable either for its respectability or emolument that it is sought for by those who have rendered service to their country in the course of the revolution either in the cabinet or the field, and so far from wanting men of respectable talents to fill places which require them that it is frequently a nice point to determine who among the applicants of this character have the best claims to public notice on account of services rendered.[45]

The services rendered by members of the Cincinnati Society during the years of Federalist ascendancy often exceeded the routine discharge of official duty. Many served as loyal and active government partisans in their home areas. After 1790 they often openly defended controversial administration policies, notably those related to foreign affairs. Near the end of the decade they supplied much of the driving force behind what formal Federalist party organization and activity existed within the South. In large measure it was the members of the Cincinnati Society, responding to the appeals and favors of both Washington and Hamilton, who initially fulfilled Hamilton's desire to build nationwide partisan interests that would defend and protect a national administration and its policies.

During the first two years of his administration Washington had the opportunity to bring many former military and political allies into the government through patronage, and he made a series of brilliant and popular appointments of

[45] Washington to Monsieur Jorré, from Philadelphia, November 15, 1791, in Fitzpatrick, ed., *Washington*, XXXI, 417–18.

southerners to important posts. In 1791 the President made a triumphant tour of the South that he fondly hoped would quell the public discontent with the policies and personnel of the national government. These significant activities represented Washington's major contributions during his term of office to the growth of partisan political interests below the Potomac.

While the final session of the Continental Congress was quietly committing the Confederation to history, Washington was besieged with requests for federal office. Until some weeks after his inauguration as President, though, he turned aside all such applications with anguished tact. After politely deferring his request, Washington told one eager officeseeker: "I cannot but feel myself disagreeably affected by having the subject even obliquely forced upon my mind."[46]

However, Washington's statements reflected careful preparation rather than hesitancy. He saw clearly that at the inception of the new government it was necessary to create an administration and judiciary of unimpeachable talent and unquestionable prestige. He also noted the necessity of binding as many former followers of 1788 as possible to the national government to insure wide acceptance and support. With the great pressures exerted upon him for patronage the implementation of such a program would be difficult. The President did not need to be reminded, as he often was, that in the matter of patronage, "there is a silent looking on from every part of the Union to see what turn that important business shall take. There are schemes and combinations innumerable to support each other, to support favorites and to establish a system of as vile corruption and intrigue as can disgrace a country."[47]

[46] To William Pierce, from Mount Vernon, January 1, 1789, *ibid.*, XXX, 175.
[47] Anonymous to Washington, from New York, n.d., Washington Papers, Vol. 243.

With these realities in mind Washington defined his patronage policy to a friend, the Charleston lawyer Edward Rutledge, several days after the inauguration. Admitting that appointments would be "one of the most difficult and delicate parts of the duty of my Office," he observed that "nothing could be more agreeable to me than to have one Candidate brought forward for every Office of such clear pretensions as to secure him against competition."[48] Unfortunately, this was seldom the case; and in being forced to reward certain men at the expense of frustrating others, the President gave the first clear definition of a national ruling interest.

The federal judiciary became his first concern. Wishing to staff it with "the first characters of the Union,"[49] Washington found many suitable individuals in the South. For the Supreme Court the President chose John Rutledge, one of the leading members of the South Carolina oligarchy, and John Blair of Virginia. District judges would be of central importance in the new government, since they were among its most direct and most important representatives within the individual states. Washington asked Edmund Pendleton to take the district judgeship for Virginia; Thomas Pinckney, a charter member of the Cincinnati Society, for South Carolina; and Nathaniel Pendleton, Edmund's nephew, for Georgia. Although Pinckney and Edmund Pendleton declined their appointments, Pinckney later accepted the prestigious ambassadorship to the Court of St. James. In further significant appointments Washington rewarded John Marshall with the federal attorneyship of the Virginia district; Matthew McAllister, at Nathaniel Pendleton's urging, was given the same post in Georgia. Edward Carrington, who was then prominent in the Virginia chapter of the

---

[48] Washington to Edward Rutledge, May 5, 1789, from New York, in Fitzpatrick, ed., *Washington*, XXX, 309–10.
[49] Washington to Madison, September 25, 1789, *ibid.*, XXX, 414.

Cincinnati Society and later served as national vice president, and Isaac Huger became federal marshals for the districts of Virginia and South Carolina, respectively. James Iredell and William Blount, both high in the leadership of their respective factions, received coveted posts when North Carolina entered the Union. Iredell obtained a Supreme Court seat, while Blount was given the governorship of the territory south of the Ohio, which allowed him to strengthen his already tight control of politics in the Tennessee country. William R. Davie was offered the district judgeship for the north state, but he declined.[50]

Southerners could not complain of lack of power in the Executive Department, either. The secretaryships of War and the Treasury went to northerners, but the portfolios of State and the Attorney Generalship were given to Virginians, Jefferson and Edmund Randolph. In the Treasury Department Nicholas Eveleigh of South Carolina was the comptroller until his death. Finally there was Washington himself, who was in the early 1790's as in 1787-1788 the symbol of national unity above sectional and local considerations. His Virginia background and the flattering deference which he received in the North briefly attenuated those sectional jealousies which existed throughout the South.[51]

Washington's astuteness and tact were not confined to the selection of appointees but pervaded his whole appointive process. He seldom made appointive decisions alone, but constantly consulted southern representatives and senators

[50] Washington to Iredell, February 13, 1790, *ibid.*, XXXI, 10-11; *State Gazette of North Carolina*, June 25, 1789; Matthew McAllister to Washington, August 26, 29, 1789, Nathaniel Pendleton to Washington, August 29, 1789, in Warren Grice, ed., "Georgia Appointments by President Washington," *Georgia Historical Quarterly*, VII (September, 1923), 187-91, Edgar Erskine Hume, *George Washington's Correspondence Concerning the Society of the Cincinnati* (Baltimore: Johns Hopkins Press, 1941), xxv; Hume, "Light Horse Harry," 277.

[51] Henry Lee to Washington, July 11, 1789, Washington Papers, Vol. 243.

in Congress, as well as leading figures in the states. When considering appointments of South Carolinians, the President relied heavily upon the Charlestonians Edward Rutledge, Cotesworth Pinckney—also a leading member of the Cincinnati Society—and, after his early retirement, John Rutledge. Senator Ralph Izard and Representative William Loughton Smith were frequently the agents through whom Washington corresponded with Rutledge and Pinckney, and by early 1793, Jefferson remarked acidly upon the effect of Izard's proximity to the presidential ear. "Izard hated Franklin with unparalleled bitterness," the Secretary noted, "but humbly adores the Presdt because he is in loco regis." The other South Carolina senator, Pierce Butler, successfully withstood the presidential influence and later moved into opposition along with Madison; but in 1790 he was proud that his strong recommendation of James Iredell for the bench had carried much weight in Washington's decision.[52]

In giving patronage favors to Virginians, Washington most frequently consulted Madison and Edmund Randolph. Washington cleared Blair's appointment with Madison before sending it to the Senate, and the President apologized to Randolph for overlooking George Wythe when selecting a Virginia district judge.[53]

North Carolina patronage was administered in cooperation with John Steele in the House and Samuel Johnston in the Senate. Steele, under strong pressure from William Blount, was instrumental in securing Blount's appointment as territorial governor south of the Ohio, while Samuel Johnston

[52] Rogers, *William Loughton Smith*, 180; Ralph Izard to Edward Rutledge, September 26, 1789, in Phillips, ed., "South Carolina Federalist Correspondence," 777; "Notes of Conversation with Other Cabinet Members," February 26, 1793, Jefferson Papers, Vol. 82; Samuel Johnston to James Iredell, from New York, March 8, 1790, Iredell Papers.

[53] Washington to Madison, September 25, 1789, to Edmund Randolph, November 30, 1789, in Fitzpatrick, ed., *Washington*, XXX, 414, 473.

joined Pierce Butler's efforts in Iredell's behalf. Johnston's pleasure at having his recommendations so quickly embraced was exceeded only by his excitement at being asked to sup at the great man's table with "Justice of Sup Ct, Atty Genl, Sec War and a number of others."[54] Unfortunately, whatever future political usefulness Johnston might have had for the Federalist cause was cut short by his retirement in 1793.

In North Carolina the President's patronage policies helped to keep some influential political leaders—notably Steele and Johnston—in the administration camp after 1790.[55] In Virginia such policies helped to lay the foundations for a future factional organization around such men as Marshall and Carrington. In South Carolina these policies aided in the maintenance of an existing organization, coterminous with the lowcountry oligarchy, which was untouched by the anti-Hamiltonian defections elsewhere in the South. In Georgia federal patronage actually stimulated the beginnings of a distinct proadministration consciousness and led to a close association of like-minded individuals who soon were to play influential roles in state politics.

Between 1789 and 1796, five influential political leaders

[54] William Blount to John Steele, April 18, 1790, in Wagstaff, ed., *John Steele*, I, 57; Johnston to Iredell, from New York, February 1, 1790, in McRee, ed., *Iredell*, II, 281; Johnston to Iredell, from New York, March 4, 1790, Iredell Papers.
[55] Along with the Constitutional amendments, national patronage policies had also helped to reconcile many North Carolina plain folk to the new government in the months just before the state's second ratifying convention was to meet. Passing through the state in October, 1789, after a fruitless attempt to negotiate with the Creeks in Georgia, David Humphreys assured Washington that "the appointments in general have met with almost universal approbation. The selection of Characters to fill the great Departments has afforded entire satisfaction particularly in the Judiciary. I heard it repeatedly said in Halifax that the Supreme Court would be the first Court in the world in point of respectability. These things cannot but auger well." October 28, 1789, from Petersburg, Washington Papers, Vol. 244. However, the government's decision the following year to hold all meetings of the district and circuit courts at New Bern angered local interests all over the state. *State Gazette of North Carolina*, August 6, 1790.

and one newspaper, the *Georgia Gazette*, energetically represented the rising partisan spirit of Federalism in the state. Of these five—Nathaniel Pendleton, Lachlan McIntosh, Anthony Wayne, Senator James Gunn, and Matthew McAllister —the first four had been in military service in the Revolution, Pendleton, McIntosh, and Wayne in the Continental Army under Washington. Wayne, Gunn, and McIntosh also were important Georgia members of the Cincinnati Society.[56] Pendleton, McIntosh, and McAllister had been given prestigious federal offices by Washington; McIntosh had won his over a rival for the collectorship of the Port of Savannah with the help of James Gunn, and Pendleton had materially aided McAllister in his quest for office.[57]

As early as 1789, Pendleton, then Chief Justice of the state, joined the editor of the *Georgia Gazette* in a propaganda campaign stressing improvements in the state and the nation resulting from the change in government and the leadership of George Washington.[58] As hostility toward the policies and leaders of the national administration later grew and hardened, friends of the government in Georgia defended it with energy, ability, and loyalty. Unfortunately, they were deficient in simple political wisdom and, above all, in integrity, and this ultimately destroyed their political effectiveness.

Such setbacks still were in the future in 1789–1790, however, and Washington could pride himself in a patronage job well done. But as opposition to the programs of the

[56] Nathaniel Pendleton to Washington, July 23, 1789, in Grice, ed., "Georgia Appointments," 193; Hume, *George Washington's Correspondence Concerning the Society of the Cincinnati*, xxv, 370. In 1784 McIntosh was cleared of a slanderous charge unjustly leveled by then Governor George Walton of Georgia in 1780. Alexander Lawrence, "General Lachlan McIntosh and his Suspension from Continental Command During the Revolution," *Georgia Historical Quarterly*, XXVIII (July, 1954), 101–41; Anthony Wayne to Sharp Delany, April 18, 1790, Wayne Papers.

[57] *Annals of Congress*, I, 60; *Georgia Gazette*, August 27, 1789.

[58] *Georgia Gazette*, February 19, 26, March 12, May 7, 14, December 3, 1789.

federal administration arose, the President did little more, either through patronage or exertion of personal influence, to halt the development of conflict within Congress between the supporters of Hamilton and those of Madison, Giles, and Jefferson. In 1791, however, the President made a final effort to regain southern support. The general had made a successful tour of the northern states during the previous year aimed at bolstering national unity. Soon after his return he determined to make a similar tour of the South. The trip proved to be profitable. Never had the President's power to evoke popular adulation been greater, and as the very symbol of the national government, Washington was able for a time to transfer personal adulation into loyalty to his administration.

Governors, mayors, aldermen, merchants, agricultural societies, and Cincinnati clubs in each town through which the President passed planned elaborate addresses and entertainments.[59] His presence produced a solemn joy among the populace, which a more complex and cynical age scarcely can comprehend and to which only contemporary newspaper accounts do justice. The President's reception at Savannah was typical of the welcomes he received.

On Thursday morning, the President of the United States arrived at Purysburg [on the Savannah River above the city] where he was received by the Committee who had been deputed [sic] by a number of the citizens of Savannah and its vicinity for that purpose. The President with the Committee, his Secretary Major Jackson, Major Butler, Gen [Anthony] Wayne and Mr. Baillie, embarked at Purysburg between ten and eleven o'clock and was [sic] rowed down by nine American Captains who were dressed in blue silk jackets, black satin breeches, white silk stockings and round hats with black ribbons, having the words "LONG LIVE THE PRESIDENT" in letters of gold. Within ten miles

[59] Most of the addresses which Washington received during his tour have been collected in the Washington Papers, Vols. 250–51.

of the city they were met by a number of gentlemen in several boats, and as the President passed by them, a band of music played the celebrated song, "HE COMES, THE HERO COMES" accompanied with several voices. On his approach to the city, the concourse on the bluff, and the crowd which had pressed into the vessels, evinced the general joy which had been inspired by this visit of the most beloved of all men, and the desire of all ranks and conditions of people to be gratified by his presence.[60]

Washington was pleased by the results of his southern trip, and he told David Humphreys soon after his return to Philadelphia that "tranquility reigns among the [southern] people, with that disposition towards the general government which is likely to preserve it."[61]

With the conclusion of his southern tour, however, Washington made no further attempts to influence, either directly or indirectly, opinion or political activity in the states. After 1790 the influence he could create through patronage was reduced, since all he could do was fill existing vacancies. Moreover, Washington turned his attention to maintaining harmony within his cabinet. Although the President steadfastly refused to make a formal commitment to one side or the other in the growing conflict between Hamilton and the Virginia-led opposition, his own early patronage policies, particularly as they benefitted his friends in the Cincinnati Society, ultimately helped to sharpen and define the developing schism as it came to affect local and state politics in the South.

Hamilton had even greater opportunities than the President to establish administration interests in the respective states at the beginning of the national experiment. Congress' successive decisions to delegate responsibility for the formu-

---

[60] From Savannah, May 19, 1791, reprinted in *North Carolina Gazette*, June 4, 1791.

[61] Washington to David Humphreys, July 20, 1791, in Fitzpatrick, ed., *Washington*, XXXI, 318–19.

The Founding of a Political Interest, 1789-1793 / 29

lation of national economic policy to the Secretary of the Treasury gave Hamilton an unparalleled opportunity to shape fiscal policies so that influential economic interests throughout the country were bound to the central government. At the same time he had the potential for a private political machine literally handed to him with his commission. The power to appoint customs officials, tax collectors, and other officers was now in the hands of a man who less than a decade before had urged that such authority be given to the national government for the express purpose of establishing local partisan interests. In fact, there were about six hundred fifty positions to be filled in the Treasury Department in 1793, according to the List of Civil Officers of the United States. These included inspectors, gaugers, weighers, measurers, and boatmen—all employed in the customs service—as well as lighthouse keepers, supervisors, inspectors of the revenue, and a plethora of clerks on several levels.[62] Obviously, Hamilton could neither ascertain nor consistently guarantee the partisan reliability and energy of the vast majority of the bureaucracy under his direction. Therefore, he chose wisely to place men of partisan reliability in certain key Treasury posts on the state and local levels in order to employ their intelligence and influence most effectively. To find and reward such men of partisan temperament in the South, Hamilton seems often to have turned—as had Washington—to the Society of the Cincinnati. Before seeking out active grassroots support in the South, however, Hamilton obtained a significant measure of southern aid within Congress.

Although the Treasury Secretary alienated most influential interests in the South by his fiscal policies, individuals in one

[62] Walter Lowrie and Walter S. Franklin, eds., *American State Papers: Miscellaneous Affairs* (2 vols.; Washington, D.C.: Gales and Seaton, 1834), I, 57–58.

critically important area stood to gain as much from funding, assumption, and the Bank as the financial and speculative groups of New England, New York, and Philadelphia. Lowcountry South Carolina planters and the merchants and financiers in Charleston persistently had pressed for assumption since 1787, and the ratification of the Constitution renewed their determination to see an assumption realized.[63] Consequently, in Congress and at home from 1790 onward, residents of lowcountry South Carolina consistently supported Hamilton's policy and thus saved the administration's economic policies from condemnation as purely sectional in nature.

South Carolina congressmen gave strong support to assumption. According to Madison, "Mass. & S. Carolina with their allies of Connecticut & New York" were the strongest pro-Hamilton delegates at New York as the second session of Congress opened.[64] Moreover, the lowcountrymen carried the support of the backcountry residents with them in this session, except for Sumter in the House. Smith, Aedanus Burke, and Izard campaigned energetically on behalf of assumption. In addition, Smith nominated himself as both unofficial whip of the state's House delegation and corresponding secretary to the legal and financial groups back home.[65]

There were some flaws in South Carolina's supposedly solid backing of Hamilton. Ralph Izard remarked that he

[63] In April of 1789 Senator Ralph Izard expressed the hope that "we shall not be wasting time with idle discussions about amendments to the Constitution, but that we shall go to work immediately about finances, and endeavor to extricate ourselves from our present embarrassed and disgraceful situation." Izard to Thomas Jefferson, April 3, 1789, in Worthington C. Ford, ed., "Letters of Ralph Izard," *South Carolina Historical and Genealogical Magazine*, II (July, 1901), 204.

[64] Madison to anonymous, April 13, 1790, Madison Papers, Vol. 13.

[65] William Loughton Smith to Edward Rutledge, February 28, May 24, June 14, 18, July 25, 30, 1790, Smith-Rutledge Correspondence; *Annals of Congress*, I, 1175, 1292–95.

The Founding of a Political Interest, 1789-1793 / 31

cared not one whit what compromise had to be made in the funding scheme, so long as assumption was assured; and, in fact, the South Carolina delegation was no happier with the funding portion of Hamilton's plan than were the congressmen from Virginia, North Carolina, and Georgia. Also, it is doubtful whether Smith at this early date had overcome wholly his initial impression of Hamilton as a boastful, disingenuous professional hero, unwilling to give the southern militia due credit for helping win the late war.[66] In the following months, however, such equivocation rapidly disappeared, and Smith became part of an increasingly well-defined pro-Hamilton faction.

So strong was the support for assumption in South Carolina itself that in February, 1790, the state legislature publicly supported the plan, an act which quickly was translated into heavy pressure on the few waverers in the state's delegation at Philadelphia.[67] As the prospect for an assumption dimmed in the spring, members of Charleston's legal and financial communities joined the legislature in pressing their congressmen on the matter, while privately expressing alarm over the fate of the Union if the states were not relieved of their debts.[68]

When the funding and assumption bills finally became law, members of the South Carolina lowcountry oligarchy felt considerable relief. Representative Smith, in obvious reference to the funding as well as the assumption bill, congratulated Gabriel Manigault, a Charleston financier, on the

[66] Smith to Cotesworth Pinckey, from New York, July 14, 1790, Pinckney Family Papers, Box 2; Smith to Edward Rutledge, December, 1789, June 14, 1790, Smith-Rutledge Correspondence.
[67] *State Gazette of North Carolina*, April 10, 1790; Smith to Rutledge, February 28, 1790, Smith-Rutledge Correspondence.
[68] Cotesworth to Harriott Pinckney, from Charleston, April 7, 1790, Pinckney Family Papers, Box 2; Smith to Gabriel Manigault, from New York, March 26, 1790, in Phillips, ed., "South Carolina Federalist Correspondence," 778.

passage of "a measure not only beneficial to the U.S. and to So. Car. particularly, but to yourself personally, a circumstance which adds much to the satisfaction I have felt." Governor Charles Pinckney informed the President in March, 1791, that assumption and the Creek Treaty of 1790, "are both measures which very highly meet the approbation, & would I am sure if necessary very chearfully [sic] receive the support of this State upon any occasion." Pinckney had expressed publicly his satisfaction several months before in his annual address to the South Carolina legislature. His elder cousin, Thomas, seems to have said little on the subject, but the fact that at the time of his appointment as Ambassador to the Court of St. James he held certificates of funded debt amounting to $6,384.57 is sufficient testimony of Thomas Pinckney's interest in and loyalty to the plan.[69]

Hamilton's Report on the Public Credit created a finely balanced coalition in Congress which became the nucleus of a well-defined Federalist interest in that body by the close of Washington's first term. Between January, 1791, and March, 1793, twelve significant votes were taken in Congress —mostly in the House—relating to the person and policies of the Secretary of the Treasury.[70] These votes have previ-

[69] Smith to Manigault, March 26, 1790, in Phillips, ed., "South Carolina Federalist Correspondence," 778–79; Charles Pinckney to Washington, from Charleston, March 29, 1791, Washington Papers, Vol. 249; John Kean to Cotesworth Pinckney, from Philadelphia, August 11, 1792, Pinckney Family Papers, Box 2; *Virginia Gazette and General Advertiser*, March 2, 1791. South Carolinians expected to benefit once more from Hamilton's 1792 plan for a further assumption of state debts. Robert Barnwell to John Rutledge, from Philadelphia, March 21, 1792, Robert Barnwell Papers, South Caroliniana Library, Columbia, S. C.

[70] These included divisions over the Excise Act, the National Bank Bill in both House and Senate, three attempts by the opposition in April and May, 1792, to destroy all or crucial portions of Hamilton's plan for further assumption of state debts (an assumption most favorable to Massachusetts, Pennsylvania, and South Carolina, *Annals of Congress*, II, 595), an attempt the following November to relieve Hamilton of the responsibility for initiating economic policy (transferring such responsibility to a House committee), and, finally, a series of divisions over several of Giles' resolutions of March,

The Founding of a Political Interest, 1789-1793

ously been summarized and categorized by Joseph Charles. Charles' primary object was to show that any attempt to pinpoint the exact time when significant and rigid party divisions came into being in Congress is "useless."[71] However, the increasing attacks upon Hamilton by well-defined groups in the House in 1792 and 1793 and the staunch defense of his policies by certain other equally well-defined groups cannot be overlooked. It is clear that even before the Giles Resolutions, Hamilton on one side and Madison on the other had captured the allegiance of most congressmen, and this was important to the subsequent fate of the Federalist interest in the South.

In general, the emerging Federalist nucleus in Congress between 1790 and 1793 centered about the New England delegations, except for Vermont (although Rhode Island and New Hampshire opposed funding and assumption, they were solidly in support of Hamilton after 1791), the representatives of the Hamilton wing in New York, and lowcountry South Carolina. These delegations either voted consistently for Hamilton's entire program or refused to oppose it publicly by abstaining from commitment on certain issues. Abstention was a favorite tactic of the South Carolinians, for instance, when the excise and bank proposals came to a vote, even though William Loughton Smith was in the majority supporting Hamilton. But the South Carolina group was explicitly and consistently pro-Hamilton on matters relating to plans for assumption and on matters in which the Treasury Secretary's personal abilities and integrity were questioned publicly.

In 1791 and after, Hamilton gained some further support from the middle and southern states when the great majority

---

1793. The votes are to be found in *Annals of Congress*, I, 1788, 1813, 1932, 2012; II, 533-35, 597, 725, 955-60.

[71] Joseph Charles, *The Origins of the American Party System* (Williamsburg, Va.: The Institute of Early American History and Culture, 1956), 93-94.

of the Pennsylvania delegation, as well as John Steele of North Carolina and Francis Willis of Georgia, backed him.[72] This support was vitally necessary on two occasions—the first in late 1792, the second the following March. In November, 1792, the Republican interest in the House openly took the offensive against Hamilton for the first time when it was proposed that questions pertaining to the redemption of the public debt be referred in the future to a special House committee rather than to the Secretary of the Treasury. This proposal was defeated thirty-two to twenty-five. Those who publicly stood with Hamilton included the entire New England delegation except Vermont, the three pro-Hamilton representatives from New York, five of the seven representatives from Pennsylvania, Steele of North Carolina, the three lowcountry South Carolina delegates, plus scattered supporters in the New Jersey and Maryland delegations. Jackson and later Baldwin of Georgia, the backcountry South Carolinians, a majority of the North Carolina contingent, all of the Virginia representatives, the three members of the Clinton-Van Rensselaer faction in New York, the Vermont, and Kentucky representatives, and most of the Maryland delegation voted in favor of a House committee. The following March, during the vote on the Giles Resolutions, Hamilton still held the support given him the previous November and added to it from among the southern delegations the partial support of Grove of North Carolina, Samuel Griffin

[72] However, Steele's loyalty to Hamilton was tinged with equivocation at this time. He wrote to a fellow North Carolinian in December, 1791, that "our evil list" of expenditures "grows on us enormously." He complained that "few in this house have seized the opty [opportunity] to apply the shears to the estimate of the Secty of the Treasury." Noting that Hamilton's estimate of expense had risen steadily and was estimated at over one million dollars for fiscal 1792, Steele concluded: "This is a thing that would not Encrease the friends to the Government in North Carolina, if publicly known, and indeed it is not a little regretted among some good Federalists here." John Steele to John Haywood, from Philadelphia, December 5, 1791, Haywood Collection.

and Richard Bland Lee of Virginia, and Francis Willis of Georgia.[73]

Despite the personal success of the President's patronage system and his southern tour, it was evident from the patterns of support for Hamilton's policies in Congress that by 1792 the administration's hold over the loyalties of most leading political interests in the South was weak. This was especially true of Virginia and North Carolina. The results of the vice presidential campaign in December gave administration leaders further cause for unease. Not only was Adams soundly repudiated in all the southern states except South Carolina—a result which may have given Hamilton either joy or sorrow, since the chief beneficiary of this reaction was his old New York enemy, George Clinton—but the names of the Vice President and Treasury Secretary were implicitly linked by a bitter southern press as coagitators for government by aristocracy and even monarchy.[74] Despite

[73] In March, 1793, John Beckley, Clerk of the House, communicated to Jefferson a list of "paper men" in Congress, i.e., hard-core supporters of Hamilton who had either directly benefitted from funding and assumption or who were directly tied to the Bank of the United States through seats on the central or divisional boards of directors. "Private Remarks," March 2, 1793, Jefferson Papers, Vol. 82. Of twenty-eight men on Beckley's list twelve were from Massachusetts and Connecticut alone; one was from New Hampshire, and three were from New York. A thin but impressively wide distribution came from the states south of New York. Two were from New Jersey, four from Pennsylvania, two from Maryland, two from North Carolina—Williamson in the House and Johnston in the Senate, both of whom retired from public life soon thereafter—and Smith and Izard from South Carolina. Hamilton's success in securing support of more than one-third of the House stimulated a Republican reaction. Beginning in November, 1791, the Republicans successfully urged a broadening of the membership of the House by decreasing the ratio of representatives to citizens. Jefferson to Thomas Mann Randolph, March 16, 1792, *ibid.*, Vol. 72. As a consequence, the number of representatives had increased from 65 to 104 when the Third Congress convened in November, 1793. Curiously, the Hamiltonians apparently did not perceive the danger to their influence in an expansion of House membership, because the issue was never debated along party lines. *Annals of Congress*, II, 191, 418.

[74] *Virginia Gazette and General Advertiser*, February 15ff., April 11, November 28, December 5, 1792; *Virginia Herald and Fredericksburg Advertiser*, February 28, 1793.

these setbacks to the popularity of his administration, Washington refused to do more to strengthen government influence in the region. Beginning as early as 1791, however, Hamilton began to employ his own resources—Treasury agents and the first Bank of the United States—in an effort to discover untapped sources of support for the government.

The encouragement of manufactures seemed to offer promise for the attachment of a sizable segment of the ambitious commonalty in and out of the South to the administration. At the close of the eighteenth century the term "manufacturer" connoted not the small New England factory owner of three decades hence, but rather the "mechanic" and artisan in the towns and cities of the country who competed against imported products. Congress' demand for a report on the current state and future prospects of manufacturing in the United States offered Hamilton the chance to gauge the extent to which this rising interest might be of political value to the government. Undoubtedly, all of the correspondence relating to this topic does not survive, but if the letters from his Treasury agents and manufacturing societies in Connecticut, New Jersey, Pennsylvania, Virginia, and South Carolina are any indication of the whole, Hamilton was exceptionally thorough in his attempts to inform ambitious entrepreneurs throughout the country that the federal government in general and the Secretary of the Treasury in particular were solicitous of their welfare.[75]

In the South, however, the response to Hamilton's efforts was discouraging. Daniel Stevens, the supervisor of the excise at Charleston, sent a circular letter to "the most lead-

[75] Brunswick Society for the Encouragement of Manufactures to Hamilton, August 9, 1791; Elisha Colt to Hamilton, August 20, 1791; Sherman Swift to John Chester, August 22, 1791; Benjamin Huntington to Chester, August 24, 1791; Constant Southworth to William Williams, September 1, 1791; Silas Condict to Aaron Dunham, August 25, 1791, in Alexander Hamilton Papers, Library of Congress, Vol. 12.

ing Characters throughout the State as per the Secretary's request" attempting to obtain as much information as possible on the state of manufactures in South Carolina, but received no reply. Stevens found that most of the state's manufactured products were swamped by a flood of cheaper importations from the North and from abroad, and local artisans were disadvantaged by "the long and general Credit given [local merchants] by the Importers." Unless import duties were significantly raised, the South Carolina mechanics and their trade would continue to languish.[76]

The outlook in Virginia was even worse. After collecting data from all over the state, Edward Carrington, the recently appointed Federal Supervisor of Revenue, wrote that the economy of Virginia was devoted so overwhelmingly to agriculture of either a subsistence or commercial nature that manufacturing could be conducted only on a domestic level— either by slaves or free artisans—and that economic self-sufficiency was therefore the logical goal of all.[77]

Undaunted that little influential support for his program could be mustered from among the southern common folk, Hamilton turned again to the financial interests of the region in his persistent attempts to build support. The chartering of the Bank of the United States offered him another opportunity to approach the southern moneyed interests. Through the financial patronage bestowed by his national bank, Hamilton insured further the perpetuation of a Federalist interest at Charleston while creating such a faction in the previously unfriendly city of Richmond.

Hamilton's immediate entree to the Charleston financial circles and to the entire lowcountry faction was through William Loughton Smith, even though Hamilton knew John

[76] Daniel Stevens to Hamilton, from Charleston, September 3, October, 1791, *ibid.*
[77] Carrington to Hamilton, from Richmond, October 4, 1791, *ibid.*

Rutledge, Cotesworth Pinckney, and other members of the South Carolina delegation at the Constitutional Convention. By 1792, Smith had become Hamilton's trusted political lieutenant in the House and his defender in the public press. In a little work entitled "The POLITICKS and VIEWS of a certain PARTY DISPLAYED," Smith fired the first shots in a pamphlet war between Federalists and Republicans that raged incessantly for the next decade. Smith first accused Madison of begetting the residence deal with Pennsylvania "in darkness . . . its Nurses were afraid of its being exposed to the light," and then of abandoning the Pennsylvania alliance in the fight over the national bank question, since the establishment of such an institution at Philadelphia might well mean the capital would remain there after 1800. Smith then turned on Jefferson, accusing the Secretary of State of opposing certain government measures because of petty fears that they would increase the power and prestige of other members of the cabinet, as well as other sections of the country, at his and his state's expense.[78]

Smith's outspoken loyalty to Hamilton guaranteed him a seat on the board of directors of the central bank. Of the twenty-five-member board, in the early 1790's only three came from the South; Smith, Samuel Johnston of North Carolina—who despite his retirement from public life in 1793 maintained sizable shareholdings in the enterprise as late as 1796—and James McClurg, a Richmond doctor.[79] Of the several branch offices of the Bank of the United States established prior to 1795, only one, at Charleston, was

[78] William Loughton Smith, "The POLITICKS and VIEWS of a certain PARTY DISPLAYED" (Philadelphia, 1792); a copy of this pamphlet may be found in the Henry E. Huntington Library, San Marino, Calif.

[79] *Virginia Herald and Fredericksburg Advertiser*, January 24, 1793; Samuel Johnston to Joseph Anthony, November 6, 1796, Preston Davie Collection, Southern Historical Collection, University of North Carolina, Chapel Hill, N.C.

The Founding of a Political Interest, 1789-1793 / 39

in the South.⁸⁰ In early 1792 the first elections for the office of deposit and discount for this branch were made by the Bank's national directors. The list of those chosen by the central board to administer the Charleston office read like a who's who of South Carolina's ruling gentry. Included were Edward Rutledge, Daniel DeSaussure, and Henry Laurens. Smith himself was a partner in the Charleston banking house of Smith, DeSaussure, and Darrell. And, as his biographer states, "When the national bank was established by Hamilton, the Charleston branch was firmly in the hands of this house. . . . Since William Smith was the only South Carolinian among the first directors of the parent bank in Philadelphia, he was obviously the channel through which bank patronage flowed."⁸¹

The structuring of a pro-Hamilton faction in Virginia proceeded along similar lines. Initially, Hamilton could count only upon his agents for information and support in this politically alien territory. His chief contact in the state prior to 1792 was William Heth, the Collector of Revenue for Bermuda Hundred. Heth was a man of acute perception and was an indefatigable researcher who sent Hamilton long, brilliant analyses of the economic structure of the Old Dominion.⁸² He and his two brothers had also been con-

---

⁸⁰ Virginia financial interests were eager from the first, however, to obtain a branch office in the state. Businessmen from Alexandria, Norfolk, and Richmond all petitioned for such a favor as soon as the Bank of the United States came into existence. "The Bank of the United States," *Virginia Magazine of History and Biography*, VIII (January, 1901), 288–95. Richmond eventually triumphed, but the branch office was not established until 1795.

⁸¹ *Georgia Gazette*, February 23, 1792; Rogers, *William Loughton Smith*, 189.

⁸² See particularly Heth to Hamilton, June 28, 1792, Hamilton Papers, Vol. 16. Hamilton in the early 1790's also received at least one exhaustive and reliable report on political conditions in Virginia and North Carolina from Daniel Huger, a staunch supporter in Georgetown, South Carolina. Huger to Hamilton, from South Carolina, June 25, 1792, *ibid.* Huger later entered Congress as a firm Federalist.

nected with the Cincinnati Society from the beginning, and in 1784 he had been treasurer of the Virginia branch of the Society.[83] As a potential political leader, however, Heth left something to be desired, because he was easily impressed by proximity to political power and the opportunity to play a minor role in its exercise. Hamilton was readily able to gain his allegiance by the most perfunctory exercise of cordiality and flattery.[84] If power shifted to another party or faction, however, such an individual might well shift with it. Moreover, Heth was not closely acquainted at the time with the commercial, financial, and speculative interests of the state.[85] As in South Carolina, someone was needed as an agent for admission into this presumably hostile group, and Edward Carrington proved to be the man.

Carrington had been tightly bound to Madison, Jefferson, and Monroe in the late 1780's, and in 1789 Madison had helped to obtain for Carrington the post of United States Marshal.[86] The first sign of a break between the two came with Madison's proposal for a discrimination in the funding plan. For if Carrington and others in Virginia roundly condemned assumption, they also claimed to see in a discrimination scheme a threat to public credit and a prejudice against the speculative interests centered in the towns.[87] Madison

[83] Hume, *George Washington's Correspondence Concerning the Society of the Cincinnati*, 228, 422.

[84] This is apparent from a reading of Heth's own entries. See the Diary of William Heth, July 19, 1792–July 3, 1793, Journals and Diaries Division, Manuscripts Department, Library of Congress.

[85] La Rochefoucauld-Liancourt noted in 1795 that these interests were neither large in number nor "opulent." Le Duc de la Rochefoucauld-Liancourt, *Travels Through the United States of North America, etc., in the Years 1795, 1796, and 1797* (2 vols.; London: T. Davison, Lombard Street, 1799), II, 32–33.

[86] Jefferson to Monroe, from Paris, August 11, 1786, in Julian P. Boyd, ed., *The Papers of Thomas Jefferson* (14 vols.; Princeton, New Jersey: Princeton University Press, 1950–1958), X, 225; Carrington to Madison, from Powhatan, April 14, 1789, from Richmond, September 9, December 20, 1789, Madison Papers, Vols. 11, 12.

[87] A discrimination "measure of the sort must necessary [sic] injure the

The Founding of a Political Interest, 1789-1793 / 41

quickly exacerbated this division by his contemptuous dismissal of such complaints. "The language of Richmond on the proposed discrimination does not surprize [sic] me," he told Randolph soon after hearing from Carrington. "It is the natural language of the towns and decides nothing."[88] Thus, the way was at least partially opened for a union between Hamilton and the few financial interests in Virginia, of which Carrington was a member. Hamilton's opportunity to perform a service for Carrington was not long in emerging. Less than a month after his criticism of the discrimination plan, Carrington complained to Madison that he was receiving but a sheriff's salary to perform a United States Marshal's job.[89] Madison's reply, if there was one, is unrecorded, but within the year Carrington had turned to Hamilton for help in securing a better position. In April, 1791, he wrote the Treasury Secretary a warm letter of thanks for setting his mind at ease about accepting the post of Supervisor of Revenue in the state while still holding down the marshal's job. That same day Washington officially appointed Carrington to the Treasury position, and thereafter the Virginian proved to be a most valuable administration worker.[90]

Carrington was immediately useful as an agent between Hamilton and the Richmond financial community. Not only was Carrington a part of this community, but his wife was John Marshall's sister-in-law; and Marshall was at the head of a Richmond faction—including Charles and Henry Lee

---

public credit which with me is the most important consideration of all." Carrington to Madison, from Richmond, March 2, 1790, Madison Papers, Vol. 12. See also anonymous to Madison, March 6, 1790; Henry Lee to Madison, March 13, 1790, *ibid*.

[88] Madison to Randolph, March 21, 1790, *ibid*.
[89] Carrington to Madison, from Richmond, April 1, 1790, *ibid*., Vol. 13.
[90] Carrington to Hamilton, April 4, 1791, Hamilton Papers, Vol. 11; Washington to Carrington, from Mount Vernon, April 4, 1791, in Fitzpatrick, ed., *Washington*, XXXI, 274.

and Wilson Cary Nicholas—which was deeply interested in obtaining funds to purchase a part of the huge Fairfax Tract for speculative purposes. The members of this faction were popular and politically influential. Henry Lee, who was a leading figure in the Cincinnati Society and who soon proved to be a staunch administration partisan, was elected governor by the General Assembly for three consecutive years in 1791, 1792, and 1793.[91] Had he so chosen, Madison might well have attracted the allegiance of at least some members of this group, but he turned them down in late 1791 by refusing to intercede with the British Minister George Hammond on the question of a possible prior claim to the Fairfax Tract by Baron Steuben.[92] The situation was ideal for Hamilton. James McClurg of Richmond was given a seat on the central board of the National Bank in December, 1792. In February, 1793, a bill passed the Virginia legislature providing for the charter of a bank in Richmond with a capital stock not to exceed $400,000. James McClurg was also a director and supervisor of this bank, along with John Marshall, William Foushee and John Harvie, two other well-

[91] Title Page, Vol. 6, John Marshall Papers, Library of Congress; "Land Papers, 1794, Survey and Letters," Wilson Cary Nicholas Papers, Drawer 277, University of Virginia Library, Charlottesville, Va.; Hardin Burnley to Madison, from Richmond, December 30, 1791, Madison Papers, Vol. 14; John Marshall to Charles Lee, from Richmond, April 20, 1797, The Adams Papers (Microfilm), Library of Congress, Reel 384; *Virginia Gazette and General Advertiser,* November 20, 1793. As late as the autumn of 1792, Henry Lee had counted himself a Madisonian. The previous February he had been instrumental in inducing Valentine Davis to publish the anti-Hamilton Cassius essays in the *Virginia Gazette and General Advertiser,* and in September he urged Madison to help defeat the plan to establish a branch office of the Bank of the United States in Virginia. Henry Lee to James Madison, from Richmond, February 6, September 10, 1792, Madison Papers, Vol. 15; *Virginia Gazette and General Advertiser,* February 8, 1792ff. Popular reaction against his beloved Washington's Neutrality Proclamation as well as government aid for his private speculative ventures seem to have been sufficient to cause Lee's shift to Federalism in 1793.

[92] Madison to Henry Lee, from Philadelphia, January 1, 1792, Madison Papers, Vol. 14.

known men who generally supported the national administration.[93] Banking obviously was booming in Richmond, even though Hamilton's Treasury agent William Heth in his long letter on the Virginia economy had doubted that this could ever be so. Hamilton was employing the same tactics in Richmond that he had used in Charleston. A "safe" and needy follower had been made the middleman between the bank at Philadelphia and needy borrowers or financial interests in the states.

But these were not the only indications of an increasingly close connection between the Richmond financial interests and the Treasury wing of the cabinet. As early as June, 1792, Jefferson learned that Hamilton already had "expressed the strongest desire that Marshall should come into Congress from Richmond, declaring that there is no other man in Virginia who [sic] he wishes to see there." Marshall had on that occasion declined Hamilton's flattering proposal.[94] A year and a half later—in December, 1793—with the Richmond financial interests already benefitting in good measure from their alliance with the Bank of the United States, Attorney General Edmund Randolph informed Wilson Cary Nicholas that he would be pleased to act as "paymaster" or "indorser or anything for your accommodation" in obtaining discounts for Nicholas' own notes from Philadelphia banks. At this time a recent yellow fever epidemic had driven the government from the city and in the process had "shattered the credit of multitudes; and generated an extreme caution in the banks in discounting."[95]

[93] *Virginia Herald and Fredericksburg Advertiser*, February 14, 1793.
[94] Jefferson to Madison, from Philadelphia, January 1, 1792, Madison Papers, Vol. 15.
[95] Randolph to Nicholas, from Germantown, December 7, 1793, Nicholas Papers, Box 1. Randolph's activity at this time on behalf of Marshall, the Bank, and doubtless Hamilton as well, is intriguing, since the Attorney General usually was found supporting Jefferson against the Secretary of the Treasury during the stormiest cabinet sessions. Further evidence of Ran-

Madison was not unaware of the growth of this Richmond-Philadelphia alliance or its implications for the emerging Republican interest. In September, 1793, he explained to Jefferson the reasons which at the time "disapate [sic] from full confidence in" Nicholas and Marshall. "It is said," Madison wrote that "Marshall, who is at the head of the great purchase from Fairfax, has lately obtained pecuniary aid from the Bank, or people connected with it. I think it is certain that he must have felt, in the amount of the purchase an absolute dependence on the monied interest, which will explain him to every one that reflects, in the active character he is assuming."[96] Marshall's "active character," to which Madison alluded, was his public and forthright defense of those administration policies most obnoxious to the Jeffersonians. By midsummer of 1793 links based on economic self-interest, previous military comeraderie, and political loyalty had been forged between the Treasury at Philadelphia and the leading financiers and speculators in Richmond.

With the creation of a distinct faction at Richmond by 1793[97] the use of patronage by Hamilton and Washington to build political strength in the South came to an end. Whatever other plans Hamilton may have had to extend government favor to certain economic interests throughout the country were never pushed thereafter, as Hamilton at last was checked by an increasingly vigorous Republican opposition in Congress. However, by the end of his first administration Washington and his Treasury Secretary had succeeded in developing loosely-structured factions within

---

dolph's increasing support of Hamilton is lacking. Probably personal friendship rather than "party" politics induced Randolph to act in Marshall's behalf. In any case, the effect on the growth of a Federalist interest in Virginia was not diminished.

[96] Madison to Jefferson, September 2, 1793, Madison Papers, Vol. 16.

[97] Members of this group gathered in amiability at· frequent intervals throughout that spring and summer. Diary of William Heth, entries of May 1, 3, June 29, 1793.

the southern states loyal to the national administration. A spirit of active loyalty to the administration flourished in the dominant lowcountry of South Carolina and in the most important city in Virginia; it was nearly extinct in North Carolina, but only because Samuel Johnston and Hugh Williamson had chosen to retire voluntarily, while John Steele temporarily had lost the confidence of the electorate; and in Georgia an ambitious group of former military commanders who now were land speculators offered hope that once the problem with the Creek Indians had been resolved, Georgia might support the administration.

Policy, patronage, and simply the passage of time made of these southern proadministration interests of 1793 something far different from the old Federalist parties which existed there in 1787 and 1788. In general, those who experienced immediate benefit from a stronger union or whose vanity was fulfilled by Washington and Hamilton willingly gave their allegiance and active support to the Constitution and its administrators. On the other hand, those whose expectations were in some way frustrated remained loyal to the Constitution while developing an inveterate opposition to its administrators.

For example, the two Georgia delegates who signed the Constitution in 1787, William Few and Abraham Baldwin, both became bitter critics of government policy after 1790, although both subsequently spent some years in national political life. The defection of young Charles Pinckney—a staunch Federalist in 1788—from the newly emerging Federalist interest of the early 1790's is considered at some length in subsequent pages. However, his voluntary withdrawal from the national government was a result of repeated personal frustrations in seeking patronage. In later years, however, young Pinckney worked strenuously in his state for the Republicans and advanced to power within the Constitutional structure that he had helped to erect at Philadelphia and had defended in Charleston a decade before. Conversely, the staunchest administration supporters in South Carolina in the early 1790's—Ralph Izard, William Loughton Smith, Edward Rutledge, and Charles Cotesworth Pinckney—all had formed close personal connections with important leaders in the national administration and had been amply rewarded. Eventually, indirect government favor was instrumental in securing for the friends of government the loyalty of the hotspur of the Antifederalist Party, Patrick Henry. Jefferson charged that Henry was won over after he had pocketed a handsome profit from Hamilton's fiscal policies.

It is important to emphasize exactly what these emerging administration interests in the South were and what they were not. In form and structure they in no way conformed to the highly institutionalized party organizations which emerged later in the eras of Jefferson and Jackson. Rather, the partisan organizational pattern stayed much the same as it had been in the colonial era, when traditional ruling elites had been bound in loose connections and cliques, by ties of interest and friendship. The only change from earlier years—and it was significant—was that now these local administration interests were part of a larger, though very loosely structured, nationwide political network, united in defense and support of a central governing and policy-making institution.

In purpose, however, the formation of these local interests was a break with tradition. Administration juntos in the South and elsewhere were expected to act as partisan groups, actively and constantly defending government policy; they were not expected to operate in an issueless vacuum. Their task, as outlined by Hamilton in 1782, was to rally support among the people for the government during times of unrest and crisis to avoid the possibility that ambitious schemers

The Founding of a Political Interest, 1789-1793 / 47

might unite them into a solid bloc of opposition. The successful fulfillment of such an assignment strongly implied the need for a more consistent and intimate contact with the electorate than ever before. It demanded flexibility and effectiveness from men who viewed the political process in traditional terms of the active and able few and the deferential and inert many. It demanded in short, at least a partial modification of the eighteenth-century American political tradition of elitist rule. Such demands were especially pressing upon friends of government in the South, where, after 1790, popular unrest and antipathy to government policy were high. They were charged with keeping at least a portion of that region firmly attached to the federal administration to avoid the destructive impression that the central government was run by and for the interests of a section rather than a nation. Unfortunately for the cause they served, nothing in their experience had prepared these proto-Federalists in the South for the responsibility of a sustained and effective confrontation with an electorate that often was sullen and suspicious.

II. *The Friends of Government,*
1789-1794

Southern supporters of the national administration during the early 1790's shared one trait: they had spent their adult lives in positions of public trust and authority. Planters, lawyers, merchants, and, in South Carolina, financiers formed the comparatively small cliques that year after year dominated public life in southern states. In an agricultural society overwhelmingly oriented toward subsistence farming, where transportation was wretched and communication slow and fitful,[1] political activity inevitably was centered in the few towns, and cities—and in the adjacent plantation regions of eastern Virginia and coastal South Carolina—where trade and social life were concentrated. Beyond these narrow spheres in each state, public life was nonexistent. Outright mistrust of vigorous government was high, even in some areas where the plantation system was well established.[2]

The members of these southern ruling classes seldom wrote or spoke extensively to justify or explain the political society which had given them such conspicuous privilege and prestige. Their elitist values had been developed instinctively from everyday experience rather than from formal training or extensive reading in eighteenth-century political theory. Background in management of extensive private enterprises, plus the existence of a political structure weighted wholly in their favor, precluded the need for philosophical speculation upon the proper relations of men to the state. Restricted franchises, extensive property qualifications for officeholding, oligarchic local governing bodies, sectionally imbalanced state legislatures with ascendant powers over the executive, all combined to restrict the exercise of political power to a privileged few.[3]

For many, the enjoyment of a commanding status had been expanded by the Revolutionary War from the legislative halls to the battlefield. An officer's commission and command of large numbers of men in action confirmed a status of social attainment previously recognized *de facto* but never *de jure*. Often those who had won their reputations in the Continental Army felt a self-conceived and self-imposed mandate to participate in political affairs as a

---

[1] Throughout the 1790's southern congressmen frequently complained that "contrary winds and bad weather" hindered their journeys and delayed important communications. Samuel Johnston to James Iredell, from New York, January 30, 1790, in Griffith J. McRee, ed., *Life and Correspondence of James Iredell* (2 vols.; New York: Peter Smith, 1947), II, 279; Ralph Izard to Edward Rutledge, from New York, December 29, 1789, in Ulrich B. Phillips, ed., "South Carolina Federalist Correspondence," *American Historical Review*, XIV (July, 1909), 777; James Jackson to John Milledge, from Philadelphia, November 12, 1794, in Harriet Milledge Salley, ed., *Correspondence of Governor John Milledge* (Columbia, S. C.: State Commercial Printing Co., 1949), 36.

[2] Le Duc de la Rochefoucauld-Liancourt, *Travels Through the United States of North America, etc., in the Years 1795, 1796, and 1797* (2 vols.; London: T. Davidson, Lombard Street, 1799), II, 24; Benjamin Harrison to Washington, from Berkeley County, October 4, 1787, Washington Papers, Vol. 239.

[3] William A. Schaper, "Sectionalism and Representation in South Carolina," *Annual Report of the American Historical Association for 1901* (2 vols.; Washington, D. C.: Government Printing Office, 1901), 245–463 *passim;* Allan Nevins, *The American States During and After the Revolution, 1775–1789* (New York: The Macmillan Company, 1927), 91–97; Fletcher M. Green, *Constitutional Development in the South Atlantic States, 1776–1860: A Study in the Evolution of Democracy* (Chapel Hill: University of North Carolina Press, 1930), 77–140 *passim;* Jackson Turner Main, *The Antifederalists: Critics of the Constitution, 1781–1788* (Chapel Hill: University of North Carolina Press, 1961), 28–30; Charles S. Sydnor, *American Revolutionaries in the Making: Political Practices in Washington's Virginia* (New York: Collier Books, 1962), 14–16.

natural continuation of an earlier public trust. It is little wonder that so many southern veterans through membership in the exclusive and unpopular Society of the Cincinnati symbolized a continuing interest in the military life and the ideal of national sovereignty.

Despite their strong elitist tendencies southern "friends of government" (as they soon began to call themselves)[4] fulfilled their partisan responsibilities to the national administration with energy and effect between 1791 and 1794 and took the first reluctant steps toward bringing a much larger proportion of the citizenry into closer contact with state and national political life. By the very prominence of their position and by occasional activities they began to bring some order to the prevailing confusion of local and state factional politics. Also, they focused the attention of the electorate upon an emerging system of polarized political conflict within which issues and individuals were far more clearly defined and definable than in the past. Most of these men did not then, or ever, significantly modify their elitist ideals, but they did ultimately realize that increasingly such ideals would have to be subverted in practice to muster the needed support for national policy.

The transformation of southern politics from the chaos of local factionalism into the comparative order of a well-defined party system had not even begun by the time of the Jay Treaty. Several events in 1795 and 1796 revealed the essential fragility and inadequacy of the factions that Hamilton and Washington had created in the southern states. But a basic "Federalist" achievement during these years cannot be denied. By their presence and occasional activities at the grassroots level the friends of government established many of the conditions for the development of a two-party system in the South.

[4] Henry Lee seems to have been the first southerner to use this phrase. Lee to Washington, July 11, 1789, Washington Papers, Vol. 243.

In 1790 no other political society in the South was as stable and well defined as that of South Carolina. The lowcountry oligarchy of planters, lawyers, and merchants enjoyed a security of status and an entrenchment of power and influence unknown to their colleagues elsewhere in the South. These friends of government in South Carolina were under the least immediate pressure of any proadministration group in the South to modify traditional principles of government by elites, though such pressure was to increase in time. Nearly all members of this immensely powerful group were bound to the national government by ties of influence and affection. Such loyalty represented one of the greatest triumphs of Washington's patronage policy and guaranteed support for early administration policies in the southern states.

In South Carolina, social and political power for years had been concentrated in the charming townhouses of Charleston and in the great rice plantations along the coastal lowcountry. Planters such as Ralph Izard, Daniel Huger, William Washington, Pierce Butler, and Robert Barnwell were united by ties of marriage and of mutual interest to a group of brilliant lawyers in Charleston led by General Charles Cotesworth Pinckney and Edward Rutledge.[5] Included in the first rank of this Charleston lawyer element were John Rutledge; Cotesworth Pinckney's younger brother, Major Thomas Pinckney; and his younger cousin Charles. Young William Loughton Smith, Jacob Read, and, soon thereafter, John Rutledge, Jr., formed a second but highly respectable rank within the bar. This alliance of lowcountry planters and Charleston lawyers was strengthened further by ties with the community of British merchants in the city,

[5] Charles Pinckney and Edward Rutledge were pointed out to the French traveler La Rochefoucauld-Liancourt as the leading Charleston lawyers in 1795. The Frenchman was told that the two earned as much as thirty-five to forty-five hundred pounds sterling a year from their legal business. La Rochefoucauld-Liancourt, *Travels Through the United States*, I, 562–63.

as well as with the local financiers headed at the time by William Henry DeSaussure and Gabriel and Louis Manigault.

The peculiar geographic and social configuration of the state, which lent special force to sectional political tensions and conflicts, greatly enhanced the influence of these wealthy lowcountrymen. Charleston was the only major city and port on the American seaboard in the more than seven hundred miles between Chesapeake Bay and East Florida. Resulting ties, both commercial and social, with individuals and business firms in Europe and with New England and the middle colonies made Charlestonians aware that they were important members of the North Atlantic civilization of the eighteenth century.[6] All the prominent Charleston lawyers not only had lived abroad extensively, but had received professional training there as well, generally at the famous Inns of Court in London, where many future rulers of the empire prepared for their careers in public life. Ralph Izard, the greatest of the lowcountry planters and the virtual political boss of St. James Goose Creek Parish, adjacent to the city, also had spent some years in England and on the Continent before and during the Revolution.[7]

The superiority and comparative isolation of the lowcountry oligarchy were confirmed by the underdevelopment of the surrounding regions. Settlement of many backcountry

[6] Carl Bridenbaugh, "Charlestonians at Newport, 1767–1775," *South Carolina Historical and Genealogical Magazine*, XLI (April, 1940), 43–47; Michael Kraus, *The Atlantic Civilization, Eighteenth Century Origins* (Ithaca: Cornell University Press, 1941); Carl Bridenbaugh, *Myths and Realities: Societies of the Colonial South* (Baton Rouge: Louisiana State University Press, 1952).

[7] In this and following pages, unless otherwise noted, the biographical material used is taken from one or both of two main sources, which shall not be cited in detail: Allen Johnson, Dumas Malone, and Harris E. Starr, eds., *The Dictionary of American Biography* (21 vols. and index; New York: Charles Scribner's Sons, 1928–1958); *The Biographical Directory of the American Congress, 1774–1961* (Washington, D. C.: Government Printing Office, 1961).

areas had not really begun much before the middle of the century; and although the rush of population into that area had been rapid, on the eve of the Revolutionary War there were few churches, no schools, and no social structure comparable to that of the lowcountry.[8] After the mid-1780's, however, the backcountry had fought for a larger share of representation in the legislature and had bitterly opposed the Constitution in 1788. Thus, the state was divided deeply, both politically and socially, between a comparatively raw, remote, provincial backcountry frontier area similar to those in Georgia and the Tennessee country and a cosmopolitian, urbanized lowcountry which resembled the urban areas of Boston, New York, and Philadelphia.

Having risen to prominence at the beginning of the Revolution, members of the oligarchy had had experience in command, both afield and in legislative chambers, by the time that Washington and Hamilton tried to gain their services and support. Cotesworth, Thomas Pinckney, and Edward Rutledge all had fought against the British during the invasion and occupation of the South in 1779–1782. Rutledge had been captured and incarcerated at St. Augustine for a year, while the service of Cotesworth and Thomas Pinckney was sufficient to earn for them the titles of general and major, respectively. John Rutledge had become so influential by 1779 that when the British appeared, the frightened legislature gave him dictatorial powers. From the vantage point of various North Carolina border towns he waged an implacable struggle to oust the English from Charleston. As a result of this determined opposition, most of the lowcountry leaders had their extensive holdings in land, slaves, and other personal property confiscated by the British. This, in effect, reemphasized to the common people

[8] Robert L. Meriwether, *The Expansion of South Carolina, 1729–1765* (Kingsport, Tennessee: Southern Publishers, Inc., 1940), 125–56.

the many sacrifices which their rulers had made on behalf of independence.[9] Despite the growth of popular political agitation, marked by the backcountry's incessant demands for more adequate representation in the legislature and by the protests of native artisans and merchants against the return of British factors in the early 1780's, members of the oligarchy continued to dominate politics and to represent South Carolina's interest in the Continental Congress throughout the Confederation era.[10]

The struggle over the adoption of the Constitution revealed the extent of the power and influence which the oligarchy could employ when aroused to united action. Disclaimers to the contrary, the Antifederalists had been actively and successfully campaigning in the backcountry prior to the meeting of the ratifying convention at Charleston.[11] Once that body convened, however, the lowcountrymen took complete command. One of the backcountry representatives, Aedanus Burke, has left a record of his impressions of those days which imparts far better than the historian can hope to do a sense of the structure of South Carolina politics, the division of popular opinion, and the overpowering influence and determined federalism of the coastal oligarchs in 1788.

It is now unnecessary perhaps to state to you the different causes, whereby the new plan has been carried in South Carolina notwithstanding 4/5 of the people do, from their souls detest it. I am convinced, from my knowledge of the country, that I am rather under, than over, that proportion. In the first place, we

[9] Charles Gregg Singer, *South Carolina in the Confederation* (Philadelphia, 1941), 11–12, 18–19.
[10] *Ibid.*, 103–105, 113, 124, 164–67; Nevins, *The American States During and After the Revolution*, 335, 401–403.
[11] Charles Cotesworth Pinckney to Rufus King, from Charleston, May 24, 1788, in Charles R. King, ed., *Life and Correspondence of Rufus King* (6 vols.; New York: G. P. Putnam's Sons, 1894–1900), I, 328–29.

in the opposition, had not, previous to our meeting, either wrote, or spoke, hardly a word against it, nor took any one step in the matter. We had no principle of concert or union, while its friends and abettors left no expedient untried to push it forward. All the rich, leading men, along the seacoast, and rice settlements; with few exceptions, lawyers, physicians and divines, the merchants, mechanicks, the populace and mob of Charleston. I think it worthy of observation that not a single instance in So. Carolina of a man formerly a Tory, or British adherent, who is not loud and zealous for the new Constitution. From the British Consul (who is the most violent man I know for it) down to the British scavenger, all are boisterous to drive it down. Add to this, the whole weight and influence of the press was in that scale. Not a printing press, in Carolina, out of the city. The printers are, in general, British journeymen, or poor citizens, who are afraid to offend the great men, or merchants, who could work their ruin. Thus, with us, the press is in the hands of a junto, and the printers, with most servile insolence discouraged opposition, and pushed forward publications in its favour; for no one wrote against it.

But the principle [sic] cause was holding the Convention in the City, where there are not fifty inhabitants who are not friendly to it. The merchants and leading men kept open houses for the back and low country members during the whole time the Convention sat. The sixth day after we sat, despatches arrived, bringing an account that Maryland had acceded to the scheme. This was a severe blow to us; for the next day, one of our best speakers in the opposition, Doctor Fousseaux, gave notice he would quit that ground, as Maryland had acceded to it.[12]

Intensive and sustained contact with the narrow ruling circles of the eighteenth-century Anglo-American world, when combined with the enjoyment and exercise of extensive political power at home, inevitably bred a strong elitist temperament among South Carolina's lowcountry oligarchs. Their lives had been passed in the houses and corridors of power among gentlemen with impeccable credentials to

[12] In George C. Rogers, Jr., *William Loughton Smith of Charleston; Evolution of a Federalist, 1758–1812* (Columbia, S. C.: University of South Carolina Press, 1962), 156. Quoted by permission of the author.

rule. Times of crisis or the quiet of private correspondence between friends often called forth expressions of exclusivist sentiment from these Charleston lawyers or their colleagues along the adjacent coast. Occasionally such views were expressed with comparative serenity, as when Cotesworth Pinckney wrote from the Philadelphia Convention that the brilliance and reputation of his fellow delegates would surely "dispose our fellow Citizens to judge favorably of such measures as we shall adopt."[13] More often, however, the tone was querulous.

Ralph Izard best typified the attitudes of this South Carolina gentry. A good friend of Edmund Burke, he shared Burke's regard for liberty and his mistrust of democracy. From his unintentional and unhappy exile in Europe, Izard called the American Revolution "the noblest" cause "that was ever contended for by a free people," and he spoke of the need "to put a proper value on the blessings of liberty." At the same time Izard expressed his dislike of democracy which placed the untrained, ignorant, and passionate masses in too close proximity to political decision-making. Soon after his return to South Carolina, the master of St. James Goose Creek complained to Thomas Jefferson that "Our governments tend too much to Democracy. A handicraftsman thinks an apprenticeship necessary to make him acquainted with his business. But our back countrymen are of opinion that a politician may be born such . . . as well as a poet."[14] Izard's antidemocratic bias carried well beyond mere words, and in the year after his letter to Jefferson, he

[13] To Harriott Pinckney, May 30, 1787, Pinckney Family Papers, Box 2.
[14] Edmund Burke to Izard, from Beaconsfield, July 20, 1777; Izard to the Duke of Richmond, November 9, 1775, to Edward Rutledge, from London, May 8, 1777, in Anne Izard Deas, ed., *Correspondence of Mr. Ralph Izard of South Carolina* (New York: Charles S. Francis & Co., 1844), 144, 280, 318–19; Izard to Thomas Jefferson, June 10, 1785, in Worthington C. Ford, ed., "Letters of Ralph Izard," *South Carolina Historical and Genealogical Magazine*, II (July, 1901), 197–98.

publicly harangued his constituents and even tried open bribery in an attempt to destroy the political career of a popular young doctor from Virginia, Thomas Tudor Tucker. When he later was chided for his actions, Izard retorted that he "'did not scruple to acknowledge what he had said, to insist on the right of saying it, and to wish every man in the parish had been present to hear it.' "[15]

As late as 1795 some lowcountry oligarchs still expressed grave doubts whether the backcountrymen and their chosen leaders possessed sufficient political maturity and wisdom to be given a majority voice in the conduct of the public business of the state. "At present," Henry William DeSaussure wrote to his Virginia colleague, Richard Bland Lee:

... the low Country ... possesses the great mass of property & information [and] has a representation proportioned to these advantages which secures a good administration on proper & federal principles. [The letter was written some months before the publication of Jay's Treaty.] Our upper country people are very unenlightened & of course rude & violent, easily misled by demagogues and governed by every passing wind—we are therefore afraid to allow any change in the representation—when they attain the Information possessed by your people in the Country above the falls of the rivers, and are guided by Men of Education & of settled principles of government, Many of our objections to encrease their representation will be done away, & we may probably follow the Example you set us of encreasing their representation by degrees.[16]

DeSaussure's remarks notwithstanding, the politically restless South Carolina backcountry developed an increasingly competent corps of leaders during the early 1790's at the same time that its economy began to expand along lines

[15] Quoted in Rogers, *William Loughton Smith*, 128.
[16] DeSaussure to Richard Bland Lee, February 14, 1795, from Charleston, R. B. Lee Papers.

similar to prevailing conditions on the coast.[17] For a time the perpetual struggles between the "upper" and "lower" interests in the Assembly aided the growth of a distinct and well-defined party in the proadministration lowcountry. Planters, merchants, and lawyers along the coast united in a self-conscious "Federalist" phalanx against the incessant assaults from the West upon their disproportionate exercise of power in the state.[18] Moreover, in order to insure their ascendancy, members of the oligarchy disregarded their elitist instincts to indulge in the "petty electioneering arts" which one of them described as "the natural growth of the fungus of all popular governments," but as such "to be tolerated" for the sake of sustained political ascendancy.[19]

At home in Charleston the Federalist oligarchs continued to flaunt their privileged status through their membership in the Chamber of Commerce and the Cincinnati Society, both of which met in the best coffeehouse in the most ex-

[17] The rapid political awakening of the backcountry and the emergence of young Robert Goodloe Harper as its chief spokesman is discussed in Schaper, "Sectionalism in South Carolina," 408. See also John Brown Cutting to Thomas Pinckney, from Columbia, December 19, 1794, Pinckney Family Papers, Box 6. According to a contemporary, as early as 1792 the backcountry began to undertake the cultivation and exportation of cotton on a "considerable" basis. David Ramsay, *History of South Carolina, from its First Settlement in 1670 to the Year 1808* (2 vols.; Charleston: David Longworth, 1809), II, 449. Meanwhile, the state increased its slave population by one-third during the final decade of the eighteenth century, as more than 38,000 Negroes were imported, while the rice industry along the coast declined steadily from the middle of this decade onward. Curtis P. Nettles, *The Emergence of a National Economy, 1775–1815*, (New York: Holt, Rinehart and Winston, 1962), 183–84, 187.

[18] In a joint letter in June, 1791, Edward Rutledge and Cotesworth Pinckney replied to Washington's repeated urgings that they accept a high government post in a tone that must have pleased Hamilton, if he had known of it. "We think we can be of more real benefit to the general government & to our own State government," they wrote, "by remaining in the [state] Legislature, than we could possibly be by accepting of any office under either which fills the public eye with the appearance of being lucrative." June 12, 1791, Washington Papers, Vol. 251.

[19] John Brown Cutting to Thomas Pinckney, from Columbia, December 19, 1794, Pinckney Family Papers, Box 6.

clusive section of the commercial district. The sailors' and mechanics' clubs—and the later Democratic-Republican Societies—also composed of sailors and mechanics plus the more modest planters, merchants, and professional people, met with equal ostentation in waterfront taverns.[20] But in Columbia the oligarchs maintained close contact and even occasionally made deals with the representatives of lower society. Such efforts were beneficial for the national administration as a whole, for the lowcountry continued to dominate the state throughout the Federalists' years in power, and excepting a brief period, the oligarchs remained loyal to that interest until the election of 1800.

Georgia, with its raw frontier setting, seemed an unlikely place for the development of a well-defined ruling group, but commerce through the port of Savannah and recurrent Indian crises on the frontier during the Confederation era brought into being a definite governing class, composed mainly of merchants and military leaders. Included in this group were Edward Telfair, William Gibbons, Sr., the Habersham brothers of Savannah, and Generals James Jackson, William Few, James Gunn, Lachlan McIntosh, and Anthony Wayne. The latter three were firm friends of government after 1790; McIntosh and Wayne had long been prominent in the Georgia chapter of the Cincinnati Society.[21]

These friends of government were faced with an early and deep opposition to the policies of the national administration both from within and without the Georgia ruling class, a radically different situation from that in South Caro-

[20] Eugene P. Link, "The Republican Societies of Charleston," *Proceedings of the South Carolina Historical Society*, 1943, p. 26.
[21] William W. Abbot, "The Structure of Politics in Georgia, 1782–1789," *William and Mary Quarterly*, Series 3, XIV (January, 1957), 47–65; James Jackson to John Milledge, from Savannah, November 4, 1793, in Salley, ed., *John Milledge*, 30; *Georgia Gazette*, July 9, 1789; Kenneth Coleman, *The American Revolution in Georgia, 1763–1789* (Athens: University of Georgia Press, 1958), 235.

lina. If Georgia—or any portion of it—was to be saved for the national administration, the practice of elitist politics, involving a measured aloofness from the populace, clearly was out of the question.[22] By 1791, with popular antipathy to various government policies running high, the friends of government obviously needed to secure an immediate mandate from the people or face extinction as a vital, influential force in the politics of the state.

In Georgia the struggle between friends and opponents of the national administration began that same year, when Anthony Wayne determined to wrest a Congressional seat from James Jackson. Wayne's decision was not the result of whim, because Jackson already had become a prominent critic of national policy and a vigorous defender of local and state rights.

Jackson was one of the earliest Congressional supporters of James Madison and as a result incurred the wrath of Hamilton's ally, William Loughton Smith.[23] The Georgia representative had complained angrily about his state's share of the assumption, and he seems to have been the first to charge that Hamilton had tipped off northern speculators to the contents of his funding scheme before public announce-

[22] It may be presumed from their status within the local ruling class and the occasional outspoken contempt which they expressed for popular opinion in the Yazoo incidents of 1789 and 1795 that the members of Georgia's pro-administration faction were strongly influenced by the eighteenth-century elitist political tradition. Supposition cannot be substantiated by hard fact, however. The several relevant manuscript collections for the time provide few clues, and whatever pertinent debates and discussions may have taken place in the ratifying convention of 1788 are lost to record.

[23] After the funding and assumption plans finally passed Congress, Smith wrote bitterly of several of the critics. "I have observed," he complained, "that Sumpter [sic] regularly votes for any thing required by Georgia or Virg^n. Burke is also a great friend to that State, notwithstanding her Members execrate us & do all the Injury they can. . . . Jackson has behaved thro' this whole business in a manner which has excited the greatest indignation in my breast." Smith to Rutledge, August 8, 1790, Smith-Rutledge Correspondence.

ment.²⁴ If Jackson could be destroyed politically, the gathering movement against current national policy possibly could receive a blow from which it might never recover.

Jackson's conduct in Congress roused Wayne's ire, but there were other reasons for his opposition to the congressman. By challenging Jackson, Wayne said, he also was opposing the adverse reaction of Goverrner Telfair to the presence of United States troops in the state, as well as the public antipathy to "the late Treaty[,] Yazoo &c."²⁵ It is significant that he chose to notify the Secretary of War—a close friend of the President—of his political intentions.

Wayne's allusion to Yazoo needs some illumination. The rescinded 1789 sale of Yazoo lands and the one carried out six years later were intertwined intimately with the fortunes of the progovernment faction in Georgia.

In 1790 Georgia was the only state in the Union not to have ceded her vast western claims—which stretched from the present-day southern Tennessee border to Spanish Florida and on out to the Mississippi River—to the central government. This explains the conflict between the state and the national governments over Indian policy and treaty-making powers; and it explains also the constant pressures upon the Georgia legislature from private sources throughout the late 1780's and early 1790's to sell this area for ventures in speculation and settlement.

Prior to the formation of the Union, Georgia had been little disturbed by speculators seeking her western claim, but in November, 1789, the representatives of four land companies appeared before the bar of the legislature. Three of these "Yazoo" companies—the South Carolina group led by Alexander Moultrie, Edward Telfair, and Isaac Huger; a

²⁴ *Annals of Congress*, I, 1132–37, 1181, 1744–52, 1760.
²⁵ Wayne to Secretary of War Henry Knox, May 12, 1790, to Richard Wayne, September 24, 1790, Wayne Papers.

company from Tennessee doubtlessly backed by William Blount; and a company from Virginia apparently led by Patrick Henry[26]—appeared at about the same time. The legislature was favorable toward selling, but wished, as one of the members said, to obtain "a good round sum down for this territory in State or other securities, so that we might pay so much of our Debt."[27] While negotiations were in progress, a fourth company, composed mainly of Georgia speculators and led by James McNeil, a state senator, made a more enticing, and more concrete offer, promising to bring in at least 40,000 settlers from Ireland, Switzerland, and sister states "within a year or two," and, perhaps even more important, guaranteeing payment of a higher price and far more of it in specie than the other companies had offered.[28] The offer of the Georgia company seemed irresistible on many obvious counts, yet by a single vote the three original companies were favored instead.[29]

Reaction was prompt, and in early January the legislative minority which had opposed the sale to the original three companies submitted a public report in the *Augusta Chronicle* which was spread quickly throughout the state. This report carefully avoided any implication that the

[26] Charles Homer Haskins, "The Yazoo Land Companies," *Papers of the American Historical Association*, V (January and April, 1891), 398–400; R. H. Lee to Patrick Henry, from New York, May 28, 1789, James C. Ballagh, ed., *The Letters of Richard Henry Lee* (2 vols.; New York: The Macmillan Company, 1914), 486–87; Alexander Moultrie to Edward Telfair, n.d., Edward Telfair Papers, Duke University Library, Durham, N. C. Pierce Butler and Ralph Izard might also have had an interest in the South Carolina Yazoo Company at this time. See Butler and Izard to anonymous, 1789, Pierce Butler Papers, South Caroliniana Library, Columbia, S. C.

[27] James to John Habersham, from Augusta, November 25, 1789, Personal Miscellany File, Library of Congress.

[28] *Georgia Gazette*, January 7, 1790; "Journal of the Georgia House of Representatives," December 8–12, 1789, in William Sumner Jenkins, ed., *Records of the States of the United States* (Microfilm, University of California Library, Berkeley).

[29] "Journal of the Georgia House of Representatives," December 8–12, 1789, in Jenkins, ed., *Records of the States.*

majority of the legislature had been bought by the three companies; it simply restated the facts, which were damning enough. It was clear that the majority had brushed aside every other issue before the legislature and every vestige of proper parliamentary procedure to insure the consummation of the sale. The report concluded by noting that sale to the Georgia company would "have given our citizens an opportunity of becoming purchasers upon equal terms with those of other states."[30] Popular response was every bit as quick and strong as the minority had hoped and the majority had doubtless feared. Letters appearing in the press reflected the "convulsion" of the public mind over the sale, and during the following summer at least two county grand juries—those of Chatham and Liberty—presented formal opposition to the sale.[31]

These tactics succeeded in uncovering the leading legislative proponent of the sale to the original companies, Lachlan McIntosh. In late January, 1790, McIntosh published a formal reply to the minority report, saying the state was to receive nearly a quarter of a million dollars for but one quarter of its western claim and also was to be relieved by the three companies of the sticky responsibility of dealing with the Spanish Intendant at New Orleans.[32] The public remained unconvinced, however.

Actually, the 1789 sale never was completed, because the companies could not meet the final payment in 1791, though they tried unsuccessfully to meet their commitment with a mixture of Georgia, South Carolina, and continental paper currency of 1776.[33] By this time the state had been divided into identifiable "Yazoo" and "anti-Yazoo" forces, with the central issue being whether the state was to retain control

[30] *Georgia Gazette*, January 7, 1790.
[31] *Ibid.*, February 4, June 17, August 12, 1790.
[32] *Ibid.*, January 28, 1790.
[33] Haskins, "Yazoo Land Companies," 407–408.

of its western lands for distribution to its own people in its own way or whether it was to relinquish this responsibility through sale to outside forces. This issue was related to the Indian problem and posed the same question: was Georgia to deal with the recurrent Indian crises, or was it to be the problem of the federal government in distant Philadelphia. Those who stood on the side of the state, the "anti-Yazooers" and anti-Creek-treaty men, soon formed an identifiable group, led by Governor Telfair, James Jackson, John Milledge, Josiah Tattnall, Seaborn Jones, and Joseph Habersham; the latter four had signed the minority report on the 1789 sale. Among those who became identified with the three land companies from other states and who favored the federal government's dealing with the Creeks were Lachlan McIntosh, Wayne, McAllister, Gunn, and the other members of the administration's patronage faction, including the editor of the *Georgia Gazette*. This distinct, fundamental cleavage in Georgia politics, so completely different from the confused situations in some other southern states, such as North Carolina, emerged in 1789–1790 and lasted until at least 1796. Nowhere else in the South during these years were proadministration interests and states-rights Republicans—for, with Jackson at its head, so this latter group soon called itself—so easily identifiable.

The Wayne-Jackson struggle of 1791 for the Congressional seat from the coast district was the first significant overt test of strength between the two parties, which they could accurately be called.

Georgia was not free from the usual sectional antagonisms which characterized the politics of the other southern states, and as might be expected, the basic division lay between the upcountry frontier counties and the little town of Augusta, on the one hand, and the seacoast planter counties and the port city of Savannah, on the other. Political issues

The Friends of Government, 1789-1794

revolved about unequal taxation and representation, with the added complaint of an alleged unjust burden placed upon the upcountry militia.[34]

In addition, as late as 1791 a profound enmity existed between so-called "Old" and "New" Georgians, and this conflict played an important role in the Wayne-Jackson election. The division was confined largely to the city of Savannah and surrounding Chatham County. Wayne, who then was a resident of Savannah, identified the Old Georgians as those who had either "basely" fled the city or had remained to cooperate actively with the enemy during the British invasion of 1780-1782. This group comprised a large proportion of the city's population, and it constantly attempted to maintain its political identity and power. In contrast, the New Georgians were those few who had taken up arms against Albion in cooperation with large numbers of "Northern veterans." After the war this element had worked magnanimously, according to Wayne, to restore the property of the Old Georgians to rightful hands. Wayne added that the Old Georgians had regained their political ascendancy along with their property and now feared that the "new" men might eclipse their power and gain the confidence of the upcountry counties, thus insuring an alliance which would obtain perpetual power.[35]

Some realignment of these interests occurred as Wayne gained the support of the "New" Georgians in Savannah and Chatham, while Jackson, though a patriot and military hero in his own right, did not discourage the support of the "Old" Georgia loyalist faction. Thus, old antagonisms played a part in the emerging party strife, and a new form of political order developed in Georgia, foreshadowing later developments in other southern states.

[34] Address of "A Planter" to the "Planters, Tradesmen, Shopkeepers and Other Voters of Chatham County," *Georgia Gazette*, October 1, 1789.
[35] Memo: "The Old Georgians Analyzed," Wayne Papers.

The campaign was quiet enough, and little space was devoted to it in the press. Wayne may or may not have soft-pedaled his support for McIntosh and the Indian policy of the federal government; this is not clear. He did win, however, a seemingly signal victory for the administration. Jackson apparently took his defeat with grace, and when he returned to Savannah in April, 1791, he accepted a memorial expressing warm appreciation for his services in Congress from Wayne's campaign manager, Mayor Thomas Gibbons.

The apparent calm was shattered in July, however, when Jackson publicly accused Wayne of rigging the election in at least two of the five counties of the district. Working quietly, Jackson had amassed evidence of bizarre corruption, including moonlight balloting and destruction of Jackson votes by a bribed county sheriff, as well as the usual charges of ballot-box stuffing.[36] Once again popular indignation quickly reached fever pitch as grand juries and public meetings supported Jackson, and prominent followers of Anthony Wayne filled the press with essays either denying participation in the fraud or threatening Jackson with personal harm.[37] Jackson was vindicated in the legislature the following November, after brushing aside a substantial bribe by the Wayne forces to forget the whole thing; and one of Wayne's aides—a justice of the state supreme court—was impeached on five counts.[38]

Georgia could not deprive Wayne of his seat in favor of Jackson, however. That was a matter for the House of Representatives in Philadelphia to decide. Jackson's de-

[36] *Georgia Gazette,* July 28, 1791.
[37] *Ibid.,* August 4, September 15, 29, October 13, 27, 1791.
[38] Jackson to Joseph Clay, Sr., from Augusta, December 2, 1791, James Jackson Papers, Duke University Library, Durham, N. C.; *Georgia Gazette,* December 8, 29, 1791, January 5, 1792; "Journal of the State Senate of Georgia," December 21, 1791, in Jenkins, ed., *Records of the States.*

termination to have Wayne's seat was well known, but Wayne was not going to give it up without a fight. He enlisted the aid of Matthew McAllister back in Georgia, hoping that a perusal of the tax lists in those counties which had gone heavily for Jackson might reveal that many voters had in fact been ineligible. However, McAllister found no such evidence.[39]

Despite personal antagonism between the two men, the Congressional investigation in February and March, 1792, proceeded smoothly in an atmosphere of "great honor."[40] However, the issue quickly became translated into partisan terms. From the first, even the staunchest supporters of the administration wisely refused to believe that Wayne had a case or could retain his seat.[41] The question was whether to give it to Jackson—an avowed follower of Madison. On March 16, Smith of South Carolina, acting for the Hamilton forces, introduced a simple resolution stating that "Anthony Wayne was not duly elected a member of this House." Three days later he inexplicably withdrew this motion, in favor of one by the Republican Representative Giles of Virginia which explicitly stated Jackson's right to Wayne's seat. After two days of debate the House deadlocked on this motion, and the Speaker broke it by voting against the resolution. Wayne lost his seat, but Jackson did not obtain it. The vote proved to be another indication of increasing party division in Congress. Of the twenty-nine voting in favor of the Giles motion, only three were later found on the list of Federalist-oriented "paper men" in Congress drawn up in March of 1793 for Jefferson's information by Madison's political lieu-

[39] Wayne to McAllister, from Philadelphia, September 7, 1791, Wayne Papers.
[40] *State Gazette of North Carolina,* March 30, 1792.
[41] William Loughton Smith to Edward Rutledge, from Philadelphia, March 24, 1792, Smith-Rutledge Correspondence.

tenant, Clerk of the House John Beckley. Of the twenty-nine voting in favor of denying Wayne's seat to Jackson by declaring it vacant, twelve—including Smith—were subsequently found on Beckley's list.[42]

Prior to Jay's Treaty the Wayne-Jackson election was the most important popular test in the South of emerging partisan strength on both sides. The administration hosts had not merely been defeated; they had been disgraced. Yet the friends of government in Georgia, undismayed, continued to battle their political opponents, as relations between the state and the federal government steadily worsened in 1793–1794. Wayne never returned to Georgia, but leadership was transferred to his friend, United States Senator James Gunn, who also took over the presidency of the Georgia Chapter of the Cincinnati Society and fought Jackson and his forces in the state legislature from 1792 onward, boasting at one point of "bursting" an unspecified "premeditated blow" aimed by Jackson.[43] The *Georgia Gazette* opened its pages to a spirited war of essays between the administration spokesman "Casca" and the Republican "Correspondent" dealing with the relative rights and responsibilities of the state and national governments to regulate affairs on the Georgia frontier, in the wake of recent Indian uprisings, white reprisals and provocations, and illegal filibustering expeditions into the interior.[44] In Decem-

[42] The entire debate and the vote were reprinted in the *Georgia Gazette*, April 26, 1792. The reasons for Smith's lapse of partisanship at one point during the course of the affair in the House is inexplicable from surviving documents, but his general determination to oppose the seating of Jackson is clear.

[43] James Jackson to John Milledge, from Augusta, November 7, 1792, Salley, ed., *John Milledge*, 25; James Gunn to Anthony Wayne, from Philadelphia, January 3, 1793, Wayne Papers, Historical Society of Pennsylvania, Philadelphia; *Georgia Gazette*, July 12, 1792.

[44] The "Casca" letters are in the issues of July 25, 1793ff. "Correspondent's" reply is in that of October 10, 1793.

ber, 1793, Gunn went one step further and opposed both George Matthews and Telfair for the governorship, but Gunn became ill before the vote was taken and was forced to withdraw. The following month Nathaniel Pendleton chaired a meeting in Savannah that expressed approbation for Washington's neutrality policy. In the autumn of 1794, Telfair and Gunn again prepared to oppose each other, this time in a contest for Gunn's seat in the United States Senate.[45] Before this election took place, however, an event of far greater consequence for the future of party politics in Georgia intervened.

The social bases of Federalist leadership in Virginia during the early 1790's were unique and reflected subtle but unmistakable changes within the governing structure of the state. For decades, as in South Carolina, political power and polite society in Virginia had been concentrated in a single section and within a single class. The large and gracious plantations which dotted the tidewater and northern neck areas of the state were the centers of a tightly woven network of political control by great families, while the vast stretch of land to the south and southwest of the James River, which belonged to the yeoman farmer prior to the nineteenth century, remained politically subordinate—and in 1788 was strongly Antifederal.[46]

By 1785, however, few of the influential members of Virginia political society were recruited from the ranks of the great planter establishment. Berkeleys, Carters, Fairfaxes, Fitzhughs—and even most of the Lees, Randolphs, and Washingtons—no longer provided the leadership in the

[45] Thomas Carnes to Seaborn Jones, from Philadelphia, January 20, 1794, Seaborn Jones Papers, Duke University Library, Durham, N. C.; *Georgia Gazette*, January 16, 1794; John Wereat to Edward Telfair, from Hardwick, Burke County, August 25, 1794, Telfair Papers.

[46] Carrington to Madison, from Richmond, April 8, 1788, Madison Papers, Vol. 9.

public life of Virginia.⁴⁷ This role had been assumed by men from somewhat lower ranks in society, and the change was to have momentous consequences for the subsequent political history of Virginia and the nation.

Eight individuals shaped the course of Virginia politics during the final decade and a half of the eighteenth century: Thomas Jefferson, James Madison, James Monroe, William Branch Giles, Wilson Cary Nicholas, Patrick Henry, Edmund Randolph, and John Marshall. These were the men who mustered support both for and against a liberalization of the state constitution in 1785, who provided the leadership for both Federalist and Antifederalist interests in 1788, and who subsequently organized and led the Federalist and Republican interests of the 1790's.

The first four formed the hard core of the Republican party leadership in the state. All had remarkably similar backgrounds, having been born into the lower-gentry class.⁴⁸ Monroe's father was a carpenter. Peter Jefferson, the elder James Madison, and William Giles all were members of the small-planter class and thus were involved intimately in the

⁴⁷ Washington never served his state in a public capacity after 1775, except at the Philadelphia Convention. His aversion to any further public service in the 1780's was well known to all and became the despair of his friends on the eve of the Constitutional Convention. See, for example, Henry Lee to Washington, November 11, 1786; Edmund Randolph to Washington, March 11, 1787; David Humphreys to Washington, April 9, 1787, in Washington Papers, Vols. 236, 238; Washington to Madison, December 16, 1786, to Randolph, December 21, 1786, in John C. Fitzpatrick, ed., *The Writings of George Washington* (39 vols.; Washington, D. C.: U. S. Government Printing Office, 1931–1944), XXIX, 115, 120.

⁴⁸ Dice Robins Anderson, *William Branch Giles: A Study in the Politics of Virginia and the Nation from 1790 to 1830* (Menasha, Wisconsin: George Banta Publishing Co., 1914), 1–9; Irving Brant, *James Madison the Virginia Revolutionary* (Indianapolis: The Bobbs-Merrill Company, 1941), 29–104 *passim;* William P. Cresson, *James Monroe* (Chapel Hill: University of North Carolina Press, 1946), 6–8; Dumas Malone, *Jefferson the Virginian* (Boston: Little, Brown and Company, 1948), 1–74; Nathan Schachner, *Thomas Jefferson: A Biography* (New York: Thomas Yoseloff, 1951), 1–31 *passim.*

cliques which consistently dominated county government. One other point is of crucial importance. All four men—and their sons after them—steadily climbed toward the top of the economic and social structure of Virginia. All increased their wealth markedly in land and slaves—and thus their social status—during their lifetimes, yet none of them ever were great planters in the traditional sense.

Thus, Jefferson and his later political allies emerged from a common social background that for its time and place might be called middle class—a background of achieved rather than ascribed status. Moreover, all four received a college education in Virginia or New Jersey or both places and chose the law rather than speculation in land, crops, and slaves as the surest means of attaining rapid social and political prominence. Not one of the four seems to have been burdened with either the elitist values of the great planters or the instinctive deferential spirit of the commonalty, both so fatal to political flexibility.

Two of the other statesmen, Nicholas and Henry, exhibited extreme equivocation with respect to emerging partisan alignments during the early 1790's. Nicholas eventually settled down as a Republican, and Henry ultimately became a Federalist. Marshall was a staunch supporter of the administration as early as 1793, and Edmund Randolph also aided the friends of government until his disgrace in the Fauchet affair in 1795. Randolph had grown up in the security of Tazewell Hall, where signs of wealth and power in the forms of land, slaves, gentlemanly living, and political responsibility had always been present. Marshall, on the other hand, despite the eventual wealth which both he and his father attained, had grown up in the atmosphere of the frontier log cabin; and knowledge of the law—a sure path to social and economic advancement—had come from fitful and often hasty individual study rather than from leisurely lectures to aspiring gentleman legalists in the halls of William and Mary or Hampden-Sydney.[49] Yet the young lawyer who worked himself up to eminence through natural ability and the member of an old and entrenched great planter family found that they shared common political interests in a mutual dedication to the cause of union and later in a partisan allegiance to the federal administration.

During the early 1790's Randolph and Henry Lee supplied the Federalist faction in Virginia with support from the declining great-planter class. John Marshall, Edward Carrington, William Heth—and Daniel Morgan and Patrick Henry somewhat later—brought the friends of government support from the rising and ambitious lower gentry element in the state. The varied social and political configuration of Federalist leadership in the Old Dominion by 1793 thus contrasted with the uniform background of the Republican leadership and implied an inevitable clash of values between members of the two factions.

Certainly, the great planter representatives had never attempted to hide their elitist beliefs. During the Revolution, Lee had played the role of the cavalier aristocrat at the head of his light cavalry squadron with dash and pomposity. Randolph had warned of the perils of democracy in the most melancholy tones while introducing the Virginia plan at Philadelphia in 1787.[50]

[49] Albert J. Beveridge, *Life of John Marshall* (4 vols.; Boston and New York: Houghton, Mifflin Company, 1916-1919), I, 1-199 *passim*. M. D. Conway's biography of Edmund Randolph, *Omitted Chapters of History Disclosed in the Life and Papers of Edmund Randolph* (New York: G. P. Putnam's Sons, 1888), is excessively partisan and simplistic. Randolph needs another and more sophisticated biographer. In the meantime I have relied primarily on the sketch in the *Dictionary of American Biography*.

[50] The biographer of the Lee family recounts that Henry Lee "delighted" in a uniform comprised of "a tall leather helmet, with horse hair plume streaming in the wind, green jacket, white lambskin breeches" and "shining boots reaching to the knees." Burton K. Hendrick, *The Lees of Virginia* (Boston: Little, Brown and Company, 1935), 336. Edmund Randolph

But for the most part the lower-gentry group among Federalist leaders in Virginia refused to contest the values of the planters. Indeed, awe of this slowly declining group, so absent among the Republicans, was still strong among the Treasury agents and influential war veterans within Virginia's Federalist ranks.[51] These men openly copied the great planters' style of living and their elitist ideals.[52] Not

---

summed up the sentiments of his class when he introduced the Virginia plan at the Philadelphia Convention. "Our chief danger," he asserted, "arises from the democratic parts of our constitutions. It is a maxim which I hold incontrovertible, that the powers of government exercised by the people swallows [sic] up the other branches. None of the [state] constitutions have provided sufficient checks against the democracy. The feeble Senate of Virginia is a phantom. Maryland has a more powerful senate, but the late distractions in that State have discovered that it is not powerful enough. The checks established in the constitution of New York and Massachusetts is [sic] yet a stronger barrier against democracy, but they all seem insufficient." Max Farrand, ed., *Records of the Federal Convention of 1787* (3 vols.; New Haven: Yale University Press, 1911), I, 26–27.

[51] Heth's deference when in the presence of men of power has already been noted. Appreciation for the favor and attention of the great planter ran deep in the Marshall family. "Thomas Marshall, the father of John Marshall, was a close friend of Washington, whom he ardently admired. They were born in the same county, and their acquaintance had begun, apparently, in their boyhood. Also . . . Thomas Marshall had for about three years been the companion of Washington, when acting as his assistant in surveying the western part of the Fairfax estate. From that time on his attachment to Washington amounted to devotion." Beveridge, *Marshall*, I, 7. Daniel Morgan, another Virginia Federalist who rose to prominence solely through his own talents, let his attachment to Washington largely shape his political commitment. Don Higginbotham, *Daniel Morgan, Revolutionary Rifleman* (Chapel Hill: University of North Carolina Press, 1961), 2–172 *passim*.

[52] Higginbotham notes the somewhat pathetic attempts of Daniel Morgan to remake himself from a "backwoods pugilist" into the image of the "military hero" he had become. *Ibid.*, 172–85, especially 172–73. Carrington's adherence to elitist ideals emerged in the wake of Shay's Rebellion. "It certainly originated," he said of the insurrection, "in the genuine baseness of the people. . . Man is impatient of restraint, nor will he conform to what is necessary to the good order of society unless he is possessed of discernment and virtue, or the Government under which he lives is efficient." Quoted in David Hackett Fischer, *The Revolution of American Conservatism; The Federalist Party in the Era of Jeffersonian Democracy* (New York: Harper & Row, 1965), 373.

even John Marshall, whose personal manners apparently were those of a democrat, was entirely free from the influence of the exclusivist political tradition. This most valuable friend of government, who had reached the top of Richmond's legal profession by 1795 at the latest,[53] reminded the Virginia ratifying convention in 1788 that the new government was "drawn from the people." But such government, he added, was to be administered by the better sort, who in America were always and should always be the ablest and most vigorous defenders of popular freedom. "The virtue and talents of the members of the general government," he assured the wavering, "will tend to the security instead of the destruction of our liberties."[54]

Thus, the formation of a proadministration interest in Virginia followed similar patterns in South Carolina and Georgia. Prominent and influential public figures strongly inclined toward the ideal of elitist governance were charged with winning public approval during times when government policy was under attack.

Friends of government in Virginia faced an early test of their political flexibility and effectiveness. In April, 1793, Genêt's appearance and Washington's Neutrality Proclamation pertaining to the recently renewed Anglo-French war divided the state as never before between the Jeffersonian friends of France and those who actively supported noninvolvement in foreign affairs. In recent years many friends of government in Virginia had attributed the developing opposition to national policy in and out of Congress to the pernicious but inevitable effects of "factionalism" and

[53] While staying at Richmond in 1795, La Rochefoucauld-Liancourt was informed that Marshall was the acknowledged leader of the Richmond bar. *Travels Through the United States,* II, 38.

[54] Jonathan Elliot, *The Debates in the Several State Conventions on the Adoption of the Federal Constitution* (5 vols.; Philadelphia: J. B. Lippincott & Co., 1941), III, 236, 420.

"wicked anarchy," and they now welcomed an opportunity to counterattack.[55]

Members of the Richmond faction committed an initial error which was to plague them many times in future years: the assumption that their own hopes and anxieties reflected public opinion. Several days before the Proclamation was issued, Carrington assured Hamilton that most Virginians desired only peace. Their attitudes were tinged strongly with Francophilism. They regarded the Treaty of 1778 as binding, Carrington admitted; but the recent execution of Louis XVI was viewed with revulsion, and many persons were decidedly in favor of perfect neutrality, if a suitable "option" in conduct was available. Even in mid-June, six weeks after the publication of the Proclamation, Henry Lee insisted that the unmistakable evidence of a surge of public reaction against the official neutrality policy was merely the work of "a set of clamorous desperadoes."[56]

Nonetheless, the members of the Federalist faction did not delay action, however much they may have deluded themselves over the real state of public opinion in Virginia. Hamilton, Jay, King, Higginson, and other leading Federalists already had begun to organize anti-Genêt meetings throughout the northern and middle states.[57] In early June Governor Henry Lee issued a public proclamation calling for support of neutrality policy, while Heth and Carrington attempted to rally popular opinion to their side through *ad hoc* county and town meetings.[58] The first was held in Richmond on August 17 with the venerable George Wythe as chairman. Marshall drafted a set of resolutions supporting

[55] Higginbotham, *Daniel Morgan*, 187.
[56] Carrington to Hamilton, from Richmond, April 26, 1793; Lee to Hamilton, from Richmond, June 15, 1793, Hamilton Papers, Vol. 19.
[57] Harry Ammon, "The Genêt Mission and the Development of American Political Parties," *Journal of American History*, LII (March, 1966), 729–30.
[58] *Virginia Gazette and General Advertiser*, June 5, 1793; Diary of William Heth, entry of June 19, 1793.

Washington's policy, and they were accepted without dissent by a large gathering. The Republicans were mortified, and Madison wrote acridly that the proceedings were no doubt dictated "by the cabal at Philadelphia," and then stressed the need for countermeetings to discover "the real sense of the people."[59]

As autumn touched the woods and gently rolling hills of Virginia, the public was aroused to an excitement unrivaled since the reception of Hamilton's fiscal plan nearly four years before. The two sides organized meetings throughout the state and collected resolutions, on the one hand praising Washington and his policy without exception and on the other hand rejecting any action which might impair the close ties existing between the world's only republics. In the battle of resolutions and meetings the friends of government seem to have won, though doubtless the decisions of many county meetings have been lost. Washington could count on support not only in Richmond, but also in the commercial towns of Williamsburg, Norfolk, Fredericksburg, and Petersburg, and in the counties of York, Fairfax, Frederick, and Fauquier. The Republicans organized successful meetings in Caroline, Shenandoah, Albemarle, and Culpeper counties.[60] Jefferson and Madison apparently

[59] *Virginia Herald and Fredericksburg Advertiser,* August 29, 1793; Madison to Jefferson, from Albemarle County, August 27, 1793, Madison Papers, Vol. 16.

[60] Robert Taylor to Washington, from Norfolk, August 31, 1793, Washington Papers, Vol. 262; Madison to Monroe, from Charlottesville, October 29, 1793, Madison Papers, Vol. 16. In his letter Madison indicated the extent to which the Richmond Federalists had activated and guided their allies in the various counties when he observed that the resolutions from Fauquier County were but a "servile echo of those in Richmond." See also *Virginia Herald and Fredericksburg Advertiser,* September 26, 1793; *Virginia Gazette and General Advertiser,* October 17, 23, 1793; Washington to Thomas G. Peach, to Ludwell Lee and R. West, October 24, 1793, to Nicholas Lewis, November 16, 1793, to Alexander White, November 23, 1793, to William A. Booth, December 18, 1793, in Fitzpatrick, ed., *Washington,* XXXIII, 101, 136–37, 153, 155, 195.

continued to cleave to the view expressed by Madison three years before that the "town interest" counted for little in the politics of the state.

The Richmond Federalists did an exceptional job in rousing favorable public opinion in a supposedly inhospitable environment. By mid-September, however, the strain was already beginning to tell, as individual members could not be everywhere at once, nor could they be sure of the stamina of their supporters. At Staunton, for example, the organizer of the administration forces, "Gl. Jones," had received letters from Marshall in Richmond urging him to organize a meeting immediately and to draft a suitable address. Unfortunately, James Monroe galloped into town soon after with a readymade address by Madison in hand and was able to "effectually change the current and give it a direction against the anti-Republican faction."[61] As winter approached it became apparent that neither side could claim a clear victory in the war of meetings and addresses.

Whatever efforts may have been made to mobilize a portion of public opinion in North Carolina on behalf of the government in the years preceding the Jay Treaty were frustrated by two factors. The first was the rapid depletion in the number of influential politicians willing to defend the national administration and its policies. The second was the disintegration once again of the structure of North Carolina politics into a welter of local and sectional conflicts with the passing of the ephemeral Federalist and Antifederalist parties of 1788 and 1789.

As late as the Congressional elections in the spring of 1791, it appeared that North Carolina's politics might retain some degree of polarity. Friends of Samuel Johnston, then believed by the public to be a tool of the national govern-

[61] Monroe to Madison, from Albemarle, September 25, 1793, Madison Papers, Vol. 16.

ment, battled outspoken opponents of Hamilton's fiscal policies for Assembly seats.[62] However, the rout of those candidates backed by Johnston signified the rapid crystallization of an anti-Hamilton consensus within the state. At about the same time several leading Federalists of the late 1780's, including Johnston himself, James Iredell, William R. Davie, and, most important of all, Archibald Maclaine, were removed from the scene by death, retirement, or appointment to high nonelective posts in the federal government.[63]

As a result of these events, North Carolina politicians once again returned to the unresolved issues that continued to pit section against section and, within the eastern interest, town against town. Thomas Blount, in a series of letters during the legislative session of 1790–1791, defined the state of North Carolina politics with clarity. The "Eastern interest," he told his brother, was "more than ever divided at a time when union was more than ever necessary." At the heart of the strife was the bitter annual struggle between the various commercial towns to obtain the legislative session for the coming year, since North Carolinians could not agree upon a permanent capital site. This struggle had hindered or enhanced political careers in the state at least since 1788.[64] Even Thomas Blount was involved in this bickering, and he predicted an early

[62] Anonymous to anonymous, from Washington County, January 22, 1791, Simpson-Bryan Papers, Southern Historical Collection, University of North Carolina, Chapel Hill, N. C. Anti-Hamilton candidates also campaigned actively for seats in the legislature during the summer of 1790. J. G. Rencher to Richard Bennehan, from Orange County, July 23, 1790, Cameron Family Papers, Southern Historical Collection, University of North Carolina, Chapel Hill, N. C.

[63] William R. Davie to Iredell, from Halifax, June 20, 1790, Iredell Papers; Iredell to Jonathan Hay, from Philadelphia, April 14, 1791; Samuel Johnston to Iredell, from New York, February 25, 1790, from Williamstown, May 9, 1793, in McRee, ed., *Iredell*, II, 281, 326, 385.

[64] Archibald Maclaine to Iredell, from Wilmington, January 15, 1788, in McRee, ed., *Iredell*, 216.

vote on this issue in one of his letters, adding that "the damned New Bernians will fix it here [Fayetteville] by their usual obstinacy." When New Bern's attempt to do that subsequently failed, Blount reported with obvious relief: "today we started Tarb[or]o (being our best nag)."

Blount was not blind to the bitter fruits of his folly and that of his colleagues within the eastern faction. "It is now plainly seen," he wrote,

that the Western members always tricked us, & could we devise ways to keep our members together we should be the strongest party on all questions; but unhappily for us that is not possible[.] they [sic] are now breaking ground daily & as soon as [the eastern] ranks are a little more thinned our Enemies will have a decided Majority & avail themselves of the opportunity of dividing 4 or 5 Counties by which means they will acquire the power of keeping us under forever.[65]

The election of a United States Senator by the state legislature in December, 1792, revealed the extent to which local and sectional influences dominated North Carolina politics in these years. No less than four candidates appeared, one of whom, John Steele, from his voting record in Congress and his patronage contacts with the administration, could be considered a moderate friend of government. All four candidates represented distinct sectional or local interests. According to William R. Davie, who confined his mild proadministration feeling to the management of Steele's interests, five ballots and much logrolling were required before Alexander Martin, who had identified himself publicly with the rising anti-Hamiltonian sentiment, was elected. Steele's election was blocked, Davie claimed, for two reasons. In the first place, Martin's supporters threat-

[65] Thomas to John Gray Blount, from Fayetteville, November 18, 27, 1790, in Alice Barnwell Keith, ed., *The John Gray Blount Papers* (2 vols.; Raleigh: State Department of Archives and History, 1952), II, 143, 146.

ened the upper Cape Fear area with perpetual opposition to Fayetteville's persistent campaign to secure the permanent capital unless that region fell into proper line politically. Secondly, a whispering campaign charging Steele with having strong bias toward Hamilton and aristocratic leanings was begun by Montfort Stokes, a delegate from Wilkes County and a front man for the determined Martin interest.[66] Thus Steele, whose Federalist proclivities were becoming increasingly apparent, was defeated by a combination of those forces—political provincialism and suspicion of the federal administration—most inimical to the creation of an effective statewide organization by the friends of government. Pro-Federalist fortunes in North Carolina seemed bleak by the end of Washington's first term.

By the end of 1793, North Carolina notwithstanding, friends of government were well established in loosely organized but easily recognizable political interest groups with some influence in three of the four southern states. The membership of these interest groups was, almost without exception, raised from the ruling classes in the region—the great land speculators of Georgia and Virginia, the wealthy planters, and the merchants and lawyers in the small cities of Virginia and South Carolina, in addition to some influential newspaper editors in Georgia, North Carolina, and Virginia.[67] The measurable public support they

[66] Davie to Steele, from Halifax, December 16, 1792, in Kemp P. Battle, ed., "Letters of William R. Davie," *James Sprunt Historical Monograph*, No. 7 (Chapel Hill: North Carolina Historical Society Publications, 1907), 24-27.

[67] Abraham Hodge, editor of the *State Gazette of North Carolina*, the state's leading paper, had been closely aligned with the Davie-Iredell-Maclaine faction since the late 1780's. Davie to Iredell, from Halifax, December 19, 1788, Iredell Papers. Throughout the early 1790's, Hodge remained a strong Federalist, as the issues of January 16, February 13, 20, September 24, 1790, March 11, 25, April 8, 1791, indicate, and also had some patronage dealings with Iredell at this time. See Hodge to Iredell, from Edenton, December 1, 1791, in McRee, ed., *Iredell*, II, 336. After the

were able to attract was meager, but in Virginia in 1793 the friends of government were able to organize large public meetings in several plantation counties near routes of trade and communication as well as in the commercial towns.

Despite their strong elitist political orientation, many friends of government in the South nonetheless energetically attempted to become a powerful influence in their respective states on behalf of the national government. As a result, they must be credited with three significant achievements as early as 1794. First, they helped to break down the political provincialism of the southern electorate, simply by relating their activities to issues of national importance. Created and sustained by the national executive department in the distant capital, Federalist groups in the South never abandoned their orientation toward national politics; and their contacts with the electorate inevitably centered around an implicit or explicit search for a mandate for existing national policy. Second, friends of government in Georgia, to some extent, and in Virginia, to a marked degree, began the process of energizing the political grassroots. In their partisan campaigns, they helped to focus popular attention upon national policy and to win a portion of the electorate to their specific goals. These two achievements are necessary prerequisites to the development of a democratic tradition and temperament within any nation, old or new.

By their efforts to reverse the tide of unfavorable public

---

spring of 1791 Hodge softened his Federalism for a time, doubtless in deference to the strong anti-Hamilton feeling among his readers; but in the later 1790's his defense of the Federalist party and its national policy again became pronounced. Valentine Davis' *Virginia Gazette and General Advertiser* at Richmond revealed a strong Federalist bias in the wake of the neutrality campaign of 1793. By the time of the Adams administration, the *Gazette* had become a strong party organ. See issues of October 9–30, November 27, 1793, and also "Old Virginia Editors," *William and Mary Quarterly*, Series 1, VII (1899), 16.

opinion in the South and to gain political power, Federalists in Virginia and Georgia also hastened the development of another crucial factor underlying sustained popular interest in politics—the formation of counterforces and the beginning of a partial polarization of state and local politics around national issues. In neither state prior to the beginning of formal political activity by friends of government had the rising opposition to the policies of the national government been expressed by an organized faction. After 1791 in Georgia and 1793 in Virginia the lines between friends and opponents of the national government were quite firmly drawn.[68]

For all their partisan activity the Federalists continued to denounce the "violent and disgusting party business which now prevails," a fact which has led even the most recent students of Federalism to conclude that its members were incapable of significant, cohesive organization prior to 1800. But with the Federalists, as with many men and organizations before and since, what was said did not always reflect what was done.[69]

The achievements of southern Federalists by 1794 represented only a modest beginning toward the building of a

[68] The development of the Republican party in Virginia in the early 1790's is traced in Harry Ammon, "The Formation of the Republican Party in Virginia," *Journal of Southern History*, XIX (August, 1953), 283–310.

[69] *Virginia Gazette and General Advertiser*, October 9, 1793. Fischer strongly intimates that George Cabot's unwillingness to admit a "legitimate role for a political party" was a belief widely shared among friends of government of the old school both above and below the Potomac. Fischer stresses that Cabot and other Federalists of the old school "recognized no legitimate role for a political party. Extra-constitutional machinery, mass meetings of the people, semi-permanent committees of correspondence smacked of subversion and the spirit of faction." Fischer, *Revolution of American Conservatism*, 5. Yet the organization of mass meetings, the establishment of semi-permanent committees of correspondence, and the creation of small but cohesive factions were precisely what the Federalists successfully set out to accomplish in several southern states between 1790 and 1793.

modern party force. Acting on the initiative of administration leaders in Philadelphia, self-conscious friends of government below the Potomac had erected informal, skeletal partisan structures and had become public defenders of administration policies at the grassroots. At the same time, however, no systematic attempts were made to build up consistent mass followings in the South, nor was any attempt made to give to the people a sense of participation in the political decision-making process. Federalist partisans employed techniques of mass appeal only when administration policies were in imminent danger of public repudiation, and even then the people were asked to ratify policies which they had no part in formulating. Moreover, these partisan appeals constituted the only form of communication between Federalist policymakers at Philadelphia and their allies in the South, on the one hand, and the southern people, on the other. Indeed, the very weakness of formal institutional structures among friends of government in the South in the early 1790's attests to the fact that the Federalist partisans were meant to serve exclusively as agents of administration propaganda, rather than as conductors of a dialogue between rulers and ruled, out of which might come a government oriented toward reflecting the will of the majority.

Because of their hesitancy in attempting to capture the emotional loyalties of the electorate, southern Federalists in the early 1790's failed to develop any of the other elements of true party organization. They did not achieve any significant range, density, or stability of popular support. They did not develop any consistent perspectives and ideologies to stir the southern voting public into a spirited defense of their policies. And they did not perform many of the critical functions of the modern party organizer and leader, conspicuously refusing to undertake any broad nominating and electioneering activity.⁷⁰ Except during the Wayne-Jackson campaign in Georgia in 1791 and the election for United States Senator involving John Steele in North Carolina the following year, a reading of contemporary correspondence and the press indicates that only one other southern election between 1791 and 1794 was tinged with the partisanship of the emerging Federalist-Republican struggle. This election, which occurred in North Carolina in 1791, involved Timothy Bloodworth, an ex-Antifederalist and currently an ally of James Madison in the House, and William Barry Grove, who was in the process of moving to a staunch proadministration position; Grove defeated Bloodworth by nearly a two to one margin.⁷¹ Even in these three elections there was no hint of party organization behind any of the candidates. The idea of mounting sustained and coordinated partisan campaigns for national offices, backed by suitable organization and propaganda, still lay well beyond the ken of southern Federalists and their opponents at the beginning of 1794.

Events in the succeeding two years, moreover, underscored how fragile and apparently ephemeral were the achievements of southern Federalists in the area of partisan organization, as the elitist temperament, with its fatal proclivity for independent political action, reemerged at a time of developing crisis in both domestic and foreign affairs. Not until 1797, when the sudden worsening of relations between France and the United States presented them with a favorable issue and an impetus to act, did southern Federalists resume their slow and never fully completed march toward party status.

[70] A sophisticated discussion of party as opposed to factional organization and activity is in William Nisbet Chambers, *Political Parties in a New Nation: The American Experience, 1776–1809* (New York: Oxford University Press, 1963), 45–48.

[71] *Fayetteville Gazette and North Carolina Chronicle*, December 13, 1790–February 7, 1791.

III. Crises and Collapse, 1795-1796

In the years 1795 and 1796 southern Federalists faced their first set of profound challenges, and they failed to resolve or to overcome any of them. The attempted purchase of the Yazoo lands in Georgia permanently linked the Federalist interest in that state with wholesale political corruption. The mass reaction against Jay's Treaty, which swept the South, carried with it Federalists as well as Republicans, especially in South Carolina, and divided the friends of government from their northern colleagues and from each other, gravely weakening their influence and effectiveness for many months. Soon after that crisis came the election of 1796, which further exacerbated the deeply rooted but previously suppressed sectional antagonisms existing within the national Federalist interest.

The Yazoo scandals in Georgia occurred within the context of incessant conflict between the state and the national government over the ultimate responsibility for the control of the vast southwestern lands and the pacification or extinction of the Creek nation, which stretched like a barrier across the western frontier of the state. From 1790 to 1793, despite the vigorous protests of the people of Georgia against it, the Treaty of New York had brought peace of a sort to the southwestern frontier. This was largely a result of the honest efforts of Alexander McGillivray, the half-breed Indian chief, to restrain the more warlike Creeks while resisting equally strong pressure from the Spanish governor at New Orleans to resume hostilities against the Americans. But in the spring of 1793 McGillivray died, and the southwest once again was plunged into crisis.

General Andrew Pickens of South Carolina, an old Indian fighter, predicted renewed hostilities between Georgia and the Creeks. "The death of Mr. McGillivray," he wrote, "is a very unfavorable event, as he constantly used his influence to maintain peace, but Galphia, his successor, is hostilely disposed." The following week, Creeks and whites clashed at a plantation in Liberty County.[1]

Georgians quickly seized the opportunity to resolve the Creek issue finally in their own way. As soon as he had been informed of McGillivray's death, Governor Telfair acted upon his own initiative. In a General Order dated April 6 to Generals Twiggs and Clark of the second and third divisions of the Georgia militia, the Governor ordered into immediate service all necessary personnel in the event of an "invasion" by the "savages."[2] Telfair then informed the President of what he had done. In a cabinet meeting of May 29 federal officials decided to allow Georgia to raise two hundred militia purely for defense,[3] while throughout the following summer Washington pondered the wisdom of sending an expedition under Pickens to subdue the refractory part of the Creek nation. Congress, however, refused to support the President, and the initiative passed to Georgia.

Having been given some power, Telfair and his allies proceeded to take much more. By late October, "A Querist" could publicly demand: "Who consulted the General Officers of this state, to have their opinion whether the instructions of the President of the United States [of May 29] authorized

[1] *Georgia Gazette,* May 9, 16, 1793.
[2] *Ibid.,* October 31, 1793.
[3] Memo, Washington Papers, Vol. 260.

an offensive war against the Creek Nation, and finding they did not think so, did nevertheless determine to raise 5,000 men, that he might exhibit his awkward figure as a General at the head of them?"⁴ "Querist" was not referring to Telfair when he spoke of an "awkward figure" at the head of the state militia, but to James Jackson, who in March had been placed in charge of the militia and who shared the Governor's eagerness to be rid of the Indian problem once and for all.⁵ In July, some of Jackson's militia had killed several Creeks who were bringing to the state officials messages indicating willingness on the part of the Creek nation to make restitution for prior depredations and, in general, to seek peace.⁶ This misfortune could not be attributed directly either to the Governor or to the general, yet that both actively wanted war with the Indians is quite obvious from Telfair's orders and from Jackson's many letters.

Telfair's decision to use McGillivray's death and the resultant fears of a Creek invasion as the pretext for an armed attack upon the Indians had immediate and widespread repercussions. Certainly Georgia's relations with the federal government worsened perceptibly. By January, 1794, Secretary of War Knox forwarded to Washington "with great pain" the first official letters "giving an account of an infamous violation of the peace with the Creeks by some of the violent frontier people of Georgia."⁷ On the next day

⁴ *Georgia Gazette*, October 31, 1793.
⁵ Jackson to Telfair, March 18, 31, 1793, in Lilla M. Hawes, ed., "Letter Book of James Jackson, 1788–1796," *Georgia Historical Quarterly*, XXXVII (March–December, 1953), 222–23, 225–26.
⁶ Jackson to anonymous (probably Brigadier General Morrison), from Savannah, July 21, 1793, *ibid.*, 305; Washington to Governor William Moultrie, August 28, 1793, in John C. Fitzpatrick, ed., *The Writings of George Washington*, (39 vols.; Washington, D. C.: U. S. Government Printing Office, 1931–1944), XXXIII, 73–74.
⁷ Memo, Knox to Washington, January 27, 1794, Washington Papers, Vol. 265.

Knox and the other cabinet members recommended that all relevant papers and letters from Georgia be laid before Congress together with a presidential message "stating the importance of Congress taking into their immediate consideration the measures requisite to prevent a repetition of and to provide adequate punishment for, such atrocious actions."[8] Washington did as suggested,[9] but Congress, absorbed with Madison's proposed discrimination law against British commerce, did nothing.

The situation soon worsened. Telfair had been replaced by George Matthews, who had promptly upheld the calling out of the state troops. Clashes on the frontier between the Creeks and the Georgians became a daily occurrence from the late autumn of 1793 onward, and the cabinet was divided over the proper course of action. Hamilton recommended that the federal government grant no further supplies to the state militia, while Knox merely urged that the President direct Matthews to reduce Georgia's forces to the number agreed upon in the instruction of the previous May 29.[10] Washington hesitated for ten long weeks. He then issued an order substantially incorporating Knox's recommendations, but it was too late. Even as Washington was signing the order, Agent James Seagrove returned to the Indian country determined to achieve peace. A meeting was arranged, but while Seagrove and the chiefs were in conversation, one hundred and fifty Georgia militiamen swept down on the camp and scattered the Indians.[11]

The persistent conflict between Georgia and the national

[8] Memo, Knox to Washington, January 28, 1794, *ibid.*
[9] "Message to the Senate and House of Representatives," January 30, 1794, in Fitzpatrick, ed., *Washington*, XXXIII, 258–59.
[10] *Georgia Gazette*, October 1–31, November 7, 14, 1793; Hamilton to Washington, with enclosure, February 12, 1794; Knox to Washington, February 19, 1794, Washington Papers, Vol. 265.
[11] Washington to Knox, May 3, 1794, *ibid.*, Vol. 266; *Virginia Herald and Fredericksburg Advertiser*, June 12, 1794.

government over Indian relations was complicated further in the spring of 1794 by the activities of General Elijah Clark, who mounted a filibustering expedition against Spanish and Indian territories on the Georgia frontier. The United States and Spain were at peace at this time, and this made Clark's activities doubly embarrassing. Knox immediately wrote to Matthews, ordering him to resist Clark, but Matthews refused to move.[12] By early June the dual crises caused by Clark's filibuster and the Georgia militia's activities against the Creeks threatened to plunge the United States into a full-scale war with the Indians and the Spaniards, and reports from Georgia invariably were grim.[13]

Washington once again asked his cabinet for advice after cease-and-desist orders were issued to Clark. The cabinet agreed on the need to stop Clark, but it was divided over the best means of doing so, should he persist. Disagreement was especially strong concerning the role Georgia should be allowed to play in the affair.[14] Then in August the administration's immediate attention shifted to the Whiskey Rebellion in western Pennsylvania. In the meantime, Seagrove's persistent attempts to recontact the Creeks had met with some success; and he told Jackson that prior incidents, coupled with the proposed establishment of several frontier posts in apparent Creek territory, were driving the Creeks toward outright war. Jackson wrote to the commander of the posts in question ordering him into inactivity for a time. A month later, while United States dragoons were fighting those Creeks who had broken the Treaty, Clark surrendered to the judges of the Indian court in Washington County. He

[12] Washington, Message to Congress, May 20, 21, 1794, in Fitzpatrick, ed., *Washington*, XXXIII, 373–74; Knox to Matthews, May 14, 1794, Seagrove to Knox, from Savannah, June 4, 1794, Washington Papers, Vol. 267.
[13] Knox to Washington, June 1, 1794, *ibid.*
[14] Memos of Alexander Hamilton, July 13, 1794, Henry Knox, July 14, 1794, and Edmund Randolph, n.d., *ibid.*, Vol. 268.

was tried immediately for breaking the treaty laws of the United States, but the local jury acquitted him.[15]

Despite some successes by the dragoons, Clark's folly led to a perpetual skirmishing on the frontier during the fall of 1794.[16] In November, with the whiskey rebels finally crushed, the administration again turned its attention to the South and endorsed Seagrove's efforts for one final attempt at peace.[17] Before such an attempt could be undertaken, however, the entire situation was altered by news of the Yazoo sale, which simplified the frontier situation for a time, even as it brought overt party conflict into sharp focus within the state.

The Yazoo purchase in December, 1794, and the subsequent exposure of fraud culminated nearly five years of steady strife between the state and federal governments and between the rival political factions in Georgia. The leading figures in the Yazoo incident apparently have left no records of their exact motives in seeking the purchase. But there were several compelling economic and political reasons for them to move at the time they did. Economically, the resumption of hostilities between France and Great Britain in 1793 reawakened interest in the rich supply of naval stores available for exploitation in the Yazoo region, while the idea of controlled settlement under the direction of private land companies had not lost its appeal.[18]

Political considerations also must have been influential, for every important member of the Federalist faction in

[15] James Jackson to James Armstrong, from Savannah, July 24, 1794, James Jackson Papers; Edward Telfair to John Wereat, from Burke County, August 23, 1794, Telfair Papers; *Georgia Gazette*, September 4, 1794.

[16] *Georgia Gazette*, October 9, November 6, 1794.

[17] Knox to Washington, November 3, 1794, Washington Papers, Vol. 269.

[18] George Ogg reported to John Gray Blount from Augusta on August 24, 1793, that there was a "pine barren [land] fever" currently raging throughout the state. Alice Barnwell Keith, ed., *The John Gray Blount Papers* (2 vols.; Raleigh: State Department of Archives and History, 1952), II, 302.

Georgia was deeply involved in the sale and, perforce, the corruption which preceded it. Prior to 1860–1861 the relations between Georgia and the federal government were never worse than in 1793–1794 when the state consistently disrupted every attempt by the national administration—and by the Creeks—to bring peace to the frontier. James Gunn and his followers probably reasoned that if the western lands could be bought from the state by a private company whose members were sympathetic to the national government's Indian policies, everyone except the Jackson-Telfair interests would benefit. The state's treasury would be replenished, the Indians presumably would be dealt with as the national government wished, and the potentially rich timber and agricultural lands of the Yazoo country would be available for exploitation by the purchasers.

As early as January, 1794, Seaborn Jones, United States Representative Thomas P. Carnes, and James Gunn had met informally to seek their own solution "for the effectual protection of our distressed frontier citizens." By the next November they and their associates had formed a Georgia Yazoo Company and were ready to approach the legislature. When they arrived at the bar of the House, however, they found that several other land companies—including one from South Carolina headed by Albert Gallatin and Alexander James Dallas, both strong Republicans—had preceded them.[19] The pretensions of these two companies were brushed aside in the final sale, and Republican politicians thus escaped any identification with the ensuing fraud.

The agent for these outside companies was revealed to

[19] Thomas Carnes to Seaborn Jones, from Philadelphia, January 20, 1794, Seaborn Jones Papers; James Gunn to Judge Wilson, from Augusta, November 28, 1794, Old Congress file, Case 1, Box 6, Gratz Collection, Historical Society of Pennsylvania, Philadelphia; "State of FACTS shewing the Right of Certain Companies to the LAND Lately Purchased By Them from the State of Georgia," Boston, 1795, pamphlet in the Henry E. Huntington Library, San Marino, Calif.

be Edward Telfair,[20] who soon afterward presented a petition of his own, cosigned by such prominent state political figures as William Few, John Wereat, and John Twiggs. In this petition Telfair and his colleagues offered to buy the Yazoo lands for a half-million dollars and to take responsibility for extinguishing all Indian claims to it. This offer proved the most favorable that the legislature had yet received, but it was turned down. Governor Matthews immediately was petitioned for an explanation, but he remained silent. The legislature then passed a most sinisterly ambiguous act which, in fact, granted the Yazoo tract to the group headed by James Gunn.[21]

At first the Governor refused to sign the act, citing eight objections to it, including opposition to the comparatively small sum offered by the Georgia Company, the small quantity of land in the tract reserved for the citizens of the state, the monopoly of landholding that would result, and the secretiveness of the sale.[22] Matthews' initial resistance encouraged the Telfair group, which on January 1, 1795, made still another proposal to the legislature to purchase the western tract.[23] Once more they were rebuffed, and Matthews then succumbed to persistent legislative pressure and signed the act of sale, though he later denied that he had any personal interest in the transaction.[24] Thus, on January 5, 1795, the vast Yazoo tract fell into the hands of the Georgia Company.

[20] Telfair to A. J. Dallas, from Augusta, January 5, 1795, Telfair Papers.

[21] "Petition of John Twiggs, et al.," December 11, 1794, ibid.; Samuel B. Adams, "The Yazoo Fraud," *Georgia Historical Quarterly*, VII (1923), 156.

[22] "A True Copy of the Dissent to the Act Entitled An Act etc. etc. to the Honorable the Speaker and Gentlemen of the [Georgia] House of Representatives," December 29, 1794, George Matthews Papers, Duke University Library, Durham, N. C.

[23] "Petition of John Wereat," January 1, 1795, Telfair Papers.

[24] "Annual Message of the Governor," January 13, 1796, in "Journal of the State Senate of Georgia," in William Sumner Jenkins, ed., *Records of the States of the United States* (Microfilm, University of California Library, Berkeley).

Gunn soon was required to give public proof of his Federalist beliefs, and he did not fail. Along with Jacob Read of South Carolina, he was the only southern senator who voted for the ratification of Jay's Treaty.[25] The other leading members of the Georgia Company also for years had been known as strong friends of government. They included Lachlan McIntosh, who had played such a significant role in the sale of 1789; Matthew McAllister, Anthony Wayne's ally in 1791; and Nathaniel Pendleton, the United States District Judge for Georgia and the organizer of the meeting and dinner in January, 1794, at which more than one hundred leading merchants of the state had proclaimed publicly their support of Washington's Neutrality Proclamation. In addition, one of the largest shareholders in the company was the budding young Federalist from South Carolina, Robert Goodloe Harper.[26]

The legislature's rigid determination to sell to the Georgia Company naturally had raised public suspicion that a sinister plot against the integrity of the state existed. Even before Governor Matthews signed the Yazoo bill, young William H. Crawford, just beginning his political career, joined other citizens of Columbia County in a remonstrance against the sale, which was sent to Augusta.[27] The next month the Grand Jury of Chatham County (Savannah)

[25] *Georgia Gazette*, July 16, 1795.

[26] A list of the leading members and shareholders of the Georgia Company of 1795 may be found in Walter Lowrie and Matthew St. Clair Clarke, eds., *American State Papers: Documents, Legislative and Executive, of the Congress of the United States*, I, Public Lands (Washington, D. C.: Gales & Seaton, 1832), 140ff. Additional evidence of Harper's close relations with the Yazoo faction may be found in Harper to Seaborn Jones, from Philadelphia, January 4, 1797, Seaborn Jones Papers; Harper to Jones, March 13, 1797, "War of 1812" file, Dreer Collection, Historical Society of Pennsylvania, Philadelphia.

[27] Charles Homer Haskins, "Yazoo Land Companies," *Papers of the American Historical Association*, V (January and April, 1891), 418; Ulrich B. Phillips, *Georgia and State Rights* (Washington, D. C.: Government Printing Office, 1901), 39–40.

also publicly opposed the sale on roughly the same grounds first expressed by Governor Matthews and congratulated the minority in the legislature which had opposed the sale.[28]

So far the only objections raised to the sale had been based upon its secretiveness and flagrant favoritism, but on March 15 a sensational new development altered the scope of the affair. Clement Lanier, a member of the House during the previous session, swore in a legal deposition that William Longstreet, state representative from Richmond County, had attempted to bribe him with land certificates from Gunn's Georgia Company while the Yazoo bill was being debated in the House.[29] From then on, evidence swiftly was uncovered which revealed that a majority of the legislature had been corrupted by the Georgia Company. The astounding extent of the bribery was matched by its crudity, and the public's fury was quickly roused. By the end of the month Madison, in Philadelphia, was aware of the magnitude of the fraud and of its political significance. After naming the two federal judges Wilson and Nathaniel Pendleton as "known adventurers" in the frauds, Madison added: "The two Senators Gun [sic] & Jackson are now pitted agst each other, and the whole State is in convulsions."[30]

The revelation of corruption placed the entire Yazoo transaction in jeopardy, and members of the Georgia Company immediately counterattacked. Never had the tendency of the elitist-minded to shade into contemptuous authoritarianism when confronted by an angry populace been more explicit than in the major defensive essay which now appeared in the leading organ of the Yazoo interest, the *Georgia Gazette*. Disdaining to deny the charge of corruption, members of the Georgia Company claimed that the people had no right to contemplate rescinding the sale, since

[28] *Georgia Gazette*, February 3, 1795.
[29] *Ibid.*, March 5, 1795.
[30] Madison to Monroe, March 27, 1795, Madison Papers, Vol. 18.

they had vested their political power wholly in the legislature, and the legislature had a constitutional right to sell. The essayist dismissed the susceptibility of the people's representatives to corruption as irrelevant, and called the popular preoccupation with this matter "strange sophistry!" He maintained that, as a result, there was ground neither for popular reversal nor legal redress. The members of the Georgia Company then reminded the people that their state had been enriched materially by the sale and that a certain portion of the tract would be set aside by the purchasers for use by Georgians. The defense then strongly intimated that Georgians should be satisfied with these advantages and not question certain aspects of public business which were none of their concern.[31]

Implicit in this argument was the concept of sanctity of contract that John Marshall invoked in his final decision on the case in 1810 and that Hamilton stressed from 1795 until his death.[32] Federalist defenses of the Yazoo sale thus were consistent and undeviating throughout.

The charge of shoddy sophistry certainly was not irrelevant when applied to the Yazoo faction's argument, and opponents of the sale were quick to point this out. It was rightly maintained that total legislative independence of the kind assumed by proponents of the sale posed a direct and eternal threat to the liberties of the people if taken as a guide to future behavior by the General Assembly of the state.[33] There was no reply to this argument.

A despised and isolated element in the state, the Yazoo faction next sought sanction for its acts from a presumably higher authority. As early as March 20, Gunn and Carnes requested aid from the federal government in arranging talks with the Creeks in an attempt to end Indian claims

[31] Letter of "Candidus," *Georgia Gazette*, April 2, 1795.
[32] Haskins, "Yazoo Land Companies," 433.
[33] "A Planter's Reply to Candidus," *Georgia Gazette*, April 9, 1795.

to the Yazoo country. Though doubtlessly grateful for Gunn's current support in the Jay Treaty crisis, Washington and his new Secretary of War, Timothy Pickering, wisely refused the request; they realized that if the request were granted, the national government might find itself at war not only with the Creeks and the Spaniards, but with Georgia as well, although this was never stated publicly.[34]

The anti-Yazoo faction, in the meantime, proceeded with plans for a rescinding act. Their first opportunity came at the constitutional convention in May, but the advantage was not pressed, probably because the anti-Yazoo forces, though excited, lacked effective leadership. James Jackson, however, was determined to play the role of the avenging angel. He attempted to return to the state in March, but poor weather kept him from reaching Savannah, and he was forced to fret in Philadelphia for several months longer while "the wicked triumph." He eventually arrived in Georgia in late October and promptly was approached by "a respectable committee from a considerable portion of the citizens of Chatham County," asking him to lead the anti-Yazoo faction. Jackson readily accepted, resigning the four remaining years of his Senate term to enter the Georgia legislature. He explained to Madison in justification of his action that Georgia was in fact a superlative arena in which to battle those speculative interests which had preyed on the democratic rights of the people ever since the introduction of the funding act.[35] The Republicans had lost a staunch friend in Congress, but they soon were to have the almost undivided loyalty of an entire state in compensation.

Despite open threats of assassination, Jackson began

[34] Pickering to Governor Matthews, reprinted in *ibid.*, April 30, 1795.
[35] Jackson to Edward Langworthy, from Philadelphia, June 10, 1795, James Jackson Papers; *Georgia Gazette,* November 5, 1795; Adams, "Yazoo Fraud," 157; Jackson to Madison, from Savannah, November 17, 1795, Madison Papers, Vol. 18.

Crises and Collapse, 1795-1796 / 97

collecting affidavits to support formal charges of corruption —a task which was almost routine to him by this time. He was so thorough that when the House considered the sale in January, 1796, some twenty "proofs relating to the fraud and corruptions practiced to obtain the act for the disposal of the western territory of the state" were produced immediately. These proofs, some truly hair-raising, established beyond doubt that Gunn, Pendleton, William Longstreet, and several others had successfully bribed a majority of the past legislature.[36] The Federalist-Yazoo party in Georgia was disgraced completely by the evidence which Jackson produced, and public humiliation was added to the popular enmity which it already had incurred.

The immediate political effects of the Yazoo fraud were immense. James Jackson, by superb leadership during the 1796 session, emerged as the undisputed leader of a politically homogeneous citizenry determined to protect state rights and property from outside encroachments from any source. Jackson personally led the parade of citizens and lawmakers which on February 9 symbolically burned the now expunged act of sale. Later in the session, "by general consent," Jackson offered a bill appropriating part of the unlocated territory of the state for the payment of the state militia. Jackson later moved, and the legislature swiftly agreed, to demand that the Governor request federal assistance against the Creeks. Jackson was determined to insure, however, that as far as possible the necessary evil of federal troops be mitigated by the existence of a friendly administration at Philadelphia. At the same time, therefore, he introduced a set of resolutions—again easily passed by the tractable legislature—providing for a revision of the electoral laws of the state so that the presidential electors might be popularly

[36] "Journal of the Georgia House of Representatives," January 25, 1796, in Jenkins, ed., *Records of the States*.

chosen. Finally, Jackson readily induced the legislature to pass a resolution condemning Jay's Treaty in the harshest terms as a servile surrender of American rights.[37] By the time that its General Assembly ended the session of 1796, Georgia was thoroughly and unequivocally Republicanized, and Jackson was its spokesman and the keeper of its public virtue.

Throughout 1795 and 1796 the Yazoo supporters continued to write angry letters to the press, but their political power had been destroyed. Only in "the little speculating town of Augusta" could Gunn, Pendleton, Carnes, Jones, and their allies find active support. As one contemporary noted, only seven members of the more than one-hundred-man legislature, three in the House and four in the Senate, opposed the rescinding act. "Nineteen-twentieths of the people throughout this state reprobate the iniquitous sale, and approve the proceedings of the Legislature in annulling the usurped act."[38] As for the individual members of the Yazoo faction, Carnes had the temerity to run for Congress once again in 1796, with the active aid of Seaborn Jones, but he was beaten by John Milledge, a young protégé of Jackson and later Jackson's successor as governor. Nathaniel Pendleton became quiescent and moved to New York by 1798 or 1799 at the latest.[39] As for James Gunn, the legislature which he had helped to corrupt had elected him for another term in the United States Senate, but his power base in the state definitely was destroyed. In later years he bound himself closer to the leaders of the national administration, ignoring as much as possible the politics and politicians of his state, until the expiration of his term in March, 1801.

[37] *Ibid.*, January 22, February 8, 21, 1796; *Georgia Gazette*, February 25, 1796.
[38] *Georgia Gazette*, March 10, 1796.
[39] Carnes to Jones, from Greensboro, September 18, 1796, Seaborn Jones Papers; Pendleton to Charles Harris, from New York, June 28, 1799, Personal Miscellany File, Library of Congress.

The Yazoo frauds brought a promising Federalist movement to an untimely end. But Georgia was not the only, nor even the major, area of concern of the friends of government in the South as an increasingly unfavorable political climate developed in the winter and spring of 1795.

The resumption of the Anglo-French war early in 1793 had altered decisively the course of American politics, and the problem of defining national policy toward these two great powers shaped the course of political strife in the country for the remainder of the decade. By the summer of 1796, Federalists and Republicans throughout the nation were clearly divided over the problem.

As their activities in Virginia in the fall of 1793 revealed, the supporters of Jefferson and Madison were displeased with Washington's policy of neutrality; but in their uncertain status they gradually, though grudgingly, accepted it. However, there was room for maneuver within this broad policy, and the Republicans took up the challenge willingly. In 1789 and again in 1794, Madison attempted to direct Congress toward a policy of commercial discrimination against Great Britain. In 1789 his view was an expression of personal judgment and prejudice, but by 1794 it was an expression of party policy and probably represented, as one recent historian has maintained, the first attempt by the Republican faction in Congress to take the political offensive.[40]

Neutrality was, of course, the expressed policy of the Federalist party. It was practiced, however, amidst a background of increasing commercial depredations on the part of Great Britain and an interference with American interests in the Ohio Valley in 1794 by the Governor-General of Canada and the Indian allies of the Crown.[41] Thus, to many neutrality seemed to represent a *de facto* preference for the

[40] Joseph Charles, *The Origins of the American Party System* (Williamsburg, Va.: The Institute of Early American History and Culture, 1956), 95.
[41] *Virginia Herald and Fredericksburg Advertiser*, December 18, 1794.

policies and interests of Great Britain over those of France.

In the South the year 1794 proved to be disastrous for the friends of government, as their once influential interests in Virginia and South Carolina either declined into apathy or were torn apart over issues relating to Anglo- and Franco-American diplomacy. In Virginia, Wilson Cary Nicholas gradually shifted to the Republican point-of-view as British seizures of American merchantmen mounted; and even Henry Lee wavered for a time, at one point contemplating the acceptance of a proferred commission as Brigadier-General in the French Army.[42] Lee's Federalist tendencies and his belief in the rectitude of neutrality were reconfirmed, however, by the flattery of political allies and by firm familial admonition not to stray from the path of political constancy. He later served effectively against the whiskey rebels in western Pennsylvania and was highly popular with his troops, despite attempts of the opposition to smear him with charges of incompetence and cowardice.[43]

Hamilton's resignation as Secretary of the Treasury and the increasingly vigorous activities of the Republicans in Virginia embittered and disheartened the friends of government, producing in them a growing lethargy that contrasted sharply with the able and energetic activities they had undertaken the year before. Carrington, for example, wrote to Hamilton and begged him not to step down simply because he had been publicly criticized in some quarters. Significantly, a week after Carrington's letter, an essay signed by "A FRIEND TO MERIT" appeared in the *Virginia Gazette,* resentfully demanding to know why the anti-

[42] Carrington to Nicholas, from Richmond, March 2, 1794, Nicholas Papers; William Lee to Henry Lee, from Green Spring, April 20, 1793, Lee Family Papers, Brock Collection, Henry E. Huntington Library, San Marino, Calif.
[43] Lee to Hamilton, from Richmond, March 6, 1794, from Shirley Hundred, January 5, 1795, Hamilton Papers, Vols. 22, 23; *Virginia Herald and Fredericksburg Advertiser,* December 25, 1794.

Hamilton forces had been gratified with a publication of Giles' Resolutions while the results of the subsequent investigation which had thoroughly exonerated Hamilton never had been printed.[44] Throughout the summer, friends of government in Virginia were alarmed that "the faction" which opposed them could only make use of "calumny and misrepresentation" in their attacks upon the government, attacks which nevertheless had succeeded in bringing "into popular disrepute and even into popular odium some of the wisest and best characters in the U. States." Federalists admitted freely that as a result of these attacks "the cause of Virtue and Talents" had been eclipsed in the state.[45]

Such concern can be justified only if it leads to increased vigor on the part of the besieged. But as late as December, Virginia Federalists remained inactive. Fully agreeing with Hamilton's observation upon "the deplorable increase of a disorganizing spirit" throughout the Union, Carrington could only "heartily re-echo your opinion, that good men should come forward and set their faces against the ills which await us, and trust it will ere long be the case in Virginia."[46] Thus, only vague hope rather than active recruitment of followers and leaders sustained the friends of government in Virginia during their months of trial.

Though lethargic and despite some defections, Virginia Federalists at least retained their cohesion throughout 1794. In South Carolina the previously solid lowcountry oligarchy was shattered into three distinct, antagonistic factions during the year. The collapse of Federalist cohesion was caused by both lofty disagreements over principle and sordid contests for public office. Internal division was preceded by the

---

[44] Carrington to Hamilton, July 9, 1794, Hamilton Papers, Vol. 22; *Virginia Gazette and General Advertiser*, July 16, 1794.
[45] Francis Corbin to Hamilton, from Buckingham, Middlesex County, July 20, 1794, Hamilton Papers, Vol. 23.
[46] Carrington to Hamilton, December 12, 1794, *ibid.*

withdrawal from the Federalist interest of two important leaders whose actions merit some notice, since both later laid implacable siege to the ideology and dominant position of the lowcountry oligarchy.

Pierce Butler could have remained as a valuable member of the Federalist lowcountry oligarchy. He had married into the native merchant aristocracy of Charleston and as a result had attained social distinction and had come within sight of a handsome fortune. However, the fiery Irishman unsuccessfully clashed with Cotesworth Pinckney on at least two occasions, and the resulting frustration had produced in him a deeply felt malice against Pinckney and the entire Charleston group. Sometime in the mid-1780's, Pinckney had blocked Butler's attempts to realize a quick profit by selling his wife's entire holdings of slaves in Georgia. In 1792, Butler and Cotesworth Pinckney clashed again over the ironclad will of a Charleston lady, a part of whose fortune Butler had hoped to obtain. Instead, the fortune went to Butler's children, and, to prevent the fortune from falling into Butler's greedy hands, the will provided that Ralph Izard and Cotesworth and Thomas Pinckney were to act as executors until the children became of age.[47] For these and other reasons, Butler withdrew from the Charleston ruling elite as early as 1789 and identified himself with the backcountry, voting in that year for the removal of the capital to Columbia.[48] After 1790 he was a strong and consistent Republican.

"A spoilsman in party politics," Charles Pinckney's withdrawal from the Federalist circle seemed to represent Wash-

[47] "Excerpts from the Recollections of John Francis Fischer, written in 1864," Pierce Butler Papers, Historical Society of Pennsylvania, Philadelphia; Cotesworth to Thomas Pinckney, from Charleston, July 14, 1792, Pinckney Family Papers, Box 3.
[48] "South Carolina House of Representatives Journal," January 23, 1789, in Jenkins, ed., *Records of the States.*

ington's greatest patronage blunder in the South. Charles Pinckney quite possibly could have obtained one of South Carolina's seats in the United States Senate in 1789; but personal and family affairs kept him tied to South Carolina, and he was forced to be content for a time with the governorship. In October, 1792, however, he wrote Washington in rather peremptory tones declaring that as his gubernatorial term was coming to a constitutional close he would gladly accept a post in the national government if the President were disposed to offer it. "If the entire confidence and approbation of my public conduct of the State I live in may be recommendation," Pinckney said, "I think I may venture to say and I believe you fully know, I possess it." Despite such bold solicitation, Pinckney was not offered a national post.[49] He retired from public life for a time and upon his return became identified with Butler and the backcountry and later the Republican interests in the state.

The initial division within the Federalist clique itself in South Carolina occurred in January, 1793, when Jacob Read, an ambitious Charleston lawyer of the second rank, determined to challenge incumbent William Loughton Smith in the forthcoming Congressional elections. This was strictly an internal struggle, as Read's Federalism had never been in doubt since 1784 and never was to be.[50] Read faced a serious challenge, for at the time the ties between the Pinckney-Rutledge faction and the Izard-Smith group were quite firm. From 1789 on, Smith and Rutledge were in

[49] Ulrich B. Phillips, "The South Carolina Federalists," *American Historical Review*, XIV (1908–1909), 739; Charles Pinckney to Rufus King, from Charleston, January 26, 1789, in Charles R. King, ed., *Life and Correspondence of Rufus King* (6 vols.; New York: G. P. Putnam's Sons, 1894–1900), I, 359; Pinckney to Washington, from Charleston, October 14, 1792, Washington Papers, Vol. 257.

[50] Read to Washington, from Annapolis, August 13, 1784, Washington Papers, Vol. 231. In 1795 Read, along with James Gunn, voted for the ratification of Jay's Treaty. See p. 93 above.

close contact whenever Congress was in session, and Smith worked assiduously to keep Rutledge informed about public business.[51] When Smith was challenged, therefore, Rutledge placed all of his considerable influence at the younger man's disposal. Read began circulating a series of unspecified "base and baseless charges" against Smith, which Rutledge successfully ridiculed, and Read was beaten. Smith was profuse in his thanks to Rutledge, and the core of the Federalist alliance in South Carolina remained firm.[52]

The Rutledge-Pinckney forces clashed with Read again in the legislative session of 1794. The first order of business involved the perpetual conflict between the coast and backcountry interests, as young Robert Goodloe Harper from Ninety-Six district led the usual upcountry attack upon the unequal representation in the legislature. Harper proposed a plan which would have "granted suffrage according to numbers without regard to color," but this scheme was rejected—by a bare five-vote margin—by the lowcountrymen as too much of an "innovation." The second important issue was the election of a governor and a United States Senator to replace Izard, who was retiring. Pinckney and Rutledge brought forward a Colonel Vanderhorst in a field of three candidates, including Read. On the first ballot Vanderhorst received a plurality but not a majority. On the second ballot Read, whose "chagrin was conspicuous" threw his votes to Vanderhorst, but he determined to salvage some influence. In so doing he gravely threatened the integrity of the lowcountry interest, for in the Senate race the defecting Charles Pinckney represented the backcountry, while Cotesworth Pinckney and Rutledge brought forward Dr. David Ramsay as the ostensible lowcountry candidate. Ramsay, however,

[51] Between 1789 and early 1794 Smith wrote thirty-eight long, informative letters to Rutledge in Charleston. Smith-Rutledge Correspondence.
[52] Smith to Rutledge, from Philadelphia, November 22, 1792, February 27, 1793, *ibid.*

was a known abolitionist, and while the two Charleston lawyers were upstairs extracting from him a promise that he never mention the subject within the borders of the state, the lowcountry rice planters nominated Read. Read and Ramsay, therefore, split the lowcountry vote on the first ballot, with Charles Pinckney close behind Read. Knowing Read's sleepless ambitions for office, Rutledge and Cotesworth Pinckney wearily threw their support to him on the next ballot to preserve lowcountry dominance, but they were not pleased with his conduct. A sense of antagonism is implicit in Cotesworth Pinckney's description of the affair.[53]

The sudden break which occurred between the Smith-Izard and Rutledge-Pinckney forces in South Carolina was far more serious than the recurrent conflicts of both these groups with the Read faction, because it reflected the growing anti-British feeling among many influential southern Federalists. This development eventually put many friends of government in the South at odds with their pro-British Yankee and Yorker colleagues and, of course, with administration policy. By 1795 and 1796 the Rutledges and the Pinckneys had almost deserted the administration over foreign policy, depriving it of inestimable power and influence in the one state that was considered to be the keystone of the Federalist arch in the South.

There are several possible explanations for this development of anti-British sentiment within ruling circles in the southern states. As is well known, southern planters were in a constant state of debt to British merchants because of the extension of long-term credit. On the other hand, ambitious native southern merchants, such as the Blounts in North Carolina, had strongly desired the reopening of trade

[53] Pinckney to Ralph Izard, December 20, 1794, Charles Cotesworth Pinckney Papers, Duke University Library, Durham, N. C.; John Brown Cutting to Thomas Pinckney, from Columbia, December 19, 1794, Pinckney Family Papers, Box 6.

with the West Indies as early as 1784 and had supported the Constitution with that end in mind. Subsequent frustration on this point, added to an increase in British seizures and impressments, produced a strong dislike of the British commercial system in the minds of John Gray and Thomas Blount, both of whom became enthusiastic supporters of Madison's plan of commercial discrimination in 1794.[54] But the intense Anglophobia shown by the Rutledges and the Pinckneys at the time of the Jay Treaty apparently was unique and likely stemmed from a growing distrust of the rising commercial and political power of the British merchant class in Charleston.

No group in the United States worked more strenuously or with greater effect at the end of the Revolution to rapidly reestablish the channels of trade with England than did South Carolina's lowcountry oligarchs. In the process they opened the city of Charleston not only to British shipping, but also to the swarm of British merchants and factors who pressed for legal residence there.[55] The resultant structure of commercial relations in South Carolina from 1783 onward thus was markedly different from what it was in New England and New York, for the resident British factors—a group largely absent from the northern seaports—soon engrossed a large proportion of South Carolina's trade and inspired a situation of perpetual conflict with the native merchants in which patriotism and self-interest were inextricably entwined.[56]

[54] Thomas to John Gray Blount, from Philadelphia, January 16, 23, March 7, 1794, in Keith, *John Gray Blount*, II, 344, 351, 372–73.

[55] George C. Rogers, Jr., *William Loughton Smith of Charleston; Evolution of a Federalist, 1758–1812* (Columbia, S. C.: University of South Carolina Press, 1962), 99–105.

[56] Contemporary statements of the influence of British commerce and merchants upon the economies and societies of South Carolina, Virginia, and Georgia may be found in the debates over Madison's 1789 proposal for a commercial discrimination against England. *Annals of Congress*, I, 192–93, 253–54.

Prior to 1789, anti-British sentiment in South Carolina could be measured along fairly well-defined class lines. The native merchants and at least most of the city's artisans and mechanics, plus most of the backcountry, bitterly resented the presence of the British factors and their influence in the local economy.[57] These were the groups which had provided much of the force for the abortive movement led by Commodore Gillon in 1783–1784 to drive the English businessmen from the city. On the other hand, the British were protected by the powerful and cohesive oligarchy.

Sometime in the 1780's or early 1790's, however, the Rutledges and the Pinckneys began to echo the anti-British feelings of the lower classes in the state, and in 1791 they informed Jefferson of their enthusiastic support of Madison's plan of commercial discrimination against British trade.[58] The motives which underlay this change are obscure; neither Edward Rutledge nor Cotesworth Pinckney expressed directly the reasons for the several shifts in his sentiments in the decade and a half after the Peace of Paris. Yet growing indications of anti-British sentiment within the Rutledge-Pinckney faction did coincide with the increasing political activities of the British factors of Charleston. And on the eve of the Jay Treaty, the Rutledges and Pinckneys openly challenged the political power of their former ally and the Congressional representative of the British commercial group, William Loughton Smith.

As Aedanus Burke indicated in his long letter outlining in detail the problems of Antifederalism in South Carolina in 1788, the British merchants and the local representatives of the British government first successfully demonstrated their political power in local American politics during the crisis over the ratification of the Constitution. After 1789

[57] *Ibid.*, 267.
[58] Edward Rutledge to Jefferson, 1791, Jefferson Papers, Vol. 59.

the British merchants of Charleston openly helped to place Smith in the United States House of Representatives and to keep him there for four terms.

As the political power of the local British merchant community grew in the early 1790's the Rutledges and the Pinckneys became ever more favorable toward Revolutionary France. But their idealism was so strongly influenced by self-deception as to suggest that hatred of the British rather than any real commitment to the French Revolution shaped their attitudes. Cotesworth Pinckney, in the fashion of the eighteenth-century elitist, spoke of "French Liberties" but never mentioned the Revolutionary ideal of equality, much less fraternity. In fact, Pinckney said he hoped that his nephew "so long in France" would "return a good Republican."[59] Pinckney and his followers were equally approving in their initial reception of Genêt, saying the young ambassador was "a very sensible, intelligent Man" when Genêt arrived in Charleston in April, 1793.[60] Despite Genêt's later *contretemps*, Pinckney and Rutledge remained loyal to France.

Their loyalty to France—though not to its Revolutionary ideals—increased not only in proportion to the growing power of the local British merchants, but in proportion to the increase in British commercial depredations as well. Cotesworth Pinckney had become so incensed by the spring of 1794 over "the wanton depredations of Great Britain" that he said openly that he hoped for further "brilliant successes" by French arms to bring Britain "to her senses." By June he noted the revival in South Carolina of "that military glow which fired our hearts in 1775," and he expressed despair

[59] Cotesworth to Thomas Pinckney, from Charleston, January 7, 1793, Pinckney Family Papers, Box 4.
[60] Cotesworth to Thomas Pinckney, April 16, 1793, James Ladson to Thomas Pinckney, July 1793, *ibid*.

concerning the Americans' ability to remain aloof from the Anglo-French conflict.⁶¹

The rising political power of the British merchants at Charleston and the increasing instances of harassment of American commerce at sea by the Royal Navy seemed to indicate a malevolent British plot to subvert the new commercial and political independence of her former colonies. In a letter to his brother on June 10, Pinckney cited several instances of preparation in the Charleston area against a possible British military invasion. In the following autumn Pinckney and Rutledge at last took the offensive against Britain's apparent political invasion of the state through the resident British merchants.

Overt conflict between the British merchants and the Rutledge-Pinckney forces was not necessarily inevitable. The two groups had cooperated in the past to advance Federalist principles, and an uneasy truce between them might have been maintained for some time. At the same time that Pinckney and Rutledge began openly to condemn Great Britain, though, Smith and his father-in-law, Ralph Izard, expressed equally strong views about the danger of the French Revolution and the need to maintain a neutrality which in practice would be favorable to England.

Izard seriously doubted the wisdom of South Carolina's slaveholders' embracing too ardently French Revolutionary dogma. "Doctrines are propagated, & attempted to be established in that Country which I believe to be erroneous, destructive of all good government & tending to make Mankind of all descriptions unhappy," he wrote. "South Carolina would be one of the first victims to the principles contained in the Rights of Man, which are applicable, without distinc-

⁶¹ *Georgia Gazette*, November 21, 1793; Cotesworth to Thomas Pinckney, from Charleston, March 29, June 10, 1794, Pinckney Family Papers, Boxes 5, 6.

tion, to persons of all Colors." Revealing his acuteness and his characteristic honesty, Izard hinted strongly that democratic ideals and a slave system could not exist in the same nation. The endemic fear of a slave rebellion, rather than any intimation of eventual civil war, clearly was motivating Izard's thinking; and although he admitted that in 1793 few shared his fears,[62] after 1796 many in South Carolina would.

Soon afterward Izard's son-in-law, William Loughton Smith, began to express anti-French sentiments in his letters to Rutledge. As spokesman and defender of the administration's neutrality policy, Smith was incensed that despite Genêt's recent humiliation, "yet a party still adheres to him, among whom are men, called by some, virtuous, respectable & the best friends of the people:—Mifflin, Dallas, Madison, Giles, Taylor Munroe [sic] &cc associate with him or dine at his house, and thus countenance his measures." Rutledge's reply, if any, is unrecorded. It must have been cool and may well have been angry, for in April, 1794, in the last extant letter which he ever wrote to Rutledge, Smith defended himself vigorously from Cotesworth Pinckney's charge that he had favored the British political system, and he charged Madison's plan of discrimination with being "founded on prejudice & ignorance & injurious to us."[63]

The break between the British merchant interest backed by Smith and Izard and the Rutledge-Pinckney group became public in the autumn of 1794 when Rutledge and Pinckney brought forward young John Rutledge, Jr., in an unsuccessful contest for Smith's Congressional seat. Like the clashes with Jacob Read, this contest too was between gentlemen who were at least nominally friends of government. Cotesworth Pinckney rejected suggestions to support

[62] Ralph Izard to Thomas Pinckney, from Boston, August 12, 1793, *ibid.*, Box 4.
[63] Smith to Rutledge, February n.d., February 15, April 28, 1794, Smith-Rutledge Correspondence.

Crises and Collapse, 1795-1796 / 111

Thomas Tudor Tucker and a Mr. Fayssoux, as he did not consider the sentiments of either to be "sufficiently federal." He hinted at the extent of the British merchants' active involvement in the state's politics when he observed that "the British Merchants & Old Tories are doing all they can" to obtain Smith's election "once more."[64] A month later Madison also commented on the Smith-Rutledge election. With young Charles Pinckney temporarily out of public life, it is possible that Madison received his information from Pierce Butler. He may, however, have received it from his friend and supporter, Edward Rutledge. In any case Madison reported that the political influence of the British merchants at Charleston during the election was not confined to the city, and the merchants "& their debtors in the country" worked to put Smith over once again.[65]

A note of caution should be injected at this point. Many of the comments concerning the political activities of the British merchants at Charleston came from Republicans, and it can be argued that they represented nothing more than partisan propaganda. Yet two facts argue against such an interpretation. First, contemporary correspondence of both Federalist and Republican leaders reveals no other explanation than anger about British commercial depredations and the political activities of the British merchants at Charleston for the gradual shift of the Rutledge-Pinckney forces to a quasi-Republican position by 1794. Secondly, neither Edward Rutledge nor Cotesworth Pinckney seem to have recognized any immediate political gain from their Republican leanings other than the opportunity to oppose openly the British merchant faction, whose activities both men obviously considered a threat to the political and economic

[64] Cotesworth to Thomas Pinckney, from Charleston, October 5, 1794, Pinckney Family Papers, Box 6.
[65] Madison to Jefferson, from Philadelphia, November 6, 1794, Madison Papers, Vol. 17.

structure of Charleston within which they had built their power and influence.

From the experiences of the Rutledges and the Pinckneys in Charleston it would seem that the presence of the politically influential British merchant class in the southern seaports, and its corresponding absence from port cities in other regions of the country, was a crucial variable in shaping the differing attitudes of southern and northern Federalists toward England in the early and mid-1790's. Other significant factors in the southerners' sterner attitude toward England were the issues of trade with the British West Indies, planters' debts to England, and growing British commercial depredations.

Northern and southern Federalists shared a concern for nationalism, as the events of the later 1790's would show, but friends of government in New England and New York could take a more detached view of British interference with American commerce because of the overall advantages they enjoyed from the close commercial ties and, because they did not have to contend with politically active resident British merchants, as did the southerners. Implicit in Cotesworth Pinckney's remarks during 1794—and those of Madison as well—is the bitter view that Americans could not call their commerce and their local politics their own so long as the British chose to intrude. The explosive reaction of the Rutledge-Pinckney circle, along with most of low and upcountry South Carolina, to the Jay Treaty the following year was a sign of Charleston's steadily rising Anglophobia. This concern was directed expressly at those provisions of the Treaty in which it seemed Great Britain undertook to further control the commercial and political life of South Carolina to her own ends.

In North Carolina, Washington's determination to maintain peace with Great Britain, even at the risk of doing damage to Franco-American relations, may actually have strengthened the Federalist cause. It is true that by 1794 the powerful Blount family ostentatiously opposed national foreign policy, but William Barry Grove and his constituents in the upper Cape Fear area entered the Federalist camp during the early months of the year and consistently supported Federalist policies during Grove's remaining nine years in Congress.

Apparently Grove was sincerely angered by the sudden attempt of the Republican forces, led by the Virginia delegation, to seize the legislative initiative during the opening days of the Third Congress. He fought vigorously, but vainly, against Madison's plan of commercial discrimination against England and grew increasingly incensed at the Republicans' arrogant assumption that those who did not support them 100 percent perforce must be opposed to them to the same degree. Grove's displeasure reflected the reaction of the independent gentleman of elitist proclivities, angered at having his and his friends' honor questioned. He defended Steele's reputation vigorously, and if he did not leave the budding Republican party, it assuredly left him.[66] Grove was certainly no Anglophile. He admitted to John Haywood that Britain's conduct toward the United States "has indeed been uncommonly tyrannical and perfidious." Along with Smith of South Carolina, however, Grove thought that only a policy of neutrality could keep the country from being destroyed by one or the other of the great powers, and he held high hopes for the success of the Jay mission.[67] Although disappointed in these hopes, Grove became independent of the Republican interest and leaned increasingly toward

[66] Grove to Steele, from Philadelphia, April 2, 1794, in Henry M. Wagstaff, ed., *The Papers of John Steele* (2 vols.; Raleigh: North Carolina Historical Commission Publications, 1924), I, 105–106.

[67] Grove to Haywood, April 24, 1794, from Philadelphia, Haywood Collection.

Federalism, becoming an ever stronger supporter as the years passed.

The outcome of the Jay mission, it appeared, would clarify public policy and political division throughout the country and, especially, the South. Jay's mission was followed eagerly and its results anticipated keenly. His strongly-worded note to Lord Grenville in November concerning the illegal seizures of American ships and seamen by the Royal Navy was given prominent space in some southern newspapers and further raised the hope, especially among Federalists, of a resultant treaty highly favorable to American commercial and frontier interests.[68] Though he did not know it, Thomas Blount was nearer the eventual truth when he condemned Jay's note to Grenville as a weak document which paved the way for a wholesale surrender of American rights. Blount mourned that "the Dignity, Honor & Interests of our Country have been entrusted to the care of such a pusillanimous wretch."[69]

With the publication of the Treaty by Republican interests in June, 1795, Blount's fears about the mission were borne out, and the friends of government immediately were faced with a crisis. During July and August, 1795, anti-Treaty meetings were held in every major port city from Boston to Savannah, and the President's desk was piled high with anti-Treaty resolutions. Jay's handiwork contained twenty-eight articles; scarcely one escaped wrathful criticism.

The Treaty particularly discriminated against southern interests, as a comparative examination of the various resolutions reveals. The Boston and New York meetings admitted the perniciousness of Articles XII and XVII and deplored

---

[68] *Virginia Gazette and General Advertiser*, April 30, September 18, October 16, November 20, 1794; *Virginia Herald and Fredericksburg Advertiser*, November 6, 1794; William R. Davie to Richard Bennehan, from Halifax, February 27, 1795, Cameron Family Papers.

[69] Thomas to John Gray Blount, from Philadelphia, November 5, 1794, in Keith, ed., *John Gray Blount*, II, 454.

the lack of any mention of the return to southern planters of Negroes taken away by the British in the late war. Nonetheless Yankees and Yorkers seemed most concerned with those articles dealing with the evacuation of the western posts and were especially critical of those clauses which guaranteed British citizens equality in the western trade.[70] The criticisms tended to be general, and there was no attempt at a detailed article-by-article criticism.

Charlestonians, led by John and Edward Rutledge, objected to the Treaty on far broader grounds, at greater length, and in greater detail. The articles upon which they concentrated and the tenor of their criticisms suggest that they saw the Treaty not so much as a single work which bartered away certain basic rights for questionable benefits, but rather as the culmination of a sustained effort by the British to reimpose domination over the commerce and the public life of the South. To be sure, Charlestonians condemned the provision of the Treaty that aided the recovery of debts by British creditors, and they complained bitterly of the lack of a provision requiring the return of the Negroes taken away by the British during the late war. But they made other and more penetrating criticisms which went far beyond what Charles Beard once suggested were the major sources of southern discontent.[71]

Most scathingly attacked were the two articles pertaining to the residence of British citizens in America—which, practically speaking, meant British factors—and to the carrying trade of the southern states. Charlestonians complained that Article II in effect "either establishes a British colony within our limits, with peculiar privileges, or, in case the

[70] "Resolutions of the meetings of the Citizens of Boston on the Late Treaty," July 13, 1795; "Resolutions of the meeting of New York," July 20, 1795, in Washington Papers, Vol. 273.
[71] Charles A. Beard, *Economic Origins of Jeffersonian Democracy* (New York: The Macmillan Co., 1915), 268–98 *passim.*

inhabitants of such colony choose to become citizens of the United States, it gives the privileges of citizens of these States to a number of men, who have been" the "most bitter and irreconcilable enemies" of the United States. The prejudices of John and Edward Rutledge against the local British merchant community had developed considerably since 1783. The two lawyers also examined Article XII carefully, perceiving not only the obvious restrictions upon trade with the British West Indies, but other restrictions upon southern carrying trade. "We are made to surrender the right of exporting in our own vessels," the resolution read, "to any part of the world, molasses, sugar, coffee and cocoa, whether productions of the British Isles or any other place; whilst the British, and all other foreign powers, have a right to send these very articles, in their own vessels, from our ports." Moreover, American shippers even were prevented from exporting cotton in their own vessels, that right also being reserved to the British by treaty.[72]

By the end of 1795, Georgia and the Carolinas seemed wholly lost to Republicanism. In South Carolina the Committee of Fifteen, which drafted the harsh Charleston Resolutions, reflected the entire political composition of the state, except, of course, the British merchants. Included within the meeting were Edward and John Rutledge, Cotesworth Pinckney, John Rutledge, Jr., Christopher Gadsden, Aedanus Burke, and Thomas Tudor Tucker. This committee in turn became the central forum for expression of popular opinion throughout the state, and anti-Treaty resolutions were sent to its members, as well as to the President, from the chairmen of meetings in Georgetown, Columbia, and Fairfield; St. John's, Christ Church, St. George, and even St. James Goose Creek parishes; and from Cheraw district.[73] For

[72] "Resolutions of the Charleston Committee of Fifteen, July 19, 1795," Washington Papers, Vol. 273.
[73] These resolutions are all in *ibid.*, Vols. 273, 274.

nearly the first time, the sectional division of the state was bridged, a circumstance which in the future would be favorable to the friends of government but which for the moment left them at the nadir of their power and influence.

Smith and Izard were silent in the face of this impressive expression of popular will, as was Jacob Read. Read, however, had publicly agreed to the Treaty in the Senate, and members of his faction naturally kept a closer and more hopeful watch on the course of public opinion. By December, William Read was telling his brother, then in Philadelphia, that it seemed as if "old E[dward] R[utledge]" had come around to a moderate course and was seeking to mitigate the actions of "the violent" members of the legislature, who were contemplating passage of an official resolution of censure against the Treaty. However, William had no kind words for young John Rutledge, Jr. "He, too, has appeared among the partizans against the President—at a committee of officers lately he taking his [glass] the President being toasted, said 'we will drink his health. He has been of some service to us.' —arrogant puppy! If the services of his whole Race & that of Washington's were put into the opposite scales, how quickly would their scale kick the Beam." While William Read obviously enjoyed releasing political frustrations in private correspondence, he apparently could not bring himself to confront the Committee of Fifteen. Later in the month Read wrote gleefully that Edward Rutledge had lost more ground than he had gained in an entire lifetime because of the stand he took on the Treaty. Read agreed with Henry DeSaussure's impression that a great reaction had occurred among many South Carolinians who believed that the state had gone too far in opposing the Treaty.[74] As events of the following year revealed, however,

[74] William to Jacob Read, from Charleston, December 18, 29, 1795, Jacob Read Papers, South Caroliniana Library, Columbia, S. C.

such opinions reflected hearsay and hope rather than reality.

North Carolina's native merchants were as violent in opposing the Treaty as was the Charleston commercial circle. In addition, speculators and many landholders in the state feared that under Article IX the large Grenville Tract, which had been sequestered during the war and opened later by the state for purchase and speculation, might be returned to the original holders.[75] In this overwhelmingly hostile atmosphere, only a few friends of government dared speak in favor of the Treaty. Grove apparently was silent, and Steele already was dickering for a government post which during the coming year would remove him from the state to become Comptroller of the national treasury.[76] William R. Davie, however, condemned "the leaders of anarchy and faction" in Congress who opposed the practical implementation of Jay's document, while at least one influential newspaper and one usually firm North Carolina House Republican supported the Treaty and defended the administration.[77]

In Georgia, too, the Treaty received its share of damnation, despite the current preoccupation with the Yazoo frauds. A large anti-Treaty meeting in Savannah was chaired by Lachlan McIntosh, while Seaborn Jones and Thomas P. Carnes signed a set of anti-Treaty resolutions drafted in Richmond County which singled out Article XII for special condemnation.[78] The anti-Yazoo forces were not fooled, however, and promptly warned the public about the

[75] *North Carolina Gazette*, October 31, 1795; Absalom Tatom to John Haywood, from Philadelphia, May 9, 1796, Haywood Papers.

[76] Wagstaff, ed., *John Steele*, I, 142–43.

[77] Davie to John Haywood, from Halifax, December 24, 1795, Haywood Papers; *North Carolina Gazette*, July 11, 1795; Alexander Martin to William Loughton Smith, from Philadelphia, June 27, 1795, William Loughton Smith Papers, Library of Congress.

[78] "Resolutions of a Meeting of the Citizens of Savannah," August 1, 1795; "Resolutions of a Meeting of Richmond County," September 1, 1795, in Washington Papers, Vols. 274–75. The citizens of Burke County also drew up a set of anti-Treaty resolutions. See *ibid.*, Vol. 275.

plot of the Yazoo men to use the condemnation of the Jay Treaty as a means of "currying favor at the next Election."[79] Georgians heeded the alarmed cries of the Jackson men and maintained their Republican consensus.

Salvaging some influence and respect for Federalist policies in the South was left to the friends of government in Virginia. As early as the spring of 1795 there were some indications that Virginia's Federalist faction was finally realizing the need to solicit directly the support of the electorate if they and their friends in Philadelphia were to stay in power. Madison at that time reported that the two districts in the state in which the Congressional elections "turned on *political* rather than *personal* considerations" were those including the towns of Alexandria and Winchester—the latter located in the northern area of the Shenandoah Valley—a source of Federalist strength in 1788. Henry Lee stood for the Alexandria seat and General Daniel Morgan for Winchester. Called by biographer J. E. Norris "the Stonewall Jackson of the Revolution," Morgan was a fiery military figure who had led the state militia under Henry Lee against the whiskey rebels; he was also a staunch supporter of President Washington. He was the first active recruit of notable stature whom Virginia Federalists enlisted after 1793, and his continual efforts in 1795 and beyond made him a valuable agent in the Winchester area. Both Lee and Morgan were defeated soundly, but they apparently gave a good account of themselves to the electorate since the opponents claimed that they left "no fraud . . . untryed." Robert Rutherford, Lee's opponent, claimed that one "Sharper" voted eight times under feigned names, and Rutherford assured his correspondent that of the five hundred votes for Light Horse Harry, no more than two hundred could be considered legal. Rutherford admitted with charm-

[79] *Georgia Gazette*, September 10, October 1, 8, 15, 1795.

ing candor that his own support was "neare mostly legal."[80]

The popular reaction against Jay's Treaty threatened to destroy even this modest beginning. Every commercial center in Virginia except Alexandria held meetings which condemned Jay's diplomacy, generally reflecting the same criticisms displayed at Charleston.[81] Jefferson told Madison that at Richmond "it is said not even Carrington undertook to defend it." Madison replied that in his knowledge only a Mr. Hopkins "and one of the Marshalls, openly espoused the treaty."[82] The nearly unanimous opposition of the Federalists in the commercial towns extended into the countryside. Burgess Ball wrote the President from near Leesburg that "the last Federalists and friends to government are pointedly oppos'd to the treaty." Norfolk citizens feared that British merchants would be able to reestablish immediately a monopoly of the West Indies trade under the provisions of the Treaty.[83] Only in the western counties of the state did the Treaty receive significant support, possibly because of its provisions regarding subsequent British evacuation of the Ohio Valley posts, and certainly because of its later tie-in with the highly favorable Pinckney Treaty in Congress.[84]

By the early autumn of 1795, however, a decided Federalist recrudescence began to be apparent in Virginia. Jefferson noted unhappily that although "the merchants were certainly (except those of them who are English) as

---

[80] J. E. Norris, *History of the Lower Shenandoah Valley* (Chicago: A. Warner & Co., Publishers, 1890), 143–46; Madison to Monroe, from Philadelphia, March 27, 1795; Rutherford to Madison, from Berkeley County, March 30, 1795, Madison Papers, Vol. 18.

[81] The resolutions are in the Washington Papers, Vol. 274.

[82] Jefferson to Madison, from Monticello, August, 1795; Madison to Jefferson, August 6, 1795, Madison Papers, Vol. 18.

[83] Ball to Washington, July 28, 1795, Washington Papers, Vol. 274; Daniel Bedinger to anonymous, November 22, 1795, Caroline Danske Dandridge Papers, Duke University Library, Durham, N. C.

[84] Arthur Campbell to Madison, from Washington County, January 24, 1796; Madison to Jefferson, from Philadelphia, April 18, 1796, Madison Papers, Vol. 19.

Crises and Collapse, 1795-1796 / 121

open-mouthed at first against the treaty as any," the enormous wave of popular indignation had "alarmed them for the strength of the government. They have feared the shock would be too great, and have chosen to tack about & support both treaty & government, rather than risk the government."[85] In early December some Federalists actually counterattacked with an *ad hoc* county meeting to condemn the opponents of Jay's Treaty.[86] Before this movement got fully started the General Assembly met, and an overt trial of party strength soon followed.

On November 20 the Republicans introduced a resolution in the lower chamber which expressed approval of the conduct of the state's senators in voting against Jay's Treaty; it passed by a 100 to 50 majority. The next day the Federalists reacted by submitting a resolution stating that the Virginia House of Delegates approved entirely Washington's motives in signing the Treaty after the Senate had ratified it. The Republicans amended this resolution to say that while the House approved of the senators' conduct in refusing to ratify the Treaty, this by no means implied a censure of Washington's determination to sign. This resolution passed 89 to 56. Once this passed, the Federalists again pressed the issue by introducing a counterresolution which stated: "That the President of the United States, for his great abilities, wisdom and integrity merits and possesses the undiminished confidence of the House." To the shock of many at the time and since, the motion lost 59 to 79, and Virginia stood on record as having publicly rebuked her most illustrious citizen.[87]

The vote, which at first glance seems to have been a clear-

[85] Jefferson to Madison, from Monticello, September 21, 1795, *ibid.,* Vol. 18.
[86] "Resolutions of a Meeting of Citizens of Frederick County, Virginia, Daniel Morgan, Chairman," December 5, 1795, in Washington Papers, Vol. 276.
[87] *Virginia Gazette and General Advertiser,* November 25, 1795.

cut repudiation, is actually somewhat ambiguous. Certainly it revealed that Virginia was strongly Republican, so much so that a majority of its representatives were willing to place themselves on public record as opposing a man who supposedly was above partisan politics and symbolized national integrity at its finest. Yet the friends of government had done little, and Republicans, with many immediate advantages, had done much to capture the popular mind. In many ways the Federalists were fortunate that there existed as strong, though usually silent, support for their leader as there appeared to be. The geographical distribution of the recorded vote showed potential Federalist strength at once extensive and thin throughout the state. Delegates from forty counties and two boroughs could be counted upon to support Washington, yet in twenty-five of the forty counties the Federalist member was opposed by one or two Republicans. Federalism seemed to have a solid majority in the towns of Richmond and Williamsburg (Alexandria was not yet incorporated), as well as in a large area of the Tidewater, up the Potomac as far as Leesburg, and inland through the northern Piedmont and valley to Frederick County. The two counties surrounding Richmond, Henrico and Hanover, as well as some scattered counties in the valley and in the extreme southwestern portion of the state, also contained some Federalist strength.[88]

Thus, while they were definitely in the minority, the friends of government in Virginia nonetheless held the potential for a rapid expansion of their influence. Realization of this potential, however, would require an active campaign for popular support. So far, except in times of im-

[88] The geographical distribution of this vote was determined from the list of names published in *ibid.*, correlated with Earl G. Swem and John W. Williams, *A Register of the General Assembly of Virginia, 1776–1918, and of the Constitutional Conventions* (Richmond: Davis Bottom, Superintendent of Public Printing, 1918), 43–45. See Appendix, Table 1.

mediate crisis, and then only fitfully, the Federalists had shown a marked disinclination to mingle with the commonalty for political advantage. The presidential and Congressional elections of 1796 offered them another opportunity to do so, but it was an opportunity unseized. In Virginia and throughout the South the Federalists' influence continued to decline as the elitist tendency toward preoccupation with men rather than measures, intrigue rather than hard politicking, continued to undermine party efficiency and influence.

A major problem was to decide whom to support for the presidency, and it was never resolved. Adams was mistrusted and disliked universally in the South. In 1792 several anti-Adams letters and essays had appeared in the Virginia press, most implying he was an avid monarchist.[89] In the election of that year Clinton, the Republican nominee, swept Georgia, North Carolina, and Virginia, while Adams won only in South Carolina.[90] This election revealed the existing configuration of party strength in the South at that time, but by 1796 it seemed highly unlikely that Adams could gain support anywhere in the region. Yet with Pennsylvania and New York uncertain, Federalists were keenly aware of the need to muster some strength in the South. To do this they either had to find a suitably attractive southerner as a running mate for Adams or ease Adams himself out of the running and seek a new candidate. The intense mutual dislike between Hamilton and Adams led the New Yorker to explore quietly the second alternative before reluctantly accepting the first.

Sometime early in April, 1796, Hamilton's ally, Rufus King, wrote John Marshall at Richmond asking him to sound out Patrick Henry on the possibility of leading the Federalist

[89] *Virginia Gazette and General Advertiser*, November 28, December 5, 1792.
[90] Edward Stanwood, *A History of the Presidency from 1788 to 1897* (Boston: Houghton, Mifflin Co., 1928), 39.

ticket that autumn. Marshall's reply was properly circumspect. He told King that he did not know Henry well enough to sound him out in a letter. Moreover, he said "I am not positively certain what course that Gentleman might take. The proposition might not only have been rejected but mentioned publicly to others in such manner as to have become an unpleasant circumstance." Marshall thus revealed the current extent of his loyalty to Hamilton. Had the Adams supporters discovered Hamilton's plot, the Federalist party would doubtless have come to an immediate end. Marshall added that "Genl Lee corresponds familiarly with Mr. H. & is in the habit of proposing offices to him." Lee, therefore, would sound Henry out first, and Marshall promised to speak to Henry when the latter was next in Richmond. "I trust it will not then be too late to bring forward to public view Mr. H. or any other gentleman who may be thought of in his stead," Marshall concluded.[91]

Henry's political attitudes had changed considerably since 1789. His long-time political enemy, Thomas Jefferson, claimed that he was "brought over to the new constitution by his Yazoo speculation." Jefferson charged that when the Georgia legislature declared the 1789 sale null and void, Henry faced ruin, as he had sunk his entire resources into depreciated state paper which the legislature would not accept. Henry was fortuitously saved from bankruptcy and even realized a modest fortune when "Hamilton's founding [sic] system came most opportunely to his relief."[92] Jefferson's interpretation of Henry's political loyalty in economic terms is intriguing. Yet it is likely that the estrangement of Madison and Jefferson from the administration was sufficient to induce Henry to view the friends of government favorably. Henry's feuds with Jefferson and Madison dated from the

[91] Marshall to King, from Richmond, April 24, 1796, Hamilton Papers, Vol. 28.
[92] Quoted in Haskins, "Yazoo Land Companies," 412.

early 1780's and involved not only profound differences over specific policies, but also Jefferson's mistrust of what he considered Henry's dictatorial ambitions.[93] Henry's duel with Madison in the state ratifying convention of 1788 confirmed their mutual dislike.

When it became apparent early in 1795 that the Jay Treaty struggle was to offer the Republicans their greatest opportunity to gain popular favor, Jefferson astutely made one gesture of conciliation toward Henry, but was summarily rebuffed.[94] Several months later Henry determined to make public his Federalism and wrote to Henry Lee assuring Lee of his respect and veneration for the President. The letter was swiftly forwarded to Philadelphia, where Washington decided to make immediate use of Henry's services.[95]

Henry's motives in this instance are obscure. He could have been either Secretary of State or Chief Justice of the Supreme Court, but turned down both offers.[96] Presumably, he was looking toward the presidency in 1796. Hamilton thought he might be and thus began arranging a droll alliance that defied every test of logic save political expediency. But Henry ultimately turned down Hamilton's offer, though just when or how is unclear. The Federalists had gained an ally of enormous influence, but neither they nor he evidently knew quite how to exploit the alliance in 1796.

With Henry apparently uninterested, Hamilton and his

[93] Dumas Malone, *Jefferson the Virginian* (Boston: Little, Brown and Company, 1948), 382.
[94] Jefferson to Archibald Stuart, April 18, 1795, quoted in William Wirt Henry, *Patrick Henry: Life, Correspondence and Speeches* (2 vols.; New York: Charles Scribner's Sons, 1891), II, 549-52.
[95] Henry to Lee, June 27, 1795; Lee to Washington, July 17, 1795, Washington Papers, Vol. 273.
[96] Washington to Edward Carrington, from Mount Vernon, October 9, 1795; Henry to Washington, October 16, 1795; Henry Lee to Henry, December 26, 1795, in Henry, *Patrick Henry: Life, Correspondence and Speeches*, II, 554-56, 558-59, 562-63; Carrington to Washington, from Richmond, October 13, 1795, Washington Papers, Vol. 275.

followers reluctantly accepted Adams' candidacy, but they still sought a suitable southerner to keep Adams from the executive chair. They soon began to speak of Thomas Pinckney, who was returning after extremely successful negotiations in Madrid, which had resulted in a treaty guaranteeing American access to the Mississippi. Pinckney was certainly a most available candidate and was perfectly acceptable to the Adams supporters as a running mate. Hamilton, however, had other, more ambitious plans for the still absent Pinckney. "I am entirely of opinion that P. H. declining Mr. P.——ought to be our man," he wrote to King in response to the latter's enthusiastic endorsement of the South Carolinian. "It is ever an idea of which I am fond in various lights—indeed on latter [sic] reflection, I rather wish to be rid of P. H. that we may be at full liberty to take up Pinckney."[97]

In contemplating a maneuver to slip Pinckney into the presidency ahead of Adams, Hamilton was playing with fire. Such an intrigue was sure to split the party in the face of a formidable Republican opposition—a fact which Hamilton seems never to have considered. Also, it would aggravate implicit sectional tensions, which already existed in full measure within the Federalist ranks. Southerners plainly were unhappy with Adams' candidacy and might well support Pinckney. New Englanders, on the other hand, were deeply embittered by the defection of Charleston and the rest of South Carolina in the Jay Treaty crisis.[98] If South Carolina and the rest of the South should abandon Adams or subordinate him to Pinckney, the Federalist interest might never be reintegrated. Finally, if Adams were able to muster

[97] King to Hamilton, from Philadelphia, May 2, 1796, Hamilton to King, May 4, 1796, from New York, Hamilton Papers, Vol. 28.
[98] Elias Boudinot to Samuel Bayard, from Rosehill, October 17, 1795, History Note Card File, Independence Hall National Park Office, Philadelphia.

some support in the South, the Federalist interest would be threatened with confusion and demoralization in that section, as supporters of Pinckney and Adams would be certain to clash. Hamilton was not to be dissuaded, however; he was determined to run Pinckney.

Unfortunately for the Federalist interest, others in the South were equally determined to champion their own candidates, and during the year four men were advanced as possible nominees. The Federalist faction at Richmond and its allies, as well as some of the older friends of government in North Carolina, hoped that the President eventually would be willing to seek a third term. Washington's battle with House Republicans over the voting of sufficient funds to carry the Jay Treaty into effect rekindled the fires of nationalism, loyalty, and affection to their chief in the hearts of many Federalists in the Richmond faction and throughout the state. By February they were carefully assessing public opinion to determine the support which might be expected for the President in Virginia, should he find it necessary to clash openly with the forces of Madison and Livingston.[99] At the same time the President's birthday brought forth the usual Federalist banquets and fervent calls for Washington to continue at the helm of state. "Your election," wrote one, "of which there can be no doubt, will demonstrate to all America that the sentiments of the people of Virginia are not understood by the temper of their representatives either in Congress, or in the State Legislature."[100]

During this election year Federalist activity in Virginia was at its peak in early spring. The President had come under sharp attack in the House for his refusal to submit

[99] Henry Lee to Washington, December, 1795; Gabriel Jones to Washington, from Rockingham County, February 8, 1796, Washington Papers, Vol. 277.

[100] H. Young to Washington, from King and Queen County, March 2, 1796, *ibid.*

to it the relevant papers regarding Jay's negotiations, and Hamilton and other Federalists determinedly organized another petition campaign, similar to that staged in the summer of 1793 in support of the neutrality policy. Although the campaign was restricted largely to the commercial centers of the North, where it was highly effective,[101] Virginia and North Carolina also strongly supported it. Marshall initially was pessimistic about its chances of success in Virginia. He deliberately held off calling a meeting at Richmond "so long as a hope remained that the house of representatives might ultimately consult the interest or honor of the nation." But with the passage of Thomas Blount's resolutions on April 6, which flatly declared the right of the House to debate the expediency of putting the treaty into effect, Marshall acted quickly. He called a meeting in the capital, which, to his obvious surprise, "was more numerous than I have ever seen at this place." Resolutions were passed by a "decided majority," which declared "that the welfare & honor of the nation required us to give full effect to the treaty negotiated with Britain."[102]

Carrington informed Washington a few days later of his alarm over the current state of public opinion, pledging himself to work actively to change it. "There never was a crisis at which the activity of the Friends of Government was more urgently called for," he said. "Some of us here have endeavored to make this impression in different parts of the Country. The events of a few days will show how successfully." The Federalists' efforts yielded surprising results,

---

[101] In New York City, for example, the Federalists went down to the docks and actually solicited the signatures of merchants and sailors on the spot to pro-Treaty petitions. This thoroughness of coverage and willingness actively to seek out popular support was never systematically attempted by any southern Federalists prior to the election of 1800. See Rufus King to Hamilton, from New York, April 20, 1796, Hamilton Papers, Vol. 28.

[102] Marshall to Hamilton, from Richmond, April 25, 1796, *ibid.*

and resolutions endorsing the President's refusal to release the Jay papers to Congress were sent to the House from meetings in Fairfax and Frederick counties, fronting the upper Potomac, both counties on the eastern shore, Fauquier in the northern Piedmont, Berkeley in the northern valley, and King William County in the Tidewater area, as well as from Richmond, Williamsburg, and Petersburg. The Petersburg meeting, Carrington remarked, was attended not only by British merchants, but by planters and farmers as well. Earlier that week Daniel Morgan informed William Loughton Smith of his success in calling a pro-Treaty meeting at Winchester.[103] The Richmond Federalists clearly had tapped a rich vein of progovernment sentiment too often ignored by them in the past. In the process they deeply alarmed their Republican opponents.[104]

In North Carolina, too, the apparent determination of the Republicans in the House to humiliate the President brought forth renewed pledges of support for the federal administration from Samuel Johnston and William R. Davie, both of whom feared for the future integrity of the Union if the opposition should persist in its obstructionist course. At least one meeting was held in the state—in April at New Bern—which publicly endorsed the President's "firm and independent temper" in his conflict with the House.[105]

The unremitting Federalist attack reached the press as well. From March to May a war of essays flared intermittent-

[103] Carrington to Washington, April 27, May 9, 1796, Washington Papers, Vol. 278; Morgan to Smith, from Winchester, April 21, 1796, William Loughton Smith Papers.

[104] Edmund Randolph to James Madison, from Richmond, April 25, 1796, Madison Papers, Vol. 19.

[105] Samuel Johnston to Iredell, from Philadelphia, April 28, May 6, 1796, Iredell Papers; Davie to John Haywood, from Halifax, March 7, 1796, Haywood Collection; "Address to the Hon. the President of the United States from the Citizens of New Bern, N. C.," April 19, 1796, Washington Papers, Vol. 278.

ly in the pages of the *Virginia Gazette*. The Federalists charged their opponents with threatening the safety of the Union and contemplating "the overthrow of the Constitution itself," an accusation without foundation but one which may have carried some weight with an impressionable and obviously excited populace.[106]

At its height the Federalist campaign in Virginia and North Carolina on behalf of the President was halted abruptly by Washington's announcement of his irrevocable determination to retire. Silence suddenly descended on the Richmond faction; the friends of government in North Carolina did not stir. The pages of the *Virginia Gazette* and Abraham Hodge's *State Gazette of North Carolina* were suddenly empty of Federalist campaign essays. Marshall, Carrington, Johnston, Davie, and the others apparently refused to commit themselves publicly to Adams or Pinckney—whether through disappointment or bewilderment or both is uncertain. All that is clear is that in North Carolina, Adams received one of the state's electoral votes—that cast by the elector from William Barry Grove's district of Fayetteville.[107]

In Virginia friends of Patrick Henry campaigned under the Federalist banner. Leven Powell, an Alexandria merchant and former Antifederalist ally of Henry, first suggested Henry's candidacy publicly in early September when he sent a circular letter around Loudoun and Fauquier counties. Powell expressed a willingness to support Adams and Pinckney as things then stood, but added: "It is now said Mr. PATRICK HENRY, of Virginia and Mr. Pinckney of South Carolina, will both be on the nomination. —Should it be so, I must declare that I feel at present disposed to vote for Mr. Henry." Powell stressed then and later that Henry's

[106] *Virginia Gazette and General Advertiser*, March 16, May 25, 1796.
[107] Henry M. Wagstaff, "Federalism in North Carolina," *The James Sprunt Historical Studies*, Vol. IX, No. 2 (Chapel Hill: University of North Carolina Publications, 1910), 28n.

candidacy would unite the country and would "do away that spirit of contention which at present rages with so much violence amongst us, and threatens destruction of the Union."[108] Three weeks later Charles Simms, declaring himself as candidate for elector representing Prince William, Stafford, and Fairfax counties, joined Powell in supporting Henry ahead of Adams, and both ahead of Jefferson.[109] No other candidates seem to have attempted to solicit any of the state's other nineteen electoral votes in behalf of the Federalist interest.

Powell waged a quixotic campaign. By October, despite his strenuous efforts, a popular enthusiasm for Henry had not materialized. Instead of redoubling his efforts to popularize his candidate Powell turned on Adams and circulated a vicious rumor that Fisher Ames, on a recent trip to Virginia, had commented upon the Vice President's marked partiality for Great Britain and the consequent need to bring Patrick Henry forward as an alternate candidate. The charge was hotly denied by an anonymous defender of the Vice President, and the populace was thus treated to a public battle within Federalist ranks.[110]

Powell's motives in placing Henry's name before the public remain a mystery. There is no evidence that either he or Simms was in any way tied to the Richmond faction, and Henry had earlier turned down Hamilton's offer of considerable support on a national scale. Whatever his reasons, Powell quickly attempted to repair the damage he had caused to party unity by inserting a strong pro-Adams essay in the *Virginia Gazette* at almost the same time that his anti-Adams essay appeared at Philadelphia. Also, some weeks

[108] This letter was reprinted in the *Virginia Gazette and General Advertiser*, September 14, 1796.

[109] *Norfolk Herald*, October 8, 1796.

[110] *North Carolina Minerva and Fayetteville Advertiser* (quoting the *Gazette of the United States*, n.d.), October 22, 1796, hereinafter cited as *North Carolina Minerva*.

later a pro-Jefferson writer charged Powell with promoting Henry's candidacy only as a means of splitting the Republican vote, thereby throwing the state to Adams. The obscurity of Powell's tactics could not materially have aided the Federalist cause. Henry refused to take public notice of the campaign being waged on his behalf until several days before the election, when he submitted a brief notice asking that his name be withdrawn. Powell made no comment on Henry's decision, but quietly cast his vote for Adams, one of the only two the Vice President received in the South in 1796. Simms was defeated.[111]

John Marshall was disgusted by the low quality of the Federalist efforts in Virginia. He informed Iredell in a retrospective critique in mid-December that the friends of government were totally disorganized during the recent campaign. Marshall clearly favored Adams over Jefferson, but did little himself to advance Adams' popularity in the state, while the Federalist candidate for presidential elector from the eastern shore was so confident of victory that he did not bother to campaign and was defeated as a result. Apparently the friends of government had high hopes of capturing the Norfolk-Princess Anne district too, but they miscalculated the sentiments of their candidate for elector, who ended by voting for Jefferson. Such miscalculations and campaign apathy were indicative of the low level of the Federalists' statewide party organization, if any at all existed.[112]

The friends of government in Virginia were far more certain of whom and what they were against than whom they were for. Their silence about the relative merits of Federalist candidates did not preclude an energetic campaign against Jefferson, which became scurrilous in the

[111] *Virginia Gazette and General Advertiser*, October 12, November 9, 1796; *Norfolk Herald*, November 2, 1796.
[112] Griffith J. McRee, ed., *Life and Correspondence of James Iredell*, (2 vols.; New York: Peter Smith, 1947), II, 425.

extreme. They charged Jefferson with political timidity and lack of personal courage, and so persistent were the Federalists in recalling to the electorate Jefferson's odd behavior as Governor during the British invasion of the state in 1781 that he was forced to procure affidavits in the middle of the campaign defending his earlier conduct.[113] Jefferson was also charged with deserting a republic in peril in 1793 to conduct a personal vendetta against the President. The Federalists also claimed that he was deeply in debt to British subjects and therefore a fair target for manipulation. Finally, Federalist propagandists maintained that Jefferson was no Christian and that "no man ought to be President who does not profess the Christian Religion."[114]

The Republicans countered by attacking Adams' alleged monarchism and urging that the people of the state protect themselves from domination by the "eastern interests" by retaining the presidency in the hands of a Virginian. These points proved far more effective, not only with the people of Virginia, but with the majority of North Carolinians as well. The results of the election indicated that the Republican bases of power were firmly anchored in these two states.

Georgia also remained firmly Republican in 1796. The Federalists, to be sure, had little chance to poll a large vote, but what opportunity they might have had was crushed by the actions of the commissioners sent down from Philadelphia in the summer of 1796 to readjust and redefine the border between Georgia and the lands belonging to the Creek nation. From the summer of 1795 on, even with the popular preoccupation with the Yazoo frauds, the people of Georgia had coveted the rich upland region which lay within

[113] Affidavits from John Blair *et al.* may be found in the Jefferson Papers, Vol. 100.
[114] *Virginia Gazette and General Advertiser*, October 12, 1796.

the Creek country between the Oconee and Ocmulgee rivers.[115] A state delegation, led by James Jackson and reinforced by the militia, therefore accompanied the United States commissioners and a body of dragoons to the conference grounds in July, 1796. To the rage of Jackson and his followers, however, the commissioners flagrantly favored the Indians, supported their determination not to sell, kept the Georgia militia away from the conference, and then upon their return to Savannah publicly lectured the people of the state on the need to deal justly with the Creeks in future years. Jackson did not miss the opportunity to translate this insult into partisan political terms, and in the fall elections only three of the state's twenty-four counties—all in the backcountry region around or near Augusta[116]—gave slim majorities to Adams. (Two others recorded tie votes.) The Yazoo faction had thus founded a small Federalist pocket, pledged to the support of a Massachusetts lawyer and aristocrat, in, of all places, frontier Georgia. However, the pocket was small, and its existence was precarious.

South Carolina politics in 1796 were ambiguous. The state went to Jefferson by a comfortable margin, but this apparently signified not a profound, enduring conversion to Republicanism, but simply a desire to see the presidency remain in the hands of a southerner—any southerner—in the wake of Jay's Treaty.

The Rutledge-Pinckney faction, which continued to dominate South Carolina politics through 1796 and beyond, still flirted with the federal administration though not with

[115] Seaborn Jones to Joseph Jones, from Augusta, July 8, 1795, Joseph Jones Papers, Duke University Library, Durham, N. C.

[116] The struggle between the United States Commissioners and the Georgia interests may be traced from the published apologia of both sides in the *Columbian Museum and Savannah Advertiser,* August 12, 1796; and the *Augusta Chronicle and Gazette of the State,* August 27, 1796; Phillips, *Georgia and State Rights,* 91.

local Federalists. Not long before the presidential campaign opened, Cotesworth Pinckney at last surrendered to the repeated pleas of the President to take a high national office and sailed for Paris to assume the critically important French ambassadorship.[117] At the same time Edward Rutledge began to shape his political strategy for the coming campaign, once he had been assured that Washington would not seek a third term. A letter which he wrote to his son in mid-July bristled with sectional consciousness and open animosity toward the "Eastern interests," which recently had tried to block Tennessee's admission to statehood and, thus, the equal political growth of the southern states within the Union. Rutledge apparently had made up his mind to secure a Jefferson-Pinckney victory in South Carolina to retain the presidency in southern hands for another four years. In this and a subsequent letter in mid-October, Rutledge indicated plainly that he wished to see Pinckney in the presidency with Jefferson as Vice President, excluding both the northern Republican, Clinton, and the northern Federalist, Adams.[118] Apparently he never deviated from this fixed plan during the campaign.

Young Robert Goodloe Harper was also active in South Carolina during the weeks preceding the 1796 election. As he represented Hamilton's interests, Harper also wished to see Pinckney brought home first. But Hamilton's public defense of the Jay Treaty and Edward Rutledge's equally public condemnation of it, precluded close contact and open alliance between Harper and Rutledge to push Pinckney into the first spot.

The Smith-Izard faction composed the third political

[117] Fitzpatrick, ed., *Washington*, XXXV, 129–31n.
[118] Edward to Henry Middleton Rutledge, from Charleston, July 21, October 20, 1796, Rutledge Papers, Dreer Collection, Historical Society of Pennsylvania, Philadelphia.

alignment in South Carolina in 1796. Its members supported the thinking of party regulars, staunchly standing by the ticket of Adams and Pinckney, in that order.

Notably absent from South Carolina in this year was a distinct Republican interest pledged to support Jefferson and Clinton. Because the Rutledge-Pinckney faction maintained obvious contacts with the administration and refused to support Jefferson for the presidency, South Carolina in 1796 still must be considered a Federalist-dominated state, one which nonetheless divided its loyalty between Pinckney and Thomas Jefferson.

The friends of government in South Carolina may have been severely divided in 1796, with some skirting close to Republicanism, but, unlike their colleagues in Virginia, North Carolina, and Georgia, they carried on an intense campaign and reawakened popular excitement over national political issues—including, for the first time, the presidential race. Harper and Rutledge could agree on one point: Pinckney was the ideal compromise candidate between Adams and Jefferson. While Harper hoped to use this argument as a means of inducing the Adams men to subordinate their candidate to Pinckney, however, Rutledge wished to see a Pinckney-Jefferson ticket and worked with ultimate success to advance the candidacies of both.[119] The only loser in this three-way battle could be Adams.

Izard and Smith did all they could for him. Edward Rutledge mentioned in the letter of November 1 to his son that "Great efforts" were being made in the state "by

---

[119] Harper to Ralph Izard, from Raleigh, November 4, 1796, in Ulrich B. Phillips, ed., "South Carolina Federalist Correspondence," *American Historical Review*, XIV (July, 1909), 783–84; Edward to Henry M. Rutledge, from Charleston, November 1, 1796, Rutledge Papers; Charleston *City Gazette and Daily Advertiser*, November 26, 1796, hereinafter cited as Charleston *City Gazette*. The anti-Adams essay of this date hammered on the old theme of the New Englander's partiality for monarchy.

certain Gentlemen for Mr. Adams." In early November, Smith sent his father-in-law, Ralph Izard, a pamphlet containing the "Phocion" letters, with the admonition that "Every man must lend his aid to save the Country at this important juncture." The younger man hoped that Izard would go to Columbia to exert his considerable influence at the right moment.[120]

Campaigning for the legislature, which was to choose the state's presidential electors, became brisk during the final month, and for the first time produced in the South an important facet of party development—the growth of ticketmaking. Numerous tickets were sent to the press from, among others, "A Merchant," "A Voter," "no party man," and "a great many MECHANICKS." One anonymous correspondent, in submitting his choices, noted how much it had become "the fashion to present the public with new lists for members of the [state] house [of representatives]." Another complained of being bombarded with such lists.[121]

The profusion of tickets was an indication both of the successes and failures of the various competing political interests in South Carolina in 1796. On the one hand, the Rutledge-Pinckney group, in particular, had been successful in arousing the grassroots. By 1796, Rutledge had established powerful support in the backcountry regions and along the coast. This aided his victory in the legislature that year and subsequently, with the support Harper added, made Federalism a statewide political force in the later 1790's.[122]

On the other hand, the very number of popular tickets, some of them varying in composition by only a name or two, reveals that the bitter divisions within South Carolina's rul-

[120] Smith to Izard, from Philadelphia, November 3, 1796, in Phillips, ed., "South Carolina Federalist Correspondence," 781–82.
[121] *South Carolina Gazette and Timothy's Daily Advertiser*, September 22, 1796; Charleston *City Gazette*, September 27, 29, October 4, 7, 8, 10, 1796.
[122] Edward to Henry Rutledge, November 1, 1796, Rutledge Papers.

ing gentry produced much popular confusion as well as excitement. The two competing electoral slates appearing in the legislature in December,[123] both containing the names of men who considered themselves loyal supporters of the federal administration, emphasized the unsettled state of South Carolina politics at the end of Washington's presidency. Federalist unity in the lowcountry and dominance of the state was for the moment at an end, but as yet there was no sign of a faction unequivocally devoted to Jeffersonian republicanism. In South Carolina the lowcountry oligarchs and the electorate alike seemed suspended between the emerging national parties after the election of 1796, but the chances for an immediate reunification of the Federalist interest seemed remote.

After the 1796 election it seemed indeed that across the South the small, but apparently active and influential, Federalist factions established earlier by Hamilton and Washington were either disbanded or dormant. Elitist political organizations so far had been incapable of expanding the interests of the friends of government. A fast-rising and vigorous, though still poorly organized, Republican interest seemed in firm control throughout most of the region. The way back to power, superficially at least, seemed long and hard for southern Federalists, and elitist political tradition offered little guidance and no consolation.

[123] On December 10, 1796, the Charleston *City Gazette* reprinted the vote for presidential electors in the legislature as follows:

"Jefferson's Ticket"		"Adams' Ticket"	
Edward Rutledge, Sen.	113 votes	A. Vanderhorst	37 votes
Genl. Pickens	112	H. W. DeSaussure	29
Judge Matthews	112	Genl. Barnwell	28
Colonel Taylor	110	Genl. [William] Washington	28
Capt. Simkins	110	David Ramsay	28
John Rutledge, Jr.	109	Robert Barnwell	28
John Chesnut	109	Nathan Russell	28
Wm. Thomas	109	John Bull	24

IV. Reconstruction, 1797

In the years after the election of 1796, Federalist leaders in the South began to rally their forces and move toward true party organization while making active efforts to enlist popular support. Their partisan politicking proved so successful that by the midterm Congressional elections of 1798 they had achieved nearly a parity of power and influence with their Republican opponents in many sections of the South. This sudden burst of political energy cannot be attributed to any discernible change in the temperament or the values of leading Federalist spokesmen in the South, but to two profoundly important developments during the final year of Washington's presidency.

The first was the increasingly rapid rise of the Republican party in and out of Congress. The campaign in the House to cripple Jay's Treaty, though in the end not successful, nonetheless frightened many Federalists. "Though the anglomen have in the end got their Treaty through," Jefferson remarked as the Fourth Congress prepared to rise,

and so far have triumphed over the cause of republicanism, yet it has been to them a dear bought victory. it [sic] has given the most radical shock to their party, which it ever received; and there is no doubt they would be glad to be replaced on the ground they possessed the instant before the nomination extraordinary. they [sic] see that nothing can support them but the colossus of the President's merits with the people and the moment that he retires, that the successor, if a Monocrat will be overborne by the republican sense of his constituents.¹

Adams' poor showing in the South the next fall seemed to support Jefferson's prediction of the eventual defeat of the "Monocrat" interest. In April the Republicans had lost their bid by only three votes to destroy the Treaty in the House; the following December they lost their attempt for the presidency by the same margin. The Federalists could count only two persistent supporters of Jay's Treaty among the southern delegations in the House during the spring; early the following winter their presidential candidate received but two southern electoral votes.² Federalist influence in the South was obviously in danger of being completely destroyed by the close of Washington's presidency. If it were thoroughly shut out of the South, Federalism was certain to perish eventually as a purely sectional interest in opposition to a national party.

Appearances were somewhat deceiving, however, and the political situation below the Potomac at the end of 1796 was neither sufficiently clear nor so disheartening as to discourage later efforts by the friends of government to gain popular favor. Despite notable victories, the Republicans had been hesitant to wage full-scale warfare against the administration, both in and out of Congress. In early

¹ Jefferson to Monroe, July 10, 1796, Jefferson Papers, Vol. 100.
² The two southern Federalists to uphold staunchly the Treaty in debate and during the crucial divisions over the Livingston and Thomas Blount resolutions were Harper and Smith of South Carolina. In the final vote on the Treaty, which was carried 51 to 48, only 4 of the 51 votes came from the southern delegations, while of the 48 representatives voting against the Treaty, no less than 33 were from the South, plus 2 more from the frontier state of Kentucky. *Annals of Congress*, IV, 438–44, 457–64, 495–500, 514, 530, 747–60, 782–83, 1289–91; Robert Goodloe Harper to his Constituents, May 2, 1796, in Elizabeth Donnan, ed., "Papers of James A. Bayard, 1796–1815," *Annual Report of the American Historical Association*, 1913 (2 vols.; Washington, D. C.: Government Printing Office, 1914), I, 21.

1796, Madison admitted uneasiness about the wisdom of continuing agitation in Congress against the Jay Treaty. He stated that his reluctance stemmed in part from strong counterreaction in favor of ratification in the northern and middle states.[3]

Madison's wish to avoid a showdown with the President and with a large portion of the electorate in the northern states obviously was shared by many of his colleagues. The results of Hamilton's pro-Treaty petition campaign in the northern and middle states and in Virginia began to flood congressmen's desks at the same time that the President's message of refusal was being considered; and as a consequence the Republicans revealed a tendency to panic and collapse.[4] Though the Republicans earlier had obtained majorities of twenty-five and twenty-two, respectively, on the Livingston and Blount resolutions, which assured the right of the House to consider controversial treaties, the party's fragile discipline disintegrated enough to allow the necessary funds for the Treaty to be voted.

During the presidential campaign Republican leaders once again refused to wage partisan warfare, and they placed national tranquility, personal honor, and friendship above party and section. When, for example, Jefferson perceived that he and Adams might tie in the Electoral College, he warned his supporters to prepare to shift their votes to the New Englander as "he has always been my Senior."[5] Moreover, even as late as 1796 the Republicans had not begun to exploit fully the vast power of public

[3] Madison to Monroe, from Philadelphia, December 20, 1795, to Jefferson, from Philadelphia, December 27, 1795, January 26, 1796, Madison Papers, Vols. 18, 19.
[4] Harper to his Constituents, May 2, 1796, in Donnan, ed., "James A. Bayard," I, 21.
[5] Quoted in Stephen G. Kurtz, *The Presidency of John Adams: The Collapse of Federalism, 1795–1800* (New York: A. S. Barnes & Company, Inc., 1961), 200.

opinion and discontent which was at their disposal. Although it sincerely disliked aristocracy and "monocracy" and was determined to reshape American institutions and values along more democratic lines, the party of Madison and Jefferson also had emerged from the elitist tradition of eighteenth-century Anglo-American parliamentary politics, where the emphasis was upon personal self-interest and loose, shifting factional coalitions. The party's eventual triumph as a truly creative political force in the United States came only after years of effort to free itself from the tight bonds of political custom. In 1796 that effort was less than half complete. Stephen Kurtz' close examination of that year's presidential campaign indicates that more often than not the results of the election in any one state were determined on the Republican—as on the Federalist—side by political factions dominated by members of the traditional ruling circles. Only Pennsylvania proved to be a clearcut exception.[6] After 1796, therefore, the friends of government did not need to feel that regaining political power in the South was an impossible task. Nor did they yet feel—as many did after 1800—that the whole political climate of the country had changed so radically because of Republican triumphs as to exclude them forevermore from a meaningful voice in the conduct of public affairs.

If the results of the presidential election in the South emphasized the Republicans' strong hold over the electorate, they also tended to mask the remaining pockets of Federalist authority within the region. The 1796-1797 Congressional elections told a different story. In Virginia, for example, the outspoken Federalist, Daniel Morgan, was elected to Congress by the citizens of Winchester district in the northern Shenandoah Valley, while in North Carolina, William Barry Grove was reelected from Fayetteville. Nor was

[6] *Ibid.*, chapters 7–9.

South Carolina a total loss for the Federalists, which it seemed to be from a perusal of the state's vote in the Electoral College. William Loughton Smith retained his Congressional seat from Charleston, while young Robert Goodloe Harper swept to an impressive victory over the older and popular Pierce Butler in the backcountry district of Ninety-Six.[7] Southern Federalists thus possessed a very slim but active cadre in public life on which they could rebuild their power when the opportunity arose.

Though many southern Federalists showed an amazing political ineptitude during the time of the Jay Treaty debate and the election of 1796, it is nevertheless true that they suffered from wretched political luck in the early 1790's. They repeatedly were identified with, and often forced to defend, policies which deeply outraged public opinion. But in December, 1796, an event in Paris gave the southern friends of government their first opportunity to exploit an issue that evoked favorable public interest. Earlier in the year Cotesworth Pinckney had reluctantly agreed to accept the French ambassadorship, thereby identifying himself with the administration's foreign policy. When Pinckney was brutally if civilly rebuffed by the Directory as he sought to press his credentials, friends of government in the South were at last handed an issue which could be used to identify Federalism with the defense of national honor and rights. A new spirit of aggressive self-confidence swept through the southern wing of the Federalist party after Pinckney's unhappy experience, and its effects were as quickly felt in Philadelphia as in Virginia and the Carolinas.

Pinckney's rebuke resulted from the French reaction to Jay's Treaty. According to an essay from Paris published in a North Carolina newspaper in February, 1798, France's

[7] Charleston *City Gazette*, October 12, 25, 1796.

objections to Jay's Treaty centered about two points: first, the Americans had no right, under the existing Franco-American Treaty of 1778, to conclude a treaty with an enemy of the Republic; and secondly, current American trade with Great Britain, which Jay's Treaty formalized and organized, was in direct opposition to Article XII of the 1778 Treaty.[8] With these complaints as a justification for action, the French as early as January, 1796, began to seize American vessels, particularly in the West Indies.[9] The American government promptly protested to the Directory over the new policy of commercial harassment, but the President had concluded by mid-1796 that his complaints were having no effect because of the mutual admiration and affection existing between Ambassador Monroe and the Directory. As a result, Pinckney was sent to France as Monroe's successor, but, upon arrival, he found that he would not be received until the Directory was given a satisfactory explanation for Monroe's recall. Pinckney acted with coolness during his dealings with intermediary agents of the Directory; but his papers were not accepted, and he eventually was forced to leave Paris for Holland, where he immediately informed his government of the incident.[10]

News of Pinckney's rejection could not have reached Philadelphia at a worse time. Adams' administration had been in office less than a week, and doubts still existed in the minds of many whether a Federalist President from New England and a Republican Vice President from Virginia would be able to work in sufficient harmony to ensure the

[8] *State Gazette of North Carolina*, February 1, 1798.

[9] Hamilton to Washington, from New York, January 19, 1796, Washington Papers, Vol. 277; J. W. G. Prescott to John Gray Blount, from Kingston, Jamaica, January 19, 1796, in William Henry Masterson, ed., *The John Gray Blount Papers*, Vol. III (Raleigh: North Carolina State Department of History and Archives, 1965), 8–9.

[10] Memo of Secretary of War McHenry to Washington, May 14, 1797, Washington Papers, Vol. 281.

continuation of the Union.[11] Moreover, many other problems plagued the new President, including relations not only with political enemies of the other party, such as Jefferson, but with antagonists in his own party, notably Hamilton.

Hamilton's position in the party at this time was at best equivocal. It was commonly known that he had tried to run Pinckney ahead of Adams the previous fall,[12] and even his staunchest ally in the House, Smith of South Carolina, had been opposed to him on this issue. By April the Hamilton-Smith collaboration seems to have been restored, as Hamilton was gratuitously offering Smith ideas, and perhaps polished speeches as well, on the current state of affairs. The alliance between the two doubtless had been weakened by Smith's apostasy in 1796, however, and Hamilton during 1797 turned more and more to Secretary of War James McHenry of Maryland as a competent aide who could be trusted to introduce Hamiltonian ideas into the Adams cabinet.[13]

Beyond the problem of dealing with real and potential enemies, the President also felt restrained by his lack of support in the South. Several weeks before his inauguration Adams told Elbridge Gerry that "information will not be easy for me to obtain especially from the Southern States, where my Friends are generally So old and so disinclined to interfere, if not so indolent, that I shall be obliged to receive it frequently from Enemies or at least from Cold

[11] Jefferson to Madison, from Monticello, January 1, 1797, Jefferson to T. M. Randolph, from Philadelphia, March 11, 1797, Jefferson Papers, Vol. 101.
[12] John Adams to Abigail Adams, from Philadelphia, January 9, 1797, Adams Papers, Reel 383.
[13] Hamilton to Smith, from New York, April 5, 1797, William Loughton Smith Papers; Hamilton to McHenry, March 22, 1797, in Bernard C. Steiner, *Life and Correspondence of James McHenry* (Cleveland: The Burrows Brothers Co., 1907), 212–13.

Friends." Also, the recent election still was an open wound. At the end of March, Adams confided to Knox his bitterness about what might have been. Had Jay or some others been the opponents in question, things might have been different, "but to see such a Character as Jefferson, and much more such an unknown being as Pinckney brought over my head and trampling on the Bellies of hundreds of other men infinitely his Superiors in Talents Services and reputation, filled me with apprehensions for the safety of us all, it demonstrated to me that if the project Succeeded our Constitution could not have lasted four years."[14] Clearly, a profound rift existed between the President from New England and the southern states as his administration began. This sense of a New England-southern political cleavage was not confined to Adams' mind alone. A fellow citizen of Massachusetts wrote to the President in May of his fears that "French politics may have contaminated the true principles of government" in the South. In late April, just before the special session of Congress met, Timothy Pickering wrote to Hamilton concerning the propriety of including Cotesworth Pinckney in a proposed three-man mission to France which Hamilton was pressing on the cabinet. Pickering saw Pinckney as at best a "neutral character" who might hold the balance if a Republican and a Federalist were nominated alongside him. He was in no way considered a staunch friend of government.[15] Such was the legacy of Hamilton's electoral scheme of 1796.

The President and others who might have foreseen the sectionalization of the Federalist party as a result of the election of 1796 did not, however, sufficiently reckon with the various pressures within southern politics at the time,

[14] Adams to Gerry, from Philadelphia, February 20, 1797, to Knox, from Philadelphia, March 30, 1797, Adams Papers, Reel 117.
[15] Joseph Ward to Adams, from Newton, May 5, 1797, *ibid.*, Reel 384; Pickering to Hamilton, April 29, 1797, Hamilton Papers, Vol. 30.

nor did they comprehend the enormous anti-French reaction which Pinckney's rebuff generated among southern political leaders. Only when Congress met in special session in mid-May to deal with the growing crisis with France, topped by the Pinckney affair, did it become obvious that a new sentiment favorable to Federalism was beginning to rise in at least three southern states.

Congress convened on May 16 and immediately heard a presidential message describing Pinckney's humiliation, a French decree of March 2 aimed at American commerce, and Adams' recommendation of a comprehensive plan for defense. Adams' plan included the creation of a navy and of coastal defenses, as well as the enlargement of the artillery and cavalry branches of the present army. The President also asked Congress to consider the establishment of a provisional army.[16]

The Federalist cause in the subsequent session was aided by Republican stupidity. Because of the insult to Pinckney and the commercial decree, Republicans would only have been following common sense had they attenuated their vociferous loyalties to France. Quite the opposite occurred, however, and, cheered on by the Vice President, the Republicans in Congress had the temerity to tack an amendment to the representatives' reply to Adams' speech, expressing a desire that the French be placed on a most-favored-nation basis commercially. While the motion passed 52 to 47, which Jefferson at the time believed was an adequate reflection of relative party strength, the first division appeared in the previously solid Virginia Republican delegation. Thomas Evans, from the district composing. York and Mathews counties and Williamsburg, voted with the minority to deny France equal commercial privileges. The following day, when the motion was reconsidered,

[16] Kurtz, *Presidency of John Adams*, 230–31.

James Machir, from the northwestern frontier counties of the state, also defected from Republican ranks and voted with Evans and Daniel Morgan, the Federalist from Winchester.[17]

In the following days the names of South Carolina Federalists began to appear in Jefferson's correspondence, as Harper and Smith led the eventually unsuccessful fight in the House to allow the arming of American merchantmen.[18] Insofar as the South Carolina delegation was concerned, however, the most significant development of the session was the conversion of John Rutledge, Jr., from a Republican to a Federalist position.

Rutledge's conversion was not the result of a passing fancy or of suave but firm pressure exerted by professional politicians on an impressionable novice. It resulted from agonized deliberation in an atmosphere of assumed crisis. John Rutledge, Jr., as well as his uncle, had in fact had very close relations with Jefferson in the past. While on a grand tour in 1788, Rutledge had stopped in Paris, where he had been warmed by Jefferson's kindly solicitude. The American ambassador had even prepared travel notes for Rutledge and his companion, Thomas Lee Shippen, Jr., and later had sent the young men useful letters of introduction. At the same time the two apparently had been received with some coolness by John Adams, for in April, 1788, Eliza Rutledge had written her son, advising him to "never let trifles affect your spirits—I mean such as John Adams insolence."[19]

Young Rutledge's generally Republican loyalty remained

[17] Jefferson to T. M. Randolph, June 1, 1797, Jefferson Papers, Vol. 101.
[18] Jefferson to Madison, from Philadelphia, June 8, 1797, Madison Papers, Vol. 20.
[19] Travel notes and letter of Jefferson to John Rutledge, Jr., from Paris, Summer, 1788; Jefferson to John Rutledge, Jr., March 25, 1789; Eliza Rutledge to John Rutledge, Jr., from Charleston, April 6, 1788, John Rutledge, Jr., Papers, Duke University Library, Durham, N. C.

intact throughout the early 1790's, aided no doubt by his uncle's cordial correspondence with Jefferson; and of course he had unsuccessfully opposed Hamilton's lieutenant, William Loughton Smith, in 1794. When he went north in early May, 1797, to take his seat in Congress, there seemed little doubt of his strong Republicanism, and his uncle sent along with him an almost adulatory letter to the Vice President.[20]

As a newcomer, nonetheless, the young man was bound to be courted by both sides. William Loughton Smith's correspondence at this time reveals a sudden and unprecedented surge of party spirit within the Congressional delegations caused by the alarming news from France and the threat of the first full-scale war the American Union ever had faced. Southern congressmen of rival political persuasions never would again amiably share a phaeton or stagecoach from their homes to Philadelphia, as Thomas Blount and William Barry Grove had done as late as December, 1795.[21] For the first time the question of who lived and dined with whom became of crucial importance. A politician's boarding house became his castle, from which he sallied forth every morning to do battle with the enemy. Rivals within the walls were to be converted at all costs, ignored if conversion failed, and opposed if they had the temerity to proselytize. According to Smith, the Republicans put Rutledge on the House select committee to reply to Adams' May 16 speech, and then "every manoeuvre was practiced to seduce Rutledge and bring him over on the Comm."ᵉ to vote for Venable's [Republican] draft, but he stood out and was decidedly for a high-toned report." Pre-

[20] Edward Rutledge to Jefferson, from Charleston, May 4, 1797, Jefferson Papers, Vol. 101.
[21] Thomas to John Gray Blount, from Philadelphia, December 11, 1795, in Alice Barnwell Keith, ed., *The John Gray Blount Papers* (2 vols.; Raleigh: State Department of Archives and History, 1952, 1959), II, 617.

sumably, Rutledge was subjected to the same partisan barrage over the evening wine and in the House during the day that Smith reports was the fate of his namesake, Major William Smith, upon his arrival.[22]

Despite these high-pressure tactics, however, Rutledge remained unimpressed. As he wrote to his "Uncle Ned," "the flattery & artfulness of S & H [Smith and Harper] can make no more impressions on me than the pressure of my little Daughters little finger would upon the Pillars of Saint Philips Church."[23] In this letter young Rutledge unloaded his contempt impartially upon not only Smith and Harper, but also Gallatin, Nicholas, and Livingston. All five "always write their Speeches and give them to the Printers," Rutledge reported scornfully.

What did impress and enrage Rutledge at this time was the attempt by the "red hot democrats" to defend Monroe at Cotesworth Pinckney's expense, saying Pinckney's incompetence was justification for his refusal by the French. If nothing else, this blind determination of the Republicans to defend the defamers of his uncle's closest friend must have caused Rutledge profound unhappiness. In fact, he told his uncle that "I had a long conversation with our friend Mr. Jefferson last Sunday about much of this business," but it was an unsatisfactory session. Adams had just decided to make one more attempt at negotiations with the French and had submitted Cotesworth Pinckney's name as one of the three commissioners. The Virginia and North Carolina Republican senators voted solidly in the minority against Pinckney, which deeply shocked Rutledge—and his entire state when the news was received. When Rutledge tried

[22] William Loughton Smith to Ralph Izard, May 23, 29, 1797, in Ulrich B. Phillips, ed., "South Carolina Federalist Correspondence," *American Historical Review*, XIV (July, 1909), 786–88.

[23] June 27, 1797, Rutledge Papers.

to draw Jefferson out on the matter, the Vice President agreed to write an explanatory letter to Charleston. Rutledge closed his letter with the ominous observation that while Jefferson was a great and good man, "the severe prosecution [sic] he has lately undergone (& which continues) has occasioned a little French bias."[24]

Like many others, young Rutledge also found himself incensed over the depredations of French cruisers and favored a stamp tax to implement the President's proposed defense system. By this time, early July, 1797, his Federalism was gradually emerging. An occurrence soon afterwards assured his conversion.

During the debate in the House on the President's message, Harper implied that Monroe had been a tool of the Directory while in France. The excited Republicans immediately concluded that Monroe had become a martyr, and when he arrived from France several days later, an ostentatious public dinner was arranged in his behalf. John Rutledge, Jr., who disliked Monroe because of his perhaps unintentional involvement in Pinckney's rebuff by the Directory, reported sadly that Jefferson had attended the dinner. The aristocratic disdain of a haughty young low-country oligarch is evident in Rutledge's secondhand description of the dinner: "Here you saw an American disorganized &c. there a blundering wild Irishman—in one corner a banished Genevan [an obvious allusion to Gallatin] & in another a french spye—on one side a greasy butcher & on another a dirty cobbler."[25] By etching his portrait of the dinner in venom, Rutledge severed all links with the Republicans. Fundamentally, by mid-1797 his quarrel with that party was over two issues: first, a fear—possibly justified—that the Republicans were preparing to sell out American

[24] *Ibid.*
[25] John Rutledge, Jr., to Edward Rutledge, July 4, 1797, *ibid.*

interests to the Directory, and second, rage at the implied humiliation meted out to Cotesworth Pinckney by Republican senators and others in the name of friendship for France.

The conversion of John Rutledge, Jr., to Federalism boosted the party's power in the southern Congressional delegations. The South Carolina delegation now consisted of three powerful Federalist members, Smith, Harper, and Rutledge. Smith soon departed for Lisbon as American ambassador to Portugal, but he was replaced, at John Rutledge, Jr.'s insistence, by Thomas Pinckney, whose equally staunch Federalism was rapidly acknowledged, even by the frequently vindictive Adams clan.[26]

The Virginia delegation during this session included three Federalists of average abilities but strong loyalties, James Machir, Daniel Morgan, and Thomas Evans.[27] Within the North Carolina delegation Grove continued to represent the Federalists in the upper Cape Fear River valley. Thus, by the opening of the first regular session of the Fifth Congress in October, 1797, Federalism had staged a spectacular revival of strength within southern Congressional delegations. This was especially true of South Carolina, whose lowcountry representatives helped to reconstruct the old Federalist Congressional alliance of New England, New York, and coastal South Carolina. Moreover, Harper, Rutledge, and Smith, and later Pinckney, were men of ability. All four energetically and effectively upheld the Federalist cause in the House during the later years of the decade,

[26] John Rutledge, Jr., to Edward Rutledge, from Philadelphia, July 7, 1797; Edward Rutledge to John Rutledge, Jr., from Charleston, August 23, 1797, *ibid.*; Thomas Simons to Jacob Read, from Charleston, August 10, 1797, Jacob Read Papers; Abigail Adams to John Quincy Adams, from Philadelphia, April 13, 1798, Adams Papers, Reel 388.

[27] All three voted with the other Federalists on the two bills of greatest importance considered during the session, those calling for the construction of six frigates and for the creation of a stamp tax to raise revenue for their construction. *Annals of Congress*, VII, 385–434.

and, in fact, in Harper and Rutledge the Federalists found their most effective floor men.

During the spring and summer of 1797, the suddenly revitalized southern wing of the Federalist party in Congress moved to reestablish cordial patronage communications with the President. William Loughton Smith quickly ingratiated himself with Adams during the special session of 1797 and increasingly sat at the President's dinner table. Considering Adams' earlier comments about his ignorance of southern politics, Smith presumably volunteered to enlighten the President about who in that region could be trusted and who could not. James Gunn, who had no significant support in his own state, made himself available as a patronage agent of the President and on at least one occasion cooperated with Henry Lee of Virginia in seeking an appointment for a deserving but obscure Savannah Federalist, Colonel Armstrong.[28]

The strongest evidence of increasing southern influence in Federalist patronage matters, however, came in June, 1797, when Adams made one more attempt to negotiate American differences with France. He decided, after consulting the cabinet, to send a three-man mission to Paris. Of the three chosen, two were southerners—Cotesworth Pinckney and John Marshall. The Republicans were not alone in opposing Pinckney. Pickering, it will be recalled, also had grave reservations about the correctness of the general's views. Most likely Smith or Rutledge set the President's mind at rest about this, which must have pleased the South Carolina Federalists—and Edward Rutledge.

Adams' selection of John Marshall was a signal victory for the Federalists of Virginia. Charles Lee had been in

[28] Smith to Ralph Izard, from Philadelphia, June 2, 1797, Phillips, ed., "South Carolina Federalist Correspondence," 790; James Gunn to John Adams, from Savannah, May 1, 1797, Adams Papers, Reel 384.

the administration as Attorney General since 1795, and with Marshall in an important post, friends of government in Virginia could feel that they once again enjoyed a sensible influence in national affairs. Adams and Marshall had not met prior to the latter's arrival in Philadelphia in preparation for his journey to Paris. However, the two quickly established a cordial, trusting relationship which endured on an official level until 1801. Writing to Gerry in early July, the President remarked that "Pinckney & marshall [sic] are able and honourable and virtuous men." After his discussions with Marshall the President was even more enthusiastic. "General Marshall took leave of me last night," the President informed Gerry; "he is a plain man, very Sensible, Cautious, guarded & learned in the Law of Nations —I think you will be pleased with him." Marshall, in turn, was pleased and impressed with Adams' character and abilities.[29] From that time on, Marshall's talents and influence were assured of prominence over a wider area than Richmond or Virginia.

While southern Federalists reestablished influence within their state Congressional delegations and restored patronage contacts with the administration, friends of government in the South on state and occasionally even local levels moved slowly toward party organization.

In Virginia, 1797 was a year of growth and consolidation for the Federalists. It opened with friends of government in an ugly mood over the results of the recent election and determined to do anything to alter their unfavorable position. Specifically, David Stuart initiated a movement to deprive "any emigrant to this Country to have the right of voting or being voted for at an election—They were by far

[29] Washington to Gerry, July 7, 17, 1797, Adams Papers, Reel 117; Marshall to Mrs. Marshall, from Philadelphia, July 2, 1797, in "Letters of John Marshall to His Wife," *William and Mary Quarterly*, Series 2, III (April, 1923), 73.

the most zealous among us, and the most influential." As early as December, 1796, Stuart was writing to friends in the Virginia Assembly hoping to get such a law passed by that body.[30] The seeds of alien and sedition legislation thus were sown early on Virginia soil.

Talk among Virginia Federalists of mounting a legislative offensive aimed at the presumed sources of Republican power was matched by a growing intimacy between Richmond and Philadelphia Federalists by the turn of the year. Randolph, who had defected to the Republicans after his disgrace as Secretary of State in the Fauchet affair, informed Madison in early January that the area of Virginia around Richmond "is very little more . . . than a colony of Philadelphia. No conversation, no object political commercial, and in many instances, legal, can occur, without looking up to that city as the standard. . . . Whatever is said in favor of the government is circulated under franks from the treasury &c. But not a Virginia eye has seen Gallatin's pamphlet, Dwight's address to the President, &c. &c."[31]

Despite Federalist attempts to make at least the Richmond area a closed society, politically speaking, the spring elections went against them as usual, though the voters did send three Federalists to Philadelphia, something never before accomplished. According to Marshall, the Republicans were able to convince many voters that current tensions with France were a result solely of the Jay Treaty. Despite the election results, however, there was strong indication that by this time Marshall and others of like philosophy throughout the state were preparing to combat actively the current Republican predominance. In separate letters to the Attorney General, Marshall and his political ally, Jonathan

[30] Stuart to Washington, from Hope Park, December 18, 1796, Washington Papers, Vol. 282.
[31] Randolph to Madison, January 8, 1797, from Richmond, Madison Papers, Vol. 20.

Hopkins, exhibited detailed knowledge of political affairs and of sources of Federalist loyalty in most of the counties east of the Blue Ridge and north of the James. Hopkins, moreover, was well aware of the Federalist leanings of Evans, Machir, and Morgan even before the three reached Philadelphia.[32]

Beyond the Richmond Federalists' increasing preoccupation with political affairs throughout the state, there were indications of widespread Federalist activity prior to the spring elections. Republicans freely admitted this. In the Congressional district of Louisa, Spotsylvania, and Orange counties, for example, rival candidates were in constant attendance at the courts and places of public meetings, "paying their respects to the freeholders so that neither will ascribe their disappointment to his indolence." Moreover, for the first time leading Republicans worried about the outcome of elections to both Assembly and Congressional seats. It is clear from contemporary correspondence that the rapid development of Republican party organization in Virginia at least was partially a reaction to a corresponding growth of Federalist spirit, harmony, and effectiveness there during and after 1797.[33]

Virginia Federalists did not cease their activities after the elections; they simply shifted the emphasis of their attack. In June, Federalist judges at Richmond "courted presentments" from their grand jury that deplored any criticism of federal officials. According to one incensed Republican, these presentments were calculated to check freedom of speech, and there seems to be litttle doubt that the Virginia Federalists at this time were attempting to promote a popular sense of unquestioned loyalty to the

[32] John Marshall to Charles Lee, from Richmond, April 20, 1797; Hopkins to Charles Lee, from Richmond, April 21, 1797, Adams Papers, Reel 384.

[33] Joseph Jones to Madison, from Charlottesville, February 5, 1797, and from Fredericksburg, March 8, 27, 1797, Madison Papers, Vol. 20.

national administration, using the growing crisis with France as the excuse.[34]

The next and most important step by Virginia Federalists to expand and strengthen their party apparatus came in the fall. According to one Republican observer, little formal party spirit existed in western Virginia even at this date, as party battles continued to be confined largely to "the great Towns" east of the Blue Ridge.[35] Therefore, it would be a great advantage if the Federalists in Virginia could unite the active supporters of Patrick Henry in 1796, who seemed to be centered in the Alexandria area, with the members of the Richmond Federalist faction. By mid-October this had been accomplished in a manner typical of Virginia Federalism: Leven Powell's relative and business agent, Burr Powell, was cut in on the spoils accruing from the Marshall-Lee Fairfax purchase.[36] Thereafter a Richmond-Alexandria Federalist axis in Virginia, led by John Marshall and Leven Powell, respectively, functioned harmoniously. When in June, 1798, Powell decided to run for Congress, he immediately informed Charles Lee of his decision and received Lee's pleased approbation in reply.[37]

The year 1797 did not bring a similar rejuvenation of Federalist fortunes in North Carolina. Davie, Johnston, and

[34] Uriah Honest to John Adams, from Georgetown, June 23, 1797, Adams Papers, Reel 384; Peregrine Fitzhugh to Jefferson, from Washington County, Maryland, June 20, 1797, Jefferson Papers, Vol. 102.

[35] Arthur Campbell to Jefferson, from Washington County, Virginia, September 30, 1797, *ibid.*

[36] Leven Powell to Burr Powell, November 21, 1790, January 30, 1791, in William E. Dodd, ed., "Correspondence of Leven Powell," *The John P. Branch Historical Papers of Randolph-Macon College* (Richmond: Everett Wadding Co., 1901), I, 224–29; agreement between Burr Powell and Charles Marshall representing James and John Marshall and Henry Lee, Marshall Family Papers, University of Virginia Library, Charlottesville, Va. James Machir was also brought into the Fairfax group sometime during the late 1790's. See indenture between John Marshall and wife and James Machir, dated May 15, 1799, *ibid.*

[37] Lee to Powell, from Philadelphia, June 6, 1798, in Dodd, ed., "Leven Powell," 230.

other veterans remained in retirement from politics, and the Blounts were now solid Republicans, apparently much to the anger of many friends of government in the state.[38] Early in the year Davie commented bitterly upon the Blounts' apostasy and also expressed uneasiness about ever-worsening Franco-American relations. "These madmen," he said of the French, "possess nothing upon which you can certainly calculate; no moral principle, no fixed political data; they seem to have no system but anarchy, no plan but plunder and military tyranny."[39] Johnston also was enraged by French conduct. "Nothing can be more odious and despicable than that Republican pride and haughtiness which they affect on all occasions," he wrote to Iredell in the spring.[40] Yet apparently the two did not transfer their anger into effective political action. According to Johnston, politics were scarcely mentioned at the spring term at Halifax Court, and the public storm which had swept through the nation seems to have passed North Carolina by. In late May, Iredell delivered a fiery, partisan charge to the District Grand Jury at Richmond, which resulted in presentments against those in any way critical of public officials. Samuel J. Cabell promptly wrote a reply, and Iredell followed just as quickly with a defense. The judge was encouraged in his struggle by both Johnston and Davie, but again, the two went no further in defense of Federalism.[41]

Though North Carolina's nominal Federalist leaders were

[38] John Gray Blount to Capt. J. L. B. Monyard, from Washington (N. C.), February 8, 1797, in Masterson, ed., *John Gray Blount*, III, 132–33. The Blounts' adherence to the Republican interest by 1796 assured that group of the undivided loyalty of the new state of Tennessee, which was virtually owned by William Blount. See *ibid.*, 63n.; and William to John Gray Blount, from Knoxville, November 7, 1797, *ibid.*, 175–76.

[39] Davie to Iredell, from Halifax, February 1, 1797, Iredell Papers.

[40] Johnston to Iredell, May 3, 1797, from Williamstown, in Griffith J. McRee, ed., *Life and Correspondence of James Iredell* (2 vols.; New York: Peter Smith, 1947), II, 503.

[41] *Ibid.*, 507–15.

publicly silent and inactive during the first year of Adams' administration, North Carolina's newspapers were not. In such a decentralized political society as that of North Carolina a vigorous, united press was the most important, cohesive element in public life. As early as the winter of 1797 the established newspapers began to move toward a position of moderate Federalism that they held throughout the presidency of John Adams and the election of 1800. Abraham Hodge's *Minerva* led the way. Hodge had been a staunch friend of government in the early 1790's, until he was apparently silenced by the huge weight of anti-administration opinion in the state. The simultaneous growth of Franco-American tensions and the intense Republican opposition to the Jay Treaty, however, reactivated his Federalist loyalties. In January, 1797, he ridiculed the French for allegedly making war on the United States as a means of chastising the Americans for their refusal to elect the tool of French interests, Thomas Jefferson. Toward the end of the year Hodge concentrated his editorial fire on the Republicans alone, charging them in what would soon become conventional party rhetoric with being "an abandoned, despicable and unprincipled faction."[42]

News of Pinckney's rebuff was enough to send the other North Carolina editors hurrying after Hodge. Allamand Hall's *Wilmington Gazette* reprinted material from the Federalist printer, Peter Porcupine, which sought to arouse American patriotism against the French.[43] In Edenton the *State Gazette of North Carolina* attempted to stir the public's anger as early as February by reprinting every available scrap of information about French seizures of American shipping, and in September reprinted rumors of secret enlistments by French agents from among the backcountrymen

[42] *North Carolina Minerva*, January 21, November 4, 1797.
[43] *Wilmington Gazette*, April 20, 1797.

of South Carolina.⁴⁴ At New Bern, Alexander Martin's *North Carolina Gazette*, in addition to publishing accounts of French commercial depredations, delivered a long tirade against the French and the party of Thomas Jefferson based upon the filibustering expedition with which William Blount was identified. Blount always had voted with the "French interest" in Congress and had been "intimate with Jefferson, Giles, Nicholas, Venable, the French minister and consul, and in fine with all the agents of the French republic." Could it not be concluded, then, that his ill-starred journey was part of a plot laid in Paris to establish a new French Republic in America? Evidence indicated that Blount had first approached the British ambassador with his scheme of a western conquest and the establishment of a new state in the Southwest, but the British ambassador had discouraged him. Evidently the French had not. Moreover, "it is said that the late president received accurate information from an authentic source in France, as long ago as the year '90 or '91 even before the death of the King, that a deep laid and well digested plan had been formed by the government of that country to establish a republic in America, to rival and balance that of the United States." The essay suggested that the Whiskey Rebellion "if not created, was at least fostered by French influence" a further reference to the Federalists' current favorite figure of scorn, Albert Gallatin.⁴⁵

Such an outpouring of contempt toward the Republicans must be balanced against the traditional Anglophobia of many North Carolinians and indeed many southerners. No editor or politician was prepared to embrace England simply as a result of rejecting France. Even the staunchest Federalist essayists pointed out that Americans should be "alive

⁴⁴ *State Gazette of North Carolina*, February 16, March 2, September 14, 1797.
⁴⁵ *North Carolina Gazette*, February 4, March 25, August 5, 1797.

to insults and injuries, from any foreign nation whatever."[46] Attacks upon French insolence and provocations were designed to reveal that at this stage of international politics, France was no better than England. Such an attitude was best expressed by "A Citizen of N. Carolina," who wrote in Hall's *Wilmington Gazette* on the eve of elections for the state Assembly. As in Virginia and elsewhere, the Franco-American crisis was forcing many North Carolina politicians to take a public stand on the issue of what the response of the individual and of the nation should be to France. "In this conjuncture of circumstances," the "Citizen" said, "it behoves [sic] us as a deliberate people to be prudent in the exercise of our rights as electors—to call up as our Representatives in Legislation true Americans, only Americans in heart and principle—Persons of known integrity and patriotism, whose interest is intimately connected with our own; and who disclaiming all foreign influence and partizanning will unite in their councils." The citizen emphasized that when he spoke of eliminating all with a tinge of foreign influence from the conduct of public policy, he meant all. Citizens of Great Britain, no matter how long their residence in North Carolina, had not been relinquished by their government, "and they cannot liberate themselves." At the same time "let us determine to exclude from our Legislative Councils as well the restless and vivacious Frenchman (though we are under never to be forgotten obligations to his country) for he may be a partizan: as the haughty and insolent Englishman, whose friendship to America we know; whose tender mercies to us have been cruelties."[47]

Such were the beginnings in 1797 of a distinct Federalist ideology in the South, which if not Hamiltonian and pro-British in tone, was certainly anti-French in emphasis.

[46] *North Carolina Minerva*, November 4, 1797.
[47] *Wilmington Gazette*, August 24, 1797.

It advocated a middle course between Jacobinism, on the one hand, and Anglomania, on the other. Its orientation was toward the development of a distinctive American consciousness and patriotism characterized by loyalty to indigenous institutions and leaders who had purged themselves of any allegiance to foreign doctrines and governments. Increasing anti-Gallican sentiments were a natural outgrowth of a preoccupation with the loyal defense of American interests.

This ideology of unreflective patriotism, coupled with a somewhat sinister hint of the need for a purge of all disloyal elements within the state, could not help but ultimately attract a significant amount of public support at a time when the country at large came to believe increasingly in the imminence of war.[48] Because it was espoused honestly, such an ideology was all the more potent.

Throughout 1797 and into 1798, as the crisis with France slowly mounted, it appeared that the Federalist editors and essayists in North Carolina were making little impression on public opinion within or beyond the borders of the state. At the same time North Carolina Republicans followed the lead of their colleagues elsewhere in maintaining an unwavering public loyalty to the French Republic.[49] Once the XYZ affair became public knowledge, however, the teachings of Hodge, Hall, Martin, and other Federalist ideologists in North Carolina began to take hold. The electorate responded to the demand that it view with malice any attempts from any quarter to subvert American honor or independence, and thus Federalist strength in North Carolina and throughout the South enjoyed an astonishing revival.

[48] Thomas to John Gray Blount, January 25, March 10, 1798, in Masterson, ed., *John Gray Blount*, III, 198, 199, 215.
[49] Thomas to John Gray Blount, March 10, 1798, *ibid.*, 215.

Federalism's fortunes in South Carolina in 1797 largely revolved about the growing estrangement of the powerful Rutledge faction from the person and policies of Thomas Jefferson. Edward Rutledge's trust in his nephew remained unshaken throughout the year, surviving even the young congressman's open break with Jefferson and his party. Moreover, the elder Rutledge admired the President's firm but prudent conduct, admitting that Adams' speech of May 16 was "substantially sound."[50] Still, his correspondence with John Rutledge, Jr., revealed a lingering hope that "harmony and Union with the French Republic might be maintained," and that resultant divisions in Congress might be closed.[51] In the latter part of the year, however, two incidents bound Rutledge in firm allegiance to Federalism. In late October a French privateer boldly penetrated the Charleston harbor and burned a British ship at anchor. Later this privateer also captured two American ships off the port. One of the captured merchantmen was from Charleston itself, the other from Savannah.[52]

In November a far more alarming incident occurred, one which certainly terrorized South Carolinians of all political persuasions in all regions of the state. A conspiracy to stage a bloody uprising in the lowcountry was uncovered among Charleston slaves. According to one of Jacob Read's acquaintances, the conspiracy was suppressed at the last moment as a result of information supplied to the whites by local Negroes. The general consensus in Charleston was that the conspiracy had originated among "French Negroes" who had come from the West India islands where unrest

[50] Edward Rutledge to Henry M. Rutledge, May 31, 1797, Rutledge Papers.
[51] Edward Rutledge to John Rutledge, Jr., from Charleston, May 19, June 2, 9, 1797, John Rutledge, Jr., Papers.
[52] Affidavit of Governor Charles Pinckney, October 22, 1797, Adams Papers, Reel 385.

among slaves was becoming endemic. Both Edward Rutledge and Read's correspondent emphasized this point.[53] Here was chilling evidence to support Ralph Izard's earlier warning that French democratic ideology constituted a direct threat to the interests and even the lives of slaveholders, not only in the lowcountry, but, increasingly, in the backcountry as well.

The foiled conspiracy made a convert of Edward Rutledge. In the legislative session in December he led the forces clamoring for a strong defense budget that would include provisions for the defense of the harbor at Charleston and the fitting out of a number of galleys for coastal defense. When the fight proved unsuccessful, Rutledge turned to his nephew at Philadelphia for aid. When this also failed, the elder Rutledge wrote sadly of finding so little inclination in Congress to defend the country. "We are in fact a much altered people," Rutledge admitted, "and are no more like what we were some twenty years ago [the date of the Franco-American Treaty] than the Italians are like the Romans."[54] Until his death two years later Edward Rutledge never again strayed from the Federalist fold.

Only in Georgia did the Federalists fail to regain strength in 1797. The public did not forget the Yazoo scandal, in which Federalist politicians were implicated deeply. Also, Georgians did not forgive the administration for its blundering activities in the summer of 1796 concerning the state's attempts to purchase large tracts of western lands from the Creeks.

[53] J. Alison to Jacob Read, from Charleston, December 5, 1797, Read Papers. Edward Rutledge to John Rutledge, Jr., from Charleston, November 21, 1797, John Rutledge, Jr., Papers.

[54] Edward Rutledge to John Rutledge, Jr., from Columbia, December 13, 1797, John Rutledge, Jr., Papers, Southern Historical Collection, University of North Carolina, Chapel Hill, N. C.; Edward Rutledge to John Rutledge, Jr., from Charleston, January 23, 1798, John Rutledge, Jr., Papers, Duke University Library, Durham, N. C.

Moreover, Georgians were not thoroughly convinced that the Jay Treaty actually had removed the British threat. The presence of warships of the Royal Navy off the southern coast of Georgia and rumors that they intended a landing at St. Augustine did nothing to calm jumpy nerves in the border state. ". . . perhaps it may appear at a future day that we had better have had no Treaty," James Habersham, a nominally Federalist Savannah merchant, wrote at the end of March. He feared that any partiality shown to Spain, France, or Great Britain by the United States would upset the uneasy balance of power existing between the three pertaining to Florida and Louisiana. Any breach of the peace in this area could only harm Georgia. In such an atmosphere most of the old Federalists were disinclined to carry on party warfare. Lachlan McIntosh claimed that he had gone "every length" to restore "what we lost by the last election," but he had received little aid; and James Gunn's unwillingness to work actively to revive Federalist fortunes in Georgia left McIntosh embittered and politically impotent.[55]

Despite the continued hostility of Georgia, Federalist strength in the South by the beginning of 1798 had improved amazingly since the election of 1796. In South Carolina and Virginia, the two most economically powerful and politically active southern states, increasingly effective Federalist factions had reemerged, composed of alert personnel and enjoying wide contacts within traditional local governing circles. In North Carolina a popular press, generally favoring Adams' brand of Federalism, was telling the electorate of the need to place American interests and honor

[55] James Habersham to Joseph Habersham, March 30, 1797, Preston Davie Papers; Lachlan McIntosh to Elisha B. Hopkins, from Louisville, Georgia, February 6, 1797, in Lilla M. Hawes, ed., "Papers of Lachlan McIntosh," *Collections of the Georgia Historical Society* (Savannah: Georgia Historical Society, 1957), XII, 161–62.

above narrow partisanship or vague allegiance to a liberal ideal of political behavior. Considering the existing political. situation, such an attitude could only benefit the Federalist cause. Within a matter of months southern Federalists would be handed an unparalleled opportunity to employ their rapidly developing skills and to exploit further popular dissatisfaction in a strong bid for dominance in the region.

V. At the Flood, 1798

In 1798 Federalism reached the apex of its influence in the southern states. State organizations were somewhat expanded in size, a large influx of more or less active followers entering Federalist ranks on county and local levels as a result of popular agitation over the XYZ crisis. Moreover, relations with the electorate were maintained on a broader, more direct and intense basis. And southern Federalists at Philadelphia participated fully and effectively in the party's struggle for national supremacy over the Jeffersonian Republicans. Of greatest importance and significance, however, was the emergence of a distinct and unmistakably favorable Federalist image in the southern mind. The disclosure of the XYZ affair further escalated Franco-American tensions, and Americans were aware that they were living in a time of extreme national peril. The earlier efforts by the friends of government to emphasize on local and state levels patriotic devotion to current national institutions and leaders now began to sway public opinion noticeably. The President's continued efforts to seek friendly relations with the Directory commensurate with the demands of national honor also had its effect, and Federalism came to symbolize responsible political conservatism in the minds of a growing number of southerners.

The revelation of the XYZ affair in March, 1798, excited public opinion in America more than any incident since the publication of Jay's Treaty some three years before. A traveler passing through central North Carolina the following July noted that in Raleigh, Fayetteville, Rockingham, and Louisbourg, "an unanimity of sentiment prevailed among all circles of the people with regard to our difference with France. All seem to regret our misunderstanding, but are ready to take up arms in defense of their country in this time of necessity." Weeks before Abigail Adams had written to her son in the same vein. Never before had her love for the people shone with such clarity and her respect for their wisdom been so clearly expressed as at this moment when they declared their unequivocal support for her husband's conduct. "The immense addresses which are raining in from all quarters," the President's lady wrote, were "like a flood from North Carolina to the province of Main [sic]. They breath [sic] one spirit, they speak one language, that of Independent Freemen, approving the measures of Government, and expressive of a full confidence in the wisdom, virtue and integrity of the Chief Magistrate."[1]

In truth, Federalists throughout the South moved swiftly to consolidate the immense advantage which Messrs. X, Y, and Z had so unwittingly handed them. Once again they used the *ad hoc* urban and county public meeting to stress their position as rightful spokesmen for the popular temperament. In Virginia, 306 persons signed a petition circulated at a meeting in Richmond, while a similar assembly in the Tidewater county of Westmoreland produced 416 signatures. As in 1795, the friends of government had tangible support outside the towns and older planter-dominated counties of the Tidewater and Potomac River areas. The President received petitions of support and approbation from citizens in Botetourt County in the south-

[1] *North Carolina Minerva*, July 7, 1798; Abigail Adams to John Quincy Adams, from Philadelphia, May 26, 1798, Adams Papers, Reel 388.

ern Shenandoah Valley and from Harrison County in the extreme northwestern portion of the state. In all there are extant addresses from citizens' meetings in Alexandria, Portsmouth, Norfolk, Petersburg, Richmond, and from nine counties scattered throughout Virginia; and in all probability Adams received some others.[2]

Virginia Federalists, by and large, were pleased with their efforts. Washington indicated his satisfaction with the apparent *volte face* in popular opinion in the state, despite receiving a few unpleasant resolutions, notably from Fredericksburg. "All the upper most populace and hardy yeomanry of this State have come, and are coming forward, with strong addresses to the Executive," Washington reported. He also underscored the growing concern of many Federalists with mustering as many expressions of popular support as possible when he complained of the lack of effective local leadership in many counties in the central portion of Virginia. Washington claimed that such lack of efficient Federalist leadership on the local level in this area prevented the impressive display of popular consensus from becoming unanimous.[3]

If the petition campaign of the spring, summer, and autumn of 1798 is any indication, the most surprising shift in public opinion toward the President and his party in the South was in North Carolina. The Adams Papers and the North Carolina press of that day contain separate addresses from eight counties and two towns, Raleigh and Fayetteville.[4] As in the case of Virginia, however, the extant petitions probably represent only a fraction of those Adams received from that state, for the public support which he won

[2] *Norfolk Herald*, May 3, 8, 10, 12, 1798; Adams Papers, Reels 119, 388.
[3] Washington to Hamilton, from Mount Vernon, May 27, 1798, Hamilton Papers, Vol. 30.
[4] Adams Papers, Reels 119, 388–89; *North Carolina Minerva*, May 19, June 16, 1798; *Wilmington Gazette*, August 30, 1798, April 4, 1799.

in the North Carolina General Assembly the following December was striking in its breadth and depth.

In South Carolina the XYZ disclosures accelerated the already existing trend toward Federalism. A meeting held in May at Charleston resulted in a pledge of support to the Constitution, the government, and the independence of the nation and castigated France for imposing "the most humiliating demands" upon the United States.[5] At the same time, however, the participants expressed displeasure at the tardiness of the national government in providing defenses for the city's unprotected harbor. Soon thereafter a committee, headed by Edward Rutledge, was formed to investigate the possibility that South Carolina might do for herself what the federal government refused to do. The President concurrently received further assurances of support from public meetings in St. Luke's Parish and Kershaw County and from the general meeting of South Carolina's Cincinnati Society.[6]

Federalist prospects revived only modestly in Georgia as a result of the XYZ affair. The prior partiality of the frontiersmen of the state to the Yazoo faction had not yet disappeared, and there is evidence that in 1798 the upcountrymen were encouraged by certain members of the federal government to oppose the leadership of James Jackson. Adams first received petitions of support from meetings in Augusta and the small village of Washington in Wilkes County, which had voted Federalist in the previous presidential election.[7] Somewhat later, meetings in St. Mary's, Glynn, and McIntosh counties expressed similar sentiments, and a traveler in the backcountry at the time observed that the entire western portions of Georgia and Tennessee supported the President's

[5] Undated address, Adams Papers, Reel 388.
[6] *Ibid.*, Reels 388, 389, 391; Charleston *City Gazette*, October 11, 1798.
[7] Adams Papers, Reels 119, 388; *Augusta Chronicle*, August 11, 1798.

foreign policy. Here was no instinctive expression of a conservative temperament, but rather a heartfelt appreciation for a carefully chosen course of action designed to warn France and her Spanish ally against taking too many liberties with American honor and rights.[8]

One Georgia Federalist attempted to capitalize on this sentiment. As a high-ranking member of the Georgia militia, James Gunn pressured all units under his command during the middle months of 1798 to send approbatory addresses to the President.[9] Gunn's motives, however, apparently were highly personal. He seems not to have coordinated his activities with McIntosh, Jones, or the other surviving members of the earlier Federalist faction in the state; rather he was concerned with demonstrating his own loyalty and efficiency to the party leaders at Philadelphia.

James Jackson sensed growing danger from another quarter, however. Since 1796 John Stith had led a group of Federalist-oriented "aristos" in Augusta in steady opposition to the Jackson Republicans in the legislature. By the autumn of 1798, Jackson indicated that Georgia's reaction to the XYZ issue had encouraged the members of this small group to make a concerted campaign to challenge Republican control of Georgia. Thus, it appeared that Stith and his allies might be the agents through which two-party politics would be reestablished within the state.[10]

There is no indication that Federalist leaders in Philadelphia carefully criticized the contents of the addresses from the southern states which arrived in such profusion after the news of the XYZ affair. In the summer of 1798

[8] *Augusta Chronicle*, September 15, 1798.
[9] Gunn to Timothy Pickering, from Savannah, October 1, 1798, Adams Papers, Reel 391.
[10] James Jackson to John Milledge, November 14, 1798, April 2, 1801, in Harriet Milledge Salley, ed., *Correspondence of Governor John Milledge* (Columbia, S. C.: State Commercial Printing Co., 1949), 58, 71.

their party was riding an unprecedented crest of popularity, and they apparently surrendered to the very human propensity not to examine the reasons for their success. Yet the tone of these petitions was unmistakably singular and should have warned party leaders against taking controversial steps. Southern citizens duly execrated French corruption and arrogance and expressed a sanguine determination to defend American honor and rights by force of arms, if necessary. Almost without exception, however, the petitioners also strongly hoped that war would not be necessary and implicitly sought to pressure the President into further negotiations with the Directory. The usual assumption in these petitions was that this in fact would be his future course of action. The emerging Federalist orientation of many southerners—as of many in the northern states—in 1798 was actually a fragile temperament requiring careful cultivation if it were to last.

There was as yet little direct indication of Federalist imprudence by the time of the off-year Congressional elections in the Carolinas and Georgia in the late summer and autumn. In North Carolina, where the decidedly progovernment bias of the press was of inestimable aid, the Federalists' popularity had continued unabated. Published letters from members of the state's Congressional delegations helped to maintain a sense of crisis after the XYZ disclosures, and astute Federalist editors printed all the wild rumors and gossip available to add to the excitement. Allamand Hall of the *Wilmington Gazette* was especially assiduous, and in August he reprinted a story from New York City, a Federalist stronghold, concerning ostensible French hopes of an uprising against the national government which was to be led by Chancellor Livingston. Frenchmen in Guadaloupe, it was further stated, were openly claiming "that there were enough Frenchmen in this country [referring to the United States] to BURN ALL OUR CITIES AND CUT THE THROATS OF ALL THE INHABITANTS—that we should therefore be afraid to do any act that might risque a war with France."[11] Such thinly veiled and vicious attacks upon the Republican opposition became more explicit later in the year when news of George Logan's private mission to the Directory was uncovered. Logan's embassy immediately was labeled an act of treason.[12]

Washington's appointment in July to command the newly created provisional army offered North Carolina Federalist editors the opportunity to exploit further the ideals of patriotism and nationalism which had brought the party its current popularity. The editor of the *State Gazette of North Carolina* was delighted at the news of Washington's return to public life. "Every American heart must leap with joy at the above nomination," he wrote. "WASHINGTON, the saviour of his country! WASHINGTON the brave, the great, who, after having, through toils, fatigues and dangers, given liberty and independence to America, and raised [her] to a rank among the nations of the earth, flew to enjoy, in the bosom of Vernon's shades, the peace he had so nobly won, is yet willing to leave those happy scenes, again to lead the armies forth." Following this strenuous exercise in reverence for the Father of his Country, the Federalist editor went on to admonish his readers to exert themselves in no less a degree:

If there is a single son of Columbia who now feels not his whole soul roused to energetic activity, whose bosom does not glow with the holy flame, let him contemplate the noble conduct of our Hero, and then, if he can suffer his musket to rust, or his

[11] *Wilmington Gazette*, May 31, August 30, 1798.
[12] *Ibid.*, November 15, 1798.

trusty blade to remain undrawn in its mouldy scabbard, let him do so, but let him also resign the honorable title of *American*.[13]

Appeals such as the above did little to boost enlistments in the new army, which never obtained its full quota of volunteers during its brief period of existence. As calls for support of the national government, however, such exhortations undoubtedly helped to produce tangible political benefits for Federalism, for the next year Jefferson found it politically necessary to set up Joseph Gales and his Republican press at Raleigh in an effort to break Federalism's stranglehold on North Carolina's newspapers.

By the time of the Congressional elections the Federalists could count upon the backing of an outspoken partisan press and popular support, not only in all of the diverse geographic areas in the state, but within nearly every socioeconomic interest group as well. The elections indicated that Federalism enjoyed still another immeasurable advantage in North Carolina. Its ranks were being infused with young blood. Indeed, some of the older party members indicated a positive disinclination to stand for high public office in this year of triumph. Johnston refused Iredell's request to seek a Congressional seat, though he later performed valuable service in the General Assembly.[14] Davie found himself under strong pressure from Grove and others to run for the governorship, but consented only grudgingly, though he eventually won. He indicated more interest in finding a high position in the provisional army. Eventually, however, Davie was able to satisfy his martial ambitions to some degree while fulfilling the desires of his friends. As governor, he became a dependable agent and

[13] *State Gazette of North Carolina*, July 18, 1798.
[14] Johnston to Iredell, July 5, November 28, 1798, in Griffith J. McRee, ed., *Life and Correspondence of James Iredell* (2 vols.; New York: Peter Smith, 1947), II, 531, 537–38.

adviser to Hamilton and Cotesworth Pinckney, helping them to staff the officer corps of the army.[15]

While older friends of government in North Carolina were seeking to evade the burden of national public office, an ambitious group of novices eagerly sought it. Soon after the results of the elections were released, one newspaper claimed seven of the state's ten representatives for Federalism. Grove himself expressed pleasure with the outcome in all districts save Hillsboro.[16] It appeared certain that the Federalists, at least initially, could now count upon the firm allegiance of William Barry Grove, as well as upon the newcomers, Joseph Dickson, William H. Hill, Archibald Henderson, David Stone, and Willis Allston. Three of the new men, Dickson, Hill, and Henderson, represented western districts. Henderson, especially, proved to be a valuable acquisition. Operating out of his home in Salisbury, which had been Steele's center of influence some years before, Henderson worked strenuously to increase Federalist influence in the western part of the state. His efforts in the Congressional campaign brought victory not only to himself, but to Dickson and Hill as well.[17]

[15] William Barry Grove to James McHenry, from Fayetteville, August 20, 1798, James McHenry Papers, Duke University Library, Durham, N. C. It may well have been, moreover, that Davie had something to do either with successfully implicating Thomas Blount in fraudulent land speculations in 1798 or at least with forming the opposition to Blount and with making the issue of Blount's alleged involvement in the land frauds a central focus of the Federalist campaign that year. See Thomas to John Gray Blount, from Philadelphia, March 10, June 21, 1798, in William Henry Masterson, ed., *The John Gray Blount Papers*, Vol. III (Raleigh: North Carolina State Department of History and Archives, 1965), 216, 237.

[16] *North Carolina Journal*, October 1, 1798; Grove to McHenry, August 20, 1798, McHenry Papers.

[17] Archibald Henderson, "A Federalist of the Old School," *The North Carolina Booklet*, XVII (July, 1917), 13. Richard Dobbs Spaight, though often considered to have had Federalist inclinations at this time, actually appears to have been an independent with strong leanings toward the Blount clan. See Spaight to John Gray Blount, from New Bern, June 26, October 18, 1798, in Masterson, ed., *John Gray Blount*, III, 239–40, 259.

The extent to which national party issues had penetrated to local levels in North Carolina by 1798 and the degree to which Federalism had captured the allegiance of the state's electorate became evident in that year's General Assembly session. Governor William R. Davie immediately gave the state legislature all the relevant material pertaining to the XYZ affair. On December 24, Samuel Johnston, as the head "of a committee to prepare an Address to the President of the U.S.," presented a draft praising Adams' moderate conduct throughout the months of crisis with France and defended the policy of American neutrality toward European politics. The address condemned, in bitter and injured tones, recent conduct of the French government toward the United States and concluded with the pledge that North Carolinians "will not patiently suffer any foreign interference with our national concerns" and would "with our lives and fortunes to the last extremity, support maintain and defend all the Constitutional measures of our Federal Government." Except for the final clause, which should have served as a warning to radical Federalists, the address was decidedly favorable to the administration. Its passage by a 51 to 38 count was a clearcut triumph for the friends of government in the state and afforded them the opportunity to assess the sources of their current strength.[18]

The fifty-one Federalist votes came from thirty-six of the fifty-eight counties represented in the General Assembly that year, fourteen of which were in the western part of the state, immediately surrounding the town of Salisbury. In 1788 this area had been thoroughly Antifederalist, and from 1790 onward it had been strongly Republican. The sudden emergence of Federalist support among the yeoman

[18] "Journal of the House of Commons of the State of North Carolina," December 11, 24, 1798, in William S. Jenkins, ed., *Records of the States of the United States* (Microfilm, University of California Library, Berkeley).

At the Flood, 1798 / 177

farmers of the west was only the most striking feature of an impressive trend, for the friends of Adams received strong support from representatives of the entire geographic and socioeconomic spectrum of the state, including the planters of the Roanoke River valley and the Albemarle and Pamlico Sound regions. Surprisingly, assemblymen from the upper Cape Fear area either voted against this resolution or abstained, indicating that at least on this one issue there was little correlation between "old Tories" and the Federalist party in North Carolina in 1798. However, the member from Fayetteville voted with the Federalists on this issue, as did the representative from Salisbury, while the representatives from Hillsboro and Edenton voted against the address, and those from Halifax, New Bern, and Wilmington abstained.[19]

For all of the new faces, the favorable press, and the significant breadth of popular support, Federalist successes in 1798 were gravely compromised by a continued lack of firm party organization. As was traditional, many who ran as Federalists entered public life at the express wish of the electorate. Henderson, for all his work on behalf of the party of order, left retirement only after being "urgently petitioned" by his personal friends to present himself as a candidate, a "step not a little contrary to his natural inclinations." Though he had never run for high public office previous to this time, Henderson was known throughout the state as a Federalist supporter.[20] Henry William Harrington of Richmond County was another "ardent" friend of government who in 1798 successfully campaigned for the state senate at the express desires of his constituents.[21] But there was no formal political machine to urge a candi-

[19] *Ibid.*, see Appendix, Table 4.
[20] Henderson, "Federalist of the Old School," 8–13.
[21] Henry M. Wagstaff, ed., "The Harrington Letters," *James Sprunt Historical Studies*, Vol. XIII, No. 2 (Chapel Hill: University of North Carolina Press, 1914), 16–17.

date on and to support him with funds and friends once he had "reluctantly" embarked upon his campaign.

Even so, several of the younger Federalists did run for Congress under the patronage of individual party elders. Willis Allston, for example, was the candidate of Abraham Hodge, who threw the entire weight of his several newspapers behind Allston's campaign. Allston defeated Thomas Blount after a filthy campaign in which the Federalists, of all people, righteously and successfully condemned Madison's lieutenant with a charge of fraud in various land speculations.[22] According to the gleeful Hodge, Blount had had a majority of more than 1,200 votes in 1796, but in 1798 he was defeated by more than 1,700 ballots, as all four of his opponents were professed Federalists. This fact in itself attests to the continued disunity of party organization among the friends of government in North Carolina, even where powerful patrons were present to aid individual candidates.[23]

Even the backing of traditional party leaders was not a sufficient guarantee that a candidate's Federalism was firm and unequivocal. A prime example was David Stone of Bertie County. Stone had read law in Davie's office and was "warmly supported by the leading Federalists" of Edenton district in his bid for a Congressional seat,[24] but Stone's public announcement of his candidacy mentioned no discernible political principles. The impression he sought to convey was that he was being pushed forward against his will, agonizingly aware that his candidacy might offend and alienate some good men.[25] By 1801 Stone had become a Republican.

[22] The decline of Thomas Blount's political fortunes in 1798 as a result of implication in land frauds within the state is traced in Masterson, ed., *John Gray Blount*, III, xv, 22n., 80n., 115, 224–59 *passim*, 582–85.
[23] *North Carolina Journal*, August 6, 20, 1798.
[24] McRee, ed., *Iredell*, II, 530n.
[25] *North Carolina Journal*, August 13, 1798.

Although Federalism had had an astonishing revival in North Carolina in the two years following Cotesworth Pinckney's rebuff by the Directory, the resurgence was more one of spirit than of form. A single set of issues revolving about Franco-American relations and sedulously cultivated by the partisan Federalist press had aroused fervent public patriotism which could only benefit those in power. Friends of government, however, could not expect to sustain their influence for any length of time on this one issue. A permanent, alert, energetic, effective, and tightly knit political organization was necessary to keep the conservative and nationalistic Federalist image and philosophy alive—not only in the minds of the North Carolina electorate, but also among the younger politicians, many of whom, it soon appeared, were pro-Federalist in 1798 largely because of the pressure of current public opinion. Such an organization, however, had not even begun to be perfected at the close of the 1798 Congressional campaigns. Instead, the Federalist style of politicking retained its traditional elitist orientation. Partisan leaders still presented themselves as reluctantly acquiescing to run for office only because of a popular draft or the backing of an influential patron. In addition, there was a conspicuous lack of communication and cooperation between friends of government in North Carolina and administration leaders at Philadelphia.[26] Because a permanent and effective party structure still was lacking, Federalist strength in North Carolina in 1798 was built on a foundation of sand.

In South Carolina also the Congressional elections of 1798 brought new power to the Federalists. The collapse

[26] For example, the efforts of Hodge and Allston to destroy the reputation of Thomas Blount were compromised by the willingness of Federalist leaders in Congress—including Harper, Bayard, and Sitgreaves—to attest publicly that the Republican representative was not implicated in the treasonous activities of his elder brother. Masterson, ed., *John Gray Blount*, III, 246.

of the XYZ negotiations heightened the sense of panic among many about the state's generally defenseless situation. By midsummer Charlestonians and the residents of "the little town of Beaufort" were busily engaged in soliciting their own funds for the construction of coastal fortifications and naval vessels.[27] Indications are, however, that not all citizens of Charleston shared in an equal feeling of loyalty to the administration. In early June, Pickering held conversations with Jacob Read in which Read confirmed Pickering's suspicion that some Charleston merchants were forcing their captains to take "deceitful oaths" concerning the nature of cargoes to French ports to make large profits in contraband.[28] Nevertheless, such instances seem to have been the exception, not the rule, for no mention of them appears in other correspondence of the day. Since Congress' failure to undertake comprehensive national defense could be blamed on the Republican faction, the Federalists had a readymade local issue.

As the autumn elections approached, it became clear that Federalists and Republicans in South Carolina were equally matched in talents, morale, and determination. As in North Carolina, however, the friends of government in South Carolina conspicuously lacked an elaborate party structure. Edward Rutledge, from his home in Charleston, became the center of Federalist strength and activity and found great demands placed upon him in the absence of young John Rutledge and Robert Goodloe Harper. Both Rutledge and Harper chose to remain with new-found friends in the North during the crucial election year rather than undertake the hazardous, fatiguing journey home to fight for their

[27] James Simons to Oliver Wolcott, from Charleston, April 10, 1798, Adams Papers, Reel 388; John Rutledge, Jr., to Benjamin Stoddert, from Newport, August 21, 1798, John Rutledge, Jr., Papers, South Caroliniana Library, Columbia, S. C.
[28] Pickering to Hamilton, June 9, 1798, Hamilton Papers, Vol. 31.

seats. Sometime in August or September, Edward Rutledge learned that his nephew would be challenged in the Orangeburg-Beaufort district by Pierce Butler. Rutledge then drafted a long "campaign letter," which he assiduously circulated throughout that district to every politically influential and significant public figure he knew and whom "my man Will" could reach.[29]

Rutledge's letter deserves examination, because it contained all of the partisan appeals and persuasions which southern Federalists had been shaping in the two years since Pinckney's humiliation in France. Rutledge first defined his nephew as a young man of honor, industry, and integrity, who was continually jealous of the national honor "and the Interest of this particular Country [South Carolina]." Moreover, Congressman Rutledge was described as a man who was always alert to outside threats of any kind to the rights of either the nation or the state. Edward Rutledge then recalled that his nephew had been a longtime friend of France and of French republicanism and had been alarmed at the efforts of the other European countries to subvert the French nation and the cause which it had espoused. But "when he saw her [France] over running innocent Countries—maintaining her armies by plunder, seducing the people from their Government; reviling this very Country, calumniating our Ministers of peace . . . searching our vessels without cause, imprisoning our seamen, & threatening to divide our Citizens from the Government, which had been fairly established by a Majority—he took fire—he manfully took his part and acted up to it."[30]

In his concluding sentences Rutledge revealed the extent to which Southern Federalists by 1798 were capable of

[29] Edward Rutledge to John Rutledge, Jr., from Charleston, October 16, 19, 1798, John Rutledge, Jr., Papers, Duke University Library, Durham, N. C.
[30] Rutledge to Captain Dunbar, n.d., John Rutledge, Jr., Papers, Southern Historical Collection, University of North Carolina, Chapel Hill, N. C.

enunciating an insinuating form of that demagoguery which they condemned in their opponents. After remarking upon the predilection of the French to attack, conquer, and plunder every nation "where the people were divided," he ended with a plea to South Carolinians: "If we keep in those who will support the Constitution & Government of our own Country," he said, the French

will have no reason to expect a successful attack, should they make it; but if they find that the Members who have supported the Measures of the present Congress are to be turned out, to make room for others, what will be the natural conclusion in their Minds? it [sic] will be this, that the People in this State Disapprove of those Measures of Congress which have been taken against France—that they approve of the Measures France has taken against this Country; and that this is the spot [i.e., South Carolina] on which they are to erect their Standard, because this is the spot on which their Friends are to be found—And should that be the case, adieu to all the happiness of life whilst they are here.

Given the recent history of slave conspiracy and the current lack of military defenses in the state, the purely emotional impact of Rutledge's dark warnings may easily be imagined.

Rutledge was not alone in warning South Carolinians of the dangers inherent in a pro-French attitude during a time of undeclared war. Harper may have been away from his backcountry constituents for too long a period, but he nonetheless sought to arouse popular fears and to shape them to partisan political advantage, just as Rutledge was doing in the lowcountry. Prior to the summer of 1798, Harper managed to keep his firm Federalist bias in check while writing his long expository letters home. He seemed to be more interested in explaining the meaning of measures and policies than with indoctrinating his constituents with the party line. Indeed, Harper's letters often assumed an implicit Federalist sentiment among his constituents which did not need further cultivation. The exposure of the XYZ affair, however, ended his restraint, and in a letter home in July, 1798, he allowed himself the luxury of a five-page fulmination against French tyranny.[31]

Despite the lack of a mature political organization and the consequent reliance upon correspondence and essays to arouse public opinion, the Federalists were not prevented from ultimately infusing excitement and purpose into the 1798 campaign in South Carolina. The elections were held in early October. As late as the end of August, Charleston newspapers—of which none are apparently extant for September—showed no signs of strenuous politicking. However, by the middle of September the Georgetown press was flooded with campaign material, much of it contributed by friends of government. "An Old Patriot" urged in the strongest terms the election only of those unalterably opposed to "the *present* system of the French Government," and a correspondent from Camden publicly admonished a friend in Charleston to "continue to send a good man from your city" to Philadelphia. These statements show a far stronger preoccupation with national, and specifically Congressional, rather than state politics. This assumption is supported when the issues of the Charleston papers are once again available. In the last days before the election the *City Gazette* was filled with tickets submitted by many persons, whose signatures identified them only as individuals from both parties who were determined not to distinguish themselves from the mass of the commonalty. These tickets were not uniform. Each party obviously agreed within itself

[31] July 23, 1798, in Elizabeth Donnan, ed., "Papers of James A. Bayard, 1796–1815," *Annual Report of the American Historical Association*, 1913 (2 vols.; Washington, D. C.: Government Printing Office, 1914), I, 64–69.

whom it supported in the Congressional races, but there was no party regularity in support of state and local officers.[32]

A highly interested contemporary observer was also impressed by the lack of rigid party divisions with respect to purely state politics at this time, as compared with New England. John Rutledge, Jr., who knew well the local politics of both sections by this time, wrote to Harrison Gray Otis, asking him to inform the President "that the political line of demarcation which separates parties here [he was writing from Newport, Rhode Island] does not extend to So. Carolina —that in this respect we have more liberality than our Eastern friends & that with us the applications for the [Republican] Governor's [patronage] recommendation . . . is a respect generally paid to the office of the Chief Magistrate without adverting to the politics or private character of the person occupying it."[33]

Taking the results of the Congressional elections as a reliable barometer of public opinion, the friends of government could be said to dominate South Carolina once more by the end of 1798. The senatorial delegation was split, with Jacob Read representing the Federalists, and Charles Pinckney, the Republicans. In the House, John Rutledge, Jr., was returned from the Orangeburg-Beaufort district, Benjamin Huger won in Georgetown, and Thomas Pinckney, despite a grave illness that often prevented him from doing any significant campaigning, was reelected in Charleston. Thus, firm and outspoken friends of government controlled the lowcountry Congressional seats in the Sixth Congress. In

[32] *Georgetown* [South Carolina] *Gazette*, September 18, 21, 28, 1798; Charleston *City Gazette*, October 5, 1798.

[33] John Rutledge, Jr., to Harrison Gray Otis, August 14, 1798, John Rutledge, Jr., Papers, Southern Historical Collection, University of North Carolina, Chapel Hill, N. C.

the backcountry Harper again was victorious in Ninety-Six. Abraham Nott from Columbia attempted to maintain a neutral position during the succeeding Congressional session, and DeSaussure complained at this time that he was no party man, but during the era of Jeffersonian democracy he proved to be a strong, though often silent, Federalist.³⁴ Only Thomas Sumter could be classified as a true Republican.

Federalists also predominated in the state legislature during the 1798 session. Led by Robert Barnwell in the House and General William Washington in the Senate, the friends of government sought to perpetuate the sense of crisis that during the previous summer had gripped even Republican leaders by introducing and pushing through bills providing for further defense measures. The Republicans, who had regained their composure by November, tried to block them. Three important divisions occurred, the most representative of which concerned the purchase by the state of an additional stand of 5,000 arms to be resold to the state militia. This imaginative proposal by the friends of government effectually destroyed the issue of the provisional army vs. the state militia while keeping alive the sense of imminent danger. It passed by a 55 to 40 vote. Federalist support came overwhelmingly from the lowcountry parishes and from the city of Charleston. Of Charleston's fourteen representatives, eleven voted for the measure and three abstained. But the friends of government also attracted a thin film of support across the arc of the backcountry, from Darlington, through Chester, Spartanburg, Pendleton, and Abbeville. If the firm hold over the lowcountry could be retained along with the thin but representative support

³⁴ David Hackett Fischer, *The Revolution of American Conservatism: The Federalist Party in the Era of Jeffersonian Democracy* (New York: Harper & Row, 1965), 405.

from the backcountry, the Federalists could not only dominate South Carolina indefinitely, but they could reasonably claim to speak for all segments of its population. Thus, as in North Carolina, Federalism in South Carolina prevailed over a wide geographic region and within diverse socioeconomic groups at the close of 1798.[35] Its supporters had appealed successfully to backcountrymen as well as lowcountry planters and urban elements. But South Carolina's Federalists had ridden to power on the strength of a single issue which could not long remain unresolved. Whether the friends of government could retain such disparate support once the crisis had eased was not clear. Their lack of a disciplined party organization and their dependence upon an influential few was not encouraging for the future.

In Georgia the Augusta Federalists overcame formidable odds and registered significant political gains at the expense of Jackson's machine. So thorough was Jackson's dominance of the press that even the *Georgia Gazette* was silent. Until just prior to the fall elections nothing relating to party politics appeared in Georgia newspapers, despite recent demonstrations of support for the President's conduct from many backcountry areas. Then on the eve of the balloting the Jackson supporters flooded at least one highly influential newspaper, the *Augusta Chronicle,* with a series of essays warning the people to beware of supporting candidates favorable to the discredited Yazoo faction of 1795.[36]

The friends of government nonetheless campaigned effectively without newspaper support. Commenting upon the newly elected legislature, Jackson told his young lieutenant, John Milledge, that "the Senate is not strong" and that John

[35] "South Carolina Journal of the House of Representatives," December 17, 1798, in Jenkins, ed., *Records of the States.* See Appendix, Table 6.
[36] *Augusta Chronicle,* November 3, 1798.

Stith's presence there posed a definite threat to Jacksonian effectiveness. "A majority in the House is of the right side," Jackson added, only "if the assiduity of the T[reasur]y department and a coalition which I am told is formed with the Augusta lads by it does not too much prevail." But whatever promising alliance might have been forged in 1798 between government officials in Philadelphia and the energetic Augusta "aristos" seems never to have materialized with sufficient force to significantly shake Jackson's hold over the state. In consequence, whatever Federalist predilections the new Georgia congressmen, Benjamin Taliaferro and James Jones, may have had were never expressed publicly. Both men voted consistently Republican during the Sixth Congress, faithfully reflecting the dominant political opinion in their state. The Jacksonians experienced a brief flutter of nerves again in the autumn of 1800 when contemplating the continued existence of the Federalist faction at Augusta. But the aristos were again apparently throttled without effort, and Georgia continued to be steadily Republican.[37]

Virginia's state and Congressional elections did not take place until the spring of 1799—six months after those in the other southern states—by which time the political climate throughout the nation had changed drastically. The grave effects upon civil liberties of the Federalists' recently passed Alien and Sedition Acts and the unfortunate influence of the Federalist-created provisional army on that party's relations with the southern electorate are discussed in a later chapter. It should be noted at this point, however, that along with their compatriots in the Carolinas, Virginia Federalists derived great and apparently lasting benefit from the XYZ issue. To some degree friends of government in Virginia

[37] Jackson to Milledge, from Louisville, Georgia, November 14, 1798; Milledge to Charles Harris of Savannah, September 11, 1800, in Salley, ed., *John Milledge*, 58, 68.

used their newly found popularity to engage in public conflict with the Republicans in the spring elections. At the same time they were constantly spurred on by administration officials in Philadelphia who were the prime movers in shaping a Federalist party ticket for the campaign. Thus, despite a mounting burden of identification with unpopular national policies, Virginia Federalists did their part to maintain the steady rise of party fortunes in the South as another presidential election year approached.

The XYZ disclosures, of course, encouraged Virginia's Federalists as much as those in other states. Adams' subsequent cautious policy proved to be popular with many Virginians, and the Federalists were able to exploit this popularity for their own ends. Robert Beverly informed young Rutledge in late spring, 1798, that even in Culpeper County, which was Jefferson's political backyard, the recent measures of the administration "have numerous and zealous advocates."[38]

By mid-autumn Virginia's Federalists had begun an active campaign among themselves to find a full slate of candidates for the forthcoming elections. Attorney General Charles Lee worked assiduously from Philadelphia to impress upon influential friends at home the need to stand for public office in a time of national peril. Lee approached Leven Powell as early as June, a full ten months before the election, and the Alexandria Federalist eventually entered the race. Marshall was urged by Washington to stand for Congress in Richmond and Henrico County, though this conflicted with his own desires; and the former Chief Executive also successfully persuaded Patrick Henry to abandon private life to bolster Federalist forces in the forthcoming General Assembly. By late September, Charles Lee informed Judge Iredell of the completion of a fairly comprehensive Federalist ticket

[38] April, 1798, John Rutledge, Jr., Papers, Southern Historical Collection, University of North Carolina, Chapel Hill, N. C.

in the state.³⁹ Thus, Federalist activities in Virginia in many ways continued to be supervised closely from Philadelphia. Since the party was active and united on the national level such supervision undoubtedly was a boon to the state party; but by the same token, when irreconcilable schisms appeared within the party hierarchy at Philadelphia, they were almost certain to divide the friends of government in Virginia as well.

Such divisions, however, had not emerged clearly prior to Adams' decision in February, 1799, to reopen negotiations with the Directory. In consequence, Federalist morale in Virginia remained high during the autumn of 1798. By mid-October party conflict in the state was "ardent," and Washington, for one declined to predict its outcome.⁴⁰ The general deplored the fact that no measure was left untried by the "democrats" to affect adversely the Federalist interests. However, the friends of government, in righteous wrath, were at that moment seeking to exclude all who professed loyalty to the Republican party from any direct connection with the defense programs of the administration.⁴¹

In this atmosphere of incessant party warfare, the increasing evidence of popular aversion to the Alien and Sedition Acts and the provisional army inevitably were ex-

³⁹ Charles Lee to Leven Powell, June 6, 1798, in William E. Dodd, ed., "Correspondence of Leven Powell," *The John P. Branch Historical Papers of Randolph-Macon College* (Richmond: Everett Wadding Co., 1901), I, 230–31; to James Iredell, from Alexandria, September 20, 1798, Iredell Papers; "John Marshall's Autobiographical Sketch," Marshall Papers; Washington to Henry, January 15, 1799; Henry to Washington, February 12, 1799, in John C. Fitzpatrick, ed., *The Writings of George Washington* (39 vols.; Washington, D. C.: U. S. Government Printing Office, 1931–1944), XXXVII, 87–90, 90n.

⁴⁰ Marshall to Pickering, from Richmond, October 1, 1798, Marshall Papers; Washington to Pickering, from Mount Vernon, October 15, 1798, in John C. Hamilton, ed., *The Works of Alexander Hamilton* (7 vols.; New York: John F. Trow, Printer, 1851), V, 367–68.

⁴¹ B. Henry Latrobe to Jefferson, from Richmond, September 22, 1798, Jefferson Papers, Vol. 104.

ploited by the followers of Jefferson when the General Assembly convened in late November. The result was the passage of Jefferson's Virginia Resolutions early the next year, along with another resolution which declared the Alien and Sedition Acts unconstitutional. A third proposal, which was considered but not passed during this session, provided that state judges could set free any person arrested under the two laws.[42]

It is not surprising that such legislation was considered and passed in a state which the friends of Jefferson and Madison had dominated for five years. Nor was the Virginia General Assembly in fact risking its existence in rejecting the Alien and Sedition Acts. The fears expressed by Virginia Republicans that Hamilton's army would be marched against them should controversial legislation be passed seems more than a bit farfetched, since Hamilton had not even begun to recruit the enlisted ranks for the proposed army.[43] More significant is the amount of opposition which these pieces of legislation aroused. The resolution which declared the Alien and Sedition Acts unconstitutional, for example, passed by a comfortable but not overwhelming margin of 100 to 63,[44] thus indicating that Federalist strength in this supposed stronghold of Republicanism was not insignificant.

The friends of government found support in forty-two of the state's ninety-seven counties, or two more than they had in 1795 in the vote on the censure of Washington's conduct relative to the Jay Treaty. At that time the Presi-

---

[42] John C. Miller, *Crisis in Freedom; The Alien and Sedition Acts* (Boston: Little, Brown and Company, 1951), 170–71.

[43] Stephen G. Kurtz, *The Presidency of John Adams: The Collapse of Federalism, 1795–1800* (New York: A. S. Barnes & Company, Inc., 1961), 337–38.

[44] "Virginia General Assembly, Journal of the House of Delegates," December 21, 1798, in Jenkins, ed., *Records of the States; Virginia Gazette and General Advertiser,* January 1, 1799.

dent's supporters had mustered fifty-nine votes—four less than Adams' supporters attracted three years later. Of the forty-two counties exhibiting Federalist strength in 1798, twenty-nine had also shown at least some Federalist tendencies in 1795. From the time of Jay's Treaty until the vote on the constitutionality of the Alien and Sedition Acts, the friends of government completely lost measurable support in twelve counties and picked up new support in thirteen. A decisive shift in the geographic and social bases of Federalist support in Virginia is apparent during the middle and later years of the decade. Of the twelve counties which moved away from Federalism between 1795 and 1798, seven were in the Tidewater region, and two others, Hanover and Henrico, surrounding the town of Richmond, bordered that area. In other words, the friends of government lost significant support in the old plantation area of the state. But at the same time, of the thirteen counties which wholly or in part shifted allegiance to the Federalist party, ten were in the area south and west of the James which had been the former stronghold of Madisonian Republicanism. Only one county in the Tidewater—New Kent—shifted somewhat in sentiment from Republicanism to Federalism in these years. In sum, of the forty-two counties which indicated entire or partial Federalist sentiment in 1798, only five were in the Tidewater region, two were on the eastern shore, four bordered the Potomac River, sixteen were in the broad area south and west of the James out to the frontier, one was in the Piedmont region directly north of the James, ten were in the Shenandoah Valley, and four were in the frontier area of the northwest around the present-day cities of Charleston and Morgantown, West Virginia.[45]

The dramatic shift in the core of Federalist strength from the counties of the Tidewater and Potomac River region to

[45] See Appendix, Table 2.

the counties of the Shenandoah Valley and the area south and west of the James River needs some examination. Can this change be explained by alteration of political loyalties on the part of influential political leaders? Certainly the transplanting of Patrick Henry's political loyalties must have carried great weight with the western yeomen, whose interests he ostentatiously had reflected and defended in previous years. This may well have been a decisive factor, but it must be remembered that by 1798, Henry had been out of active public life for nearly a decade, while new issues and younger men had dominated state and national politics. His reputation, while still impressive, might not have carried quite the same weight with the farmers of southern and western Virginia as it had ten years before. Another probable influence was the sectional struggle between western and Tidewater counties for control of the General Assembly. Professor Kurtz has discovered some indications that during the 1796 election Federalist writers in the Northern Neck area used the issue of sectional representation as a bludgeon against the Republicans, who were accused of promoting the continuation of an unjust sectional imbalance in the state legislature even while prattling of democracy and popular rights.[46] The Federalists may have been supported as a negative reference group by some in the west who identified Madison, Jefferson, and other Republican leaders with the despised older ruling group of the Tidewater.

Three facts argue against accepting the issue of sectional representation as a major explanation of Federalist strength in Virginia, however. First, the most prominent Virginia Federalists usually were content to take their identification and their issues from the party leadership in Philadelphia. There is no indication that Marshall, Carrington, Heth, Lee, or others in Virginia exploited the issue of sectional repre-

[46] Kurtz, *Presidency of John Adams*, 165-66.

sentation for the benefit of the Federalist interest. Secondly, had this issue played a significant role in determining the patterns of partisan allegiance in the state, it might have been expected to influence the vote on Washington's conduct in the 1795 Assembly and the outcome of the 1796 election. Yet at neither time did the friends of government appear to obtain significant support either in the counties of the Shenandoah Valley or in those below and to the west of the James River. Finally, many of the counties below the James, where Federalist sentiment was strong in 1798, were in the eastern and central portions of the state and would naturally be identified, and probably aligned themselves, with the "Tidewater" interest on questions of sectional representation.

The conversion of many yeoman farmers of southern and western Virginia to the Federalist party in 1798 can be viewed meaningfully only as part of the larger trend which ran through the entire southern backcountry during that year. There is much room for conjecture, but little concrete evidence available, for an exact evaluation of the sources of this major shift.

Certainly, one important factor was the rise of an active cadre of Federalist leaders throughout the area, including Henry in Virginia, Archibald Henderson in North Carolina, and Robert Goodloe Harper in South Carolina. Also noteworthy in South Carolina was the growing interest shown by the lowcountry's Federalist-oriented oligarchs in binding the backcountry area to the coast politically as well as economically, an interest first displayed during the Jay Treaty controversy in 1795.

Another possible explanation for the shift of the southern backcountry to Federalism in 1798 relates to ethnic politics. The region was settled heavily by Germans and Scots-Irish during the middle decades of the century. It might be assumed that these groups remained comparative strangers in the land and that their social distinctiveness bred a political particularism which manifested itself in 1798 in extreme patriotism—representing an eager attempt by first- and second-generation immigrants to prove that their "Americanism" was as legitimate as that claimed by the longer established Anglo-Saxon groups around them. This explanation loses much of its force in light of the recent findings of the historical geographer, Harry Roy Merrens, who concludes from a study of eighteenth-century North Carolina that Protestant Germans and Scots-Irish, unlike later immigrants to the United States, were quickly and easily assimilated into the social structure of North Carolina and that, indeed, it is extremely difficult even to trace any distinct settlement patterns for these folk.[47]

A final, more satisfactory explanation is simply that a peculiar convergence of circumstances caused backcountrymen from Georgia to Virginia to fear physical attack from the "savages" around them should war with France come. This fear explains their excitement, their willingness to take up arms, and yet their urgent desire that Adams would maintain his position of armed watchfulness with hopes of an eventual settlement with the Directory. The "savages" from whom the backcountry residents feared violence and atrocity were the Negro slaves and the Indians. The South Carolina upcountry, as has been noted, began to import large numbers of Negroes during the middle and later years of the decade, and the social structure of the region had begun to take on a cast similar to that of the lowcountry slave-plantation region. By 1798, it would seem that many upcountrymen would be as susceptible to fears of a French invasion and a resultant slave rebellion as their brethren along the coast.

[47] Harry Roy Merrens, *Colonial North Carolina in the Eighteenth Century* (Chapel Hill: University of North Carolina Press, 1964), 55–76.

In backcountry Virginia and Georgia, white settlers feared not the Negro slaves, of whom there were comparatively few, but the Indians. The tense situation with the Creeks in Georgia remained unresolved, while in southwestern Virginia, Indian massacres of isolated families and individuals were a part of very recent history.[48] A French war, which Adams seemingly had averted by his prudent response to the XYZ incident, might prove catastrophic. Should the French actually invade the South, as Washington thought they would, then they might contact and rouse the Indian tribes of the southwest to the same pitch of barbarity as earlier French governments had done with many of the tribes of New York and New England throughout nearly a century of colonial warfare. Even without an actual invasion of the coastal South, the French might work through the pliant Spanish and their empire in Florida and Louisiana. All of these factors doubtless played a part in reshaping markedly the political response of the southern backcountry in 1798, and, along with the simple emotional response to an insult to national honor, gave the Federalists an unparalleled opportunity to make inroads into a formerly hostile region.

In 1798 partisan newspapers and *ad hoc* public meetings —the traditional agencies of Federalist contact with the grassroots—were vigorously utilized by the friends of government to emphasize further the new, favorable public image of the national administration. In particular, the Federalist press in North Carolina went far beyond previous efforts; even earlier than the emergence of the XYZ affair, North Carolina editors began formulation of a simplistic, conservative political ideology, stressing unreflective patriotism and unquestioned loyalty to the existing political leadership and institutions. In the remaining period of Federalist pop-

[48] Lewis Preston Summers, *Annals of Southwest Virginia, 1769–1800* (Abingdon, Virginia: Lewis Preston Summers, 1929), 1495–1513.

ularity this ideological theme became a touchstone of the party's campaigns for the loyalty of the southern electorate. At the same time it appears that newly active partisans of the federal administration were behind many, if not all, of the mass meetings which were called on local and county levels throughout the South to affirm public allegiance to the national government after the insulting attempt to bribe the American mission. Beyond these traditional means of contact with the people, in Virginia there was growing evidence that by the latter half of the year a few Federalist leaders were at last contemplating a united partisan campaign for public office. Such campaigning surely would entail some active solicitation of popular support; eventually it might even result in the establishment of a meaningful two-way communication between local spokesmen of the federal administration and the southern grassroots.

Despite these achievements, Federalism's apex of popularity in the South in 1798 was more the result of a single favorable issue, which was exploited well by partisan leaders and a partisan press, than of a notable expansion of party organization. By the end of the year the reconstruction of Federalist organizations in the South had reached a level first achieved in 1793, but it proceeded little further. The very number of *ad hoc* county and town meetings called to applaud Adams' foreign policy argues that under the impact of the maritime crisis with France, the Federalists in the South had attracted a growing number of active followers on local and county levels. It is equally clear, however, that these new and active recruits received little sustained encouragement or direct supervision from older Federalist leaders. Moreover, contact with the electorate continued to be maintained only through the traditional elitist channels of indoctrination—the partisan newspaper and the public meeting—while party organization remained loosely structured, centering on informal factions composed of a select few gentleman politicians who seldom worked in close cooperation or attempted to coordinate policy. Virginia seemed an exception only because the national party leadership took the initiative and exercised a strong, persistent influence upon the Federalist factions at Richmond and Alexandria.

Burdened by continuing organizational weaknesses, southern Federalists soon began to feel the effects of another disturbing development in national affairs. As the year waned, there were increasing signs that Federalist harmony on the national level was breaking down and that at least one of the emerging factions was pursuing policies radical enough to destroy the Federalist image as a party of prudence and preservation in the southern mind. Not until this development reached disastrous proportions on the eve of the presidential election of 1800, however, did many friends of government at the southern grassroots make a desperate attempt to organize a modern party system to save themselves from political ruin.

During the Congressional session of 1797–1798 there had been little indication that the Federalist party was in the process of destroying its popularity. As in the southern states, the Federalist interest in Congress rode the crest of successive triumphs which seemed to assure the perpetuation of the party on a national level for years to come.

Congressional Federalists entered the year 1798 as a united, though somewhat apprehensive, phalanx. Southern Federalists reported that the persistent lack of news from the three-man mission which Adams had dispatched to Paris had set Congressional nerves on edge.[49] On January 30

[49] Thomas Pinckney to Edward Rutledge, November 24, 1797, January 6, 1798, Thomas Pinckney Letterbook, 1791–1798, South Caroliniana Library, Columbia, S. C.; Jefferson to Thomas Mann Randolph, from Philadelphia, January 11, February 15, 1798, Jefferson Papers, Vol. 102; John Rutledge, Jr., to Bishop Smith, from Philadelphia, January 3, 1798, John Rutledge, Jr., Papers, Southern Historical Collection, University of North Carolina, Chapel Hill, N. C.

tensions exploded momentarily in the House as a result of "one of the most Savage Acts that ever disgraced any Publick Body."[50] The resolution of the Lyon-Griswold feud, in which a Republican representative had spat in the face of a Federalist opponent and had in turn been caned, became the initial test of party unity and loyalty in the First Session of the Fifth Congress. While Jefferson unhappily noted the absence of several leading members of the Republican party, the Federalists, led by Harper and Sewall, managed to have Lyon expelled by a 52 to 44 count.[51] The Federalists gained an important new recruit at this juncture; appearing in the list against Lyon, along with Harper and Rutledge of South Carolina, Grove of North Carolina, and Evans, Morgan, and Machir of Virginia, was Josiah Parker, representative from Norfolk, one of Madison's earliest and staunchest allies and the only Republican representative of Virginia's urban interests.[52] Parker's vote marked the beginning of his and Norfolk's shift to Federalism and meant that for a time the friends of government could claim dominance in every urban center in Virginia.

With the news of the failure of the XYZ mission and the subsequent Republican blunder in wishing to know the exact reasons for its collapse, the Federalist party in Congress, led by able southern members, attacked vigorously. According to Jefferson, South Carolina's two Federalist representatives, "Mr. Harper and Mr. Pinckney pronounced bitter phillipics against France, selecting such circumstances & aggravations as to give the worst picture they could present." Jefferson added acidly that Pinckney "on this, as in the affair

[50] James Gunn to Seaborn Jones, from Philadelphia, January 30, 1798, History Note Card File, Independence Hall National Park Office, Philadelphia; Thomas to John Gray Blount, from Philadelphia, February 8, 16, 1798, in Masterson, ed., *John Gray Blount*, III, 206, 209–10.

[51] Madison to Jefferson, from Orange, March 4, 1798, Madison Papers, Vol. 20.

[52] *Annals of Congress*, V, 1008–1009.

of Lyon and Griswold, went far beyond that moderation he has on other occasions recommended." So deep was Jefferson's bitterness against Pinckney that by early April the Vice President was accusing him of being at the head of a distinctly pro-Hamilton faction in Congress.[53] In the meantime, all of the "waverers" in the House went over to the Federalist side, while the demoralized Republican interests disintegrated, with five members immediately departing for home. "We now expect to lose every question which shall be proposed," the Vice President mourned.[54] By late May he was in despair. "The war-men," he reported, "have been indefatigable in the use they have made of [the XYZ dispatches] with the people, who are not in the habit of analyzing things of that kind."[55]

The Federalists pressed their advantage cruelly. Between May 17 and July 10, 1798, they passed what may be called the first positive legislative program of a well-defined political party in American history. Included in this program were the Alien and Sedition Acts, a bill to suspend all commercial intercourse with France, and legislation to create a provisional army of ten thousand men—though the original figure proposed was twenty thousand—and to increase the navy to a respectable size. Of equal importance to the friends of government was the overwhelming defeat on July 3 of a motion proposed by Edward Livingston requesting the House to address Adams on the desirability of Gerry's remaining at Paris to negotiate further with the French government.[56] On all of the crucial divisions southern Fed-

[53] Jefferson to Madison, from Philadelphia, March 29, April 5, 1798, Madison Papers, Vol. 20.
[54] Jefferson to Thomas Mann Randolph, from Philadelphia, April 19, 26, 1798, Jefferson Papers, Vol. 103.
[55] Jefferson to T. M. Randolph, from Philadelphia, May 24, 1798, *ibid.*, Vol. 104.
[56] *Annals of Congress*, V, 1553, 1769–70, 1772, 1831, 1865–66, 2028–29, 2086–87, 2171.

eralists showed disciplined fidelity to party interests.[57]

However, sectional and factional tensions were never absent from Federalist councils, even during the party's months of greatest national supremacy. The failure of the American mission to Paris prompted many friends of government to fear imminent armed conflict and to desire to establish an efficient war cabinet. Jefferson informed Madison that if war should take place, Federalists were agreed on the need to dispose of the notoriously inefficient Secretary of War, James McHenry. The party was sharply divided over Secretary of State Timothy Pickering, however, whose distrust of southern Federalists had not abated. According to the Vice President, the solid bloc of New England Federalists was determined that Pickering be retained, while the resurgent southern wing of the party was equally determined to be rid of the Secretary of State, whose suspicions were corroding party harmony.[58]

Thus, the interests and prejudices of the President and of the members of his party's southern wing converged during the spring and summer of 1798. Adams' steadily ripening mistrust of the military ambitions of Hamilton and his allies —who included Pickering—found support among leading southern Federalists who wanted to purge their party of those possessed of dangerous passions.

In October the growing estrangement between members of the high Federalist faction and more moderate southern Federalists was dramatized in an exchange of letters between Pickering and John Marshall. Marshall had returned to New York in mid-June, apparently hoping to dampen the war spirit in the United States until further indications of

[57] Manning J. Dauer, *The Adams Federalists* (Baltimore: Johns Hopkins Press, 1953), has analyzed exhaustively the voting behavior of each representative during the Fourth, Fifth, and Sixth Congresses. (Appendix III, 288–326.)

[58] Jefferson to Madison, March 15, 1798, Madison Papers, Vol. 20.

French enmity rendered the crisis insoluble. According to the ubiquitous Vice President, Edward Livingston met Marshall when he landed and received assurances that France had no desire for war at the moment. Once Marshall reached Philadelphia, however, he was engulfed by the hawks, with the Secretary of State at their head. Bells were rung in the capital upon the Virginian's arrival "& immense crouds [sic] were collected to see & make part of the shew, which was circuitously paraded through the streets before he was set down at the city tavern." Jefferson's alarm at the uses made of the envoy's person by the excited high Federalists was obvious. "Since his arrival I can hear of nothing directly from him," the Vice President wrote, "while they are disseminating through the town things, as from him, diametrically opposed to what he said to Livingston."[59]

Marshall never again allowed himself to be used in such a fashion by the Hamiltonian Federalists. When four months later Pickering and other high Federalists sought to blacken Gerry's name and to stimulate patriotic ardor and enlistments in the new army, they asked Marshall to write an inflammatory essay on the entire XYZ affair. In his two replies, Marshall was cordial but stubbornly evasive. He made clear his anti-French bias and his unhappiness with Gerry's conduct in remaining in Paris to negotiate with Talleyrand. But he turned down the request, pleading the press of personal business and his apprehension at the possibility of being dragged into "news paper altercations."[60] Pickering clearly was displeased, but there was little he could do to budge the stubborn Virginian. Adams thus could expect no hindrance from Marshall in his attempts to further conciliate the Directory. In fact, as the rift be-

[59] Jefferson to Madison, June 21, 1798, *ibid.*
[60] Pickering to Marshall, from Trenton, October 4, 18, 1798; Marshall to Pickering, from Richmond, October 15, 22, 1798; Marshall to Elbridge Gerry, from Richmond, November 12, 1798, Marshall Papers.

tween Adams and the pro-Hamilton Federalists widened, Marshall identified himself completely with the President and his foreign policy.

By the end of the year all indications pointed to a firm alliance between the President, a large bloc of moderate supporters among the southern electorate, and the southern wing of the Federalist party, against the militaristic ambitions of the high Federalist faction, on the one hand, and the naked Francophilism of the Republican opposition, on the other.[61]

The next year most southern Federalists began to deviate somewhat from the moderate policies pursued by the President. Under the steady pressure of Republican opposition, many of them defended the Alien and Sedition Acts; many more eagerly participated in the recruitment of a suitable officer corps for the provisional army, which was viewed as a bulwark against all threats to the government from within and without. Such discrepancies in temperament between the President and his southern followers, however, were not of major importance in the long run. They did not signal a break in relations nor should they be taken as an indication that most southern Federalists finally approved Hamilton's

[61] Although implicated in the military ambitions of the high Federalists, Washington himself cogently expressed the mature development of this moderate strain in Federalist thinking which appealed to so many southerners. He wrote bluntly to Lafayette in December, 1798: "That there are many among us, who wish to see this Country embroiled on the side of Great Britain, and others who are anxious that we should take part with France against her, admits of no doubt. But it is a fact on which you may entirely and absolutely rely, that the Governing powers of the Country, and a large part of the people, are truly Americans in principle, attached to the interest of it; And unwilling under any circumstances whatsoever to participate in the Politics or Contests of Europe: Much less since they have found that France, having foresaken the ground she first took, is interfering in the internal concerns of all nations, Neutral as well as Belligerent, and setting the world in an uproar." From Mount Vernon, December 25, 1798, in Fitzpatrick, ed., *Washington*, XXXVII, 69.

bizarre schemes for the eventual use of the army. With the exception of Attorney General Charles Lee, who could not escape its implications, southern Federalists generally waited watchfully and remained independent in the acrid struggle between Adams and the high Federalist faction within the party. Not until the President abruptly dismissed his Secretaries of State and War in March, 1800, did southern Federalists feel any intense pressure to make an explicit choice of sides. Although the conflict between Adams and the high Federalists became profound and bitter, especially after February, 1799, from the perspective of southern Federalism it seems to have been largely a battle at court, to be evaded by those that were there and to be regarded as a conflict fought in a distant capital by those who were not.[62] The few further Federalist gains in the South in 1799 were largely unequivocal victories. Those who won them apparently were willing to support any self-professed friend

[62] John Rutledge, Jr., seems to have been the only southern Federalist to align himself publicly with Hamilton's clique. In December, 1799, he noted caustically that Adams' recent dispatch of yet another peace mission to the Directory and the President's "modus rei . . . have laid the roots of bitterness firm and deep" within the Federalist faction in Congress. Harper's circumspection was far more representative of the attitude of most southern Federalist congressmen. "I always thought the mission an ill-judged and unlucky measure," he wrote in August, "but having been adopted, I think that the policy and dignity of the Government equally require, that it should be pressed in the spirit of firmness and good faith." Josiah Parker, the Norfolk Federalist, chose another way of expressing ostentatious neutrality during the troublesome months when the conflict between the President and the high Federalists came to a climax. He closed a letter to Hamilton's lackey, McHenry, with the bland request that the Secretary of War should send his warmest regards on to the President upon the next meeting! John Rutledge, Jr., to Bishop Smith, from Philadelphia, December 7, 1799, John Rutledge, Jr., Papers, Southern Historical Collection, University of North Carolina, Chapel Hill, N. C.; Harper to McHenry, August 2, 1799, Harper Papers, LC; Josiah Parker to McHenry, from Norfolk, April 29, 1799, in Bernard C. Steiner, ed., "Correspondence of James McHenry," *William and Mary Quarterly*, Series 1, XIII (October, 1904), 102–107.

of government, be it Hamilton, Adams, or an agent of one or the other, against the hated Republican leaders. Prior to the spring of 1800, therefore, Federalist triumphs in the South served to emphasize party unity and strength rather than deep internal divisions.

VI. *Defense and Diversion,*
1799

From the close of 1798 until the end of 1799 a perceptible decline in Federalist activity was discernible at the state and local levels throughout much of the South. In Virginia, Federalists did register some gains both in popular strength and in modest expansion of organization and activity during the period. Federalists throughout the South now were willing to bow to the demands of party regularity as they energetically, if not always brilliantly, defended the controversial legislative programs passed by their congressmen the previous summer. There are strong indications, moreover, that the friends of government in the South did not suffer a precipitate drop in popularity because of their determined support of party policy.

At the same time many Federalists, especially in the Carolinas, allowed their energies to be diverted from the problems of expanding their political organization by the endless difficulties involved in the organization of the provisional army, and this proved to be a serious mistake. The army, either as an institution or an issue, would do the Federalists little good in the presidential campaign of 1800. In choosing to turn away from their constituents and immerse themselves in an enterprise far removed from popular favor or interest, many southern Federalists built a barrier between themselves and the people, thus contributing to their ultimate downfall.

Directly upon its passage into legal existence the provisional army took fatal hold over the attentions of far too many friends of government in both the North and the South, whether or not they were personal allies of Hamilton. Both Adams and Washington were determined that southern Federalists should play a key role in the formation of the provisional army, and they met a ready response. When the President submitted to Washington his controversial list of candidates for the three-man general staff in the summer of 1798, four of the fifteen men mentioned were southerners. Three were from Virginia—Daniel Morgan, Henry Lee, and Edward Carrington. The other was Cotesworth Pinckney.[1] Washington, too, was aware of the importance of retaining the loyalty of his fellow southerners, and his determination to give them a fair place in the hierarchy of command led to a minor crisis in military and party politics.

Immediately after his appointment Washington frankly informed one of Hamilton's most fervent allies, Secretary of State Pickering, that Cotesworth Pinckney must, if he wished to take it, be given the powerful number two post of Inspector General. If the French should be so mad as to attack the United States directly, Washington remarked,

I conceive there can hardly be two opinions respecting their Plan and that their operations will commence in the Southern quarter—1. because it is the weakest.—2. because they will expect, from the tenor of the debates in Congress, to find more friends there.—3. because there can be no doubt of their arming our own Negroes against us—and 4. because they will be more contiguous to their Islands; and to Louisiana, if they should be possessed thereof.

Washington added that Pinckney "is an officer of high military reputation—fond of the profession, —spirited, —active,

[1] Adams to McHenry, July 6, 1798, Adams Papers, Reel 117.

—and judicious—and much advanced in the estimation of the Public by his late conduct as Minister and Envoy at Paris." This being the case, Washington was "morally Certain" that Pinckney—then still in Europe—would not accept a position junior to Hamilton. If he were forced to it, the general hinted at unpleasant political repercussions. "Disgust would follow, and its influence would spread where most to be deprecated, as his connections are numerous, powerful, and more influential than any other in the 3 Southern States." The conclusion was obvious. "It would be impolitic, and might be dangerous" to force Hamilton's pretensions ahead of those of Pinckney.[2]

When Hamilton and his allies nevertheless refused to end their incessant conspiring, Adams joined Washington in demanding that Pinckney be given the first chance at the post of Inspector General.[3] Washington never showed the same consideration for Adams' anti-Hamiltonian prejudices as he did for Pinckney's pretensions, however. Most likely Washington at this time deeply feared an imminent French invasion of the South—a fear which some southern Federalists sought to keep alive as much as a year later.[4]

By August, 1798, therefore, profound schisms within the Federalist party already were becoming apparent. Hamilton was besieged. Knox already had refused to take a subordinate role to the former colonel from New York, despite Hamilton's strong insistence that he must.[5] Now it appeared that some southern Federalists as well might turn aside in bitterness. Fortunately for the army faction and

[2] Washington to Pickering, from Mount Vernon, July 11, 1798, Hamilton Papers, Vol. 31.
[3] Adams to McHenry, from Quincy, August 14, 1798, Adams Papers, Reel 118.
[4] Jacob Read to James Jackson, from Philadelphia, March 22, 1799, Jacob Read Papers, South Caroliniana Library, Columbia, S. C.
[5] Hamilton to Washington, from New York, August 20, 1798, Hamilton Papers, Vol. 31.

the future of party harmony, Pinckney chose not to provoke existing antagonisms further. He had had hatred of France driven deep into his soul by his unhappy experiences in Paris during the previous two years. He returned to Philadelphia in October, highly abusive of any further attempts at reconciliation and quickly agreed to accept a position on the general staff subordinate to Hamilton.[6]

With the Pinckney crisis resolved, and with Adams' subsequent attempts to block Hamilton's accession to the Inspector Generalship frustrated, southern Federalists willingly helped to recruit a suitable officer corps. In the Senate, James Gunn of Georgia, cut off from all hope of further political influence after March 1801, led the Federalist forces who wanted to establish an effective army rapidly. Gunn had been a well-known military leader during the Revolution, and Hamilton sought him out as a potential ally when Congress reconvened in December. Gunn quickly agreed. When the new Inspector General wrote expressing a desire ultimately to see the Georgia senator in a field command, Gunn responded with flattery. "I am persuaded it can be no part of your plan merely to execute the feeble arrangements of other men," he wrote. After observing that Hamilton would have charge of running the army in the absence of actual war, Gunn implicitly committed himself to help the Inspector General find "the Legislative aid necessary for the Support of that department."[7]

By late January, Gunn had more than fulfilled his com-

[6] Pinckney to McHenry, from Trenton, October 31, 1798, in John C. Hamilton, ed., *The Works of Alexander Hamilton* (7 vols.; New York: John F. Trow, Printer, 1851), VI, 373; "Personal Memo," January 14, 1799, Jefferson Papers, Vol. 105.

[7] Hamilton to Gunn, from New York, December 16, 1798; Gunn to Hamilton, from Philadelphia, December 19, 1798, Hamilton Papers, Vol. 33; Hamilton to Gunn, December 22, 1798, in Bernard C. Steiner, *The Life and Correspondence of James McHenry* (Cleveland: The Burrows Brothers Company, 1907), 360–61.

mitment. Working through McHenry, he sponsored supplementary bills to the army legislation in the Senate with such haste and enthusiasm that at one point Hamilton complained he could not keep up with Gunn's demands for the drafts of fresh bills or amendments to existing ones.[8]

Robert Goodloe Harper was another nationally prominent Federalist from the South who did not attempt to disguise his eagerness to seek "the bubble reputation, even in the cannon's mouth." In the summer of 1799 he applied both to McHenry and to Cotesworth Pinckney for permission to raise a brigade in the South Carolina backcountry. McHenry sent Harper's letter on with the remark that the South Carolina congressman's talents "are splendid, and he has usefully employed a fund of information, and solidarity of argument in our public councils." Pinckney, however, turned Harper's request aside for the moment with the observation that raising private military units was not authorized under existing legislation until an invasion actually took place.[9] Harper's ambitions later were satisfied by his appointment as Washington's aide-de-camp, a post which would not interfere with his Congressional duties except upon the outbreak of actual hostilities.[10]

In the southern states the practical job of recruitment was begun in the winter of 1798–1799 and was undertaken by friends of government prominent on both national and local levels. Overall direction was delegated to Cotesworth Pinckney and Brigadier General William Washington of South

[8] Hamilton to McHenry, January 14, 1799, *ibid.*, 366; Gunn to Hamilton, January 23, 1799, Hamilton Papers, Vol. 33.

[9] Harper to McHenry, from Baltimore, July 29, 1799, Robert Goodloe Harper Papers, South Caroliniana Library, Columbia, S. C.; Cotesworth Pinckney to Harper, from Charleston, June 13, 1799; McHenry to Harper, from Philadelphia, August 7, 1799, Harper Papers, LC.

[10] Stephen G. Kurtz, *The Presidency of John Adams: The Collapse of Federalism, 1795–1800* (New York: A. S. Barnes & Company, Inc., 1961), 330.

Carolina and William R. Davie of North Carolina.[11] In Virginia, Washington himself handled recruitment with the aid of Daniel Morgan, Henry Lee, John Marshall, William Heth, and Edward Carrington; the entire hard-core Virginia Federalist faction of earlier years openly identified itself with the army.[12]

In the matter of actual recruitment Virginia Federalists were as careful to insure the political reliability of potential officers as were Federalists in New England and the middle states. In May, 1799, John Nicholas, unsuccessful Federalist Congressional candidate from Madison's district, assured the Secretary of War that he was aware of "the propriety of the govt's giving incouragement [sic] to federalism in this quarter of the Union, where its sparks, I am sorry to say, are too rare." In this spirit, Nicholas added, he called the volunteer corps of riflemen of Albemarle County for active service.[13] William Heth reopened his formerly close contact with Hamilton concerning the choice of a suitable aide-de-camp for the Inspector General. Certainly he and Carrington were quite aware of Hamilton's privately expressed wish "of appointing friends of the government to military stations."[14]

In North Carolina, William R. Davie was given some aid in his recruiting drive by William Barry Grove.[15] Davie

[11] Washington to Davie, from Mount Vernon, December 28, 1798, William R. Davie Papers; Washington to Brigadier General William Washington, from Mount Vernon, December 28, 1798, in John C. Fitzpatrick, ed., *The Writings of George Washington* (39 vols.; Washington, D. C.: U. S. Government Printing Office, 1931–1944), XXXVII, 74.

[12] Washington to McHenry, from Mount Vernon, May 13, 1799, in Fitzpatrick, ed., *Washington*, XXXVII, 207.

[13] Nicholas to McHenry, May 13, 1799, in Steiner, *Life and Correspondence of McHenry*, 388.

[14] Heth to Hamilton, from Petersburg, July 8, 1798, Hamilton Papers, Vol. 31; Hamilton to McHenry, February 6, 1799, in Steiner, *Life and Correspondence of McHenry*, 368.

[15] Grove to McHenry, from Raleigh, September 5, 1799, James McHenry Papers.

seemed as determined as his Virginia colleagues to weed out politically questionable candidates. In December, 1798, he forwarded to Washington "the names of those Gentlemen of whose character I was fully satisfied and whose willingness to serve had been ascertained."[16]

Little is known of military patronage in South Carolina; of Georgia, nothing except that, in Pinckney's words, "merely a Colonel of Infantry" was to be appointed.[17] Patronage in South Carolina was under the direct supervision of Pinckney and William Washington, however, which undoubtedly meant that eager, loyal young Federalists from the area were given every consideration. In early 1800, Hamilton appointed young Captain Izard as one of his aides, thereby enlisting a powerful South Carolina name, if not personality, to the Federalist cause.[18]

Some friends of government in the South indicated less enthusiasm for the Alien and Sedition Acts, which had been initiated and drafted largely at the instigation of Senator Lloyd of Maryland and Representative Harper of South Carolina.[19] Soon after the Sedition Act passed Congress, Edward Rutledge informed his nephew John, who had voted for the bill, that in his opinion the provisions of the act "are carried . . . much too far." The older man admitted, however, that in South Carolina "so anxious are we for Union & the Benefits of self-government, that those who see, or think they see the Errors of the Bill . . . discuss the propriety of it with the calmness of Philosophy rather than with the ardor of Politicians."[20] In Virginia, John Marshall fell under

[16] December 3, 1798, from Halifax, William R. Davie Papers.
[17] Pinckney to Harper, June 13, 1799, Harper Papers, LC.
[18] Hamilton to William Loughton Smith, from New York, March 11, 1800, in Hamilton, ed., *Works of Hamilton*, VI, 432.
[19] John C. Miller, *The Federalist Era, 1789–1801* (New York: Harper & Brothers, 1960), 229–30.
[20] Edward to John Rutledge, Jr., July 29, 1798, John Rutledge, Jr., Papers, Southern Historical Collection, University of North Carolina, Chapel

personal attack because of popular agitation over the laws and chose to condemn them publicly, though his private attitude apparently was somewhat different.[21] The North Carolina House of Representatives condemned the laws with the same breath used to praise the President's conduct toward France, certain proof of the decidedly moderate nature of the Federalist impulse in the state. The vote was a crushing 58 to 21.[22]

Yet many southern Federalists chose to defend the laws, thus indicating that the party continued to generate measurable enthusiasm throughout the region. Twenty-one North Carolina representatives did go on public record in defense of the Alien and Sedition Acts, while at the same time the upper house of the legislature contemptuously tabled the Kentucky Resolutions when they were introduced by a Republican senator. One observer added that "in the temper" the North Carolina Senate was in, it "might easily have been prevailed on to throw them in the fire."[23]

In the early months of 1799 leading Republicans believed that South Carolina was coming under their influence once

---

Hill, N. C. In the spring of 1799, Timothy Pickering and the South Carolina Federalists, led by Cotesworth Pinckney and Henry William DeSaussure, attempted to use the so-called "tub plot," wherein the French were alleged to have sent agents to Charleston to stir up further slave unrest, as a means of reconciling the people of the state to the Alien and Sedition laws. The Federalists bungled the affair, however, and the Republicans were able to prove that the "plot" had been a partisan fabrication. Cotesworth Pinckney and John Marshall suffered personal ridicule as a result. The entire affair is discussed in John C. Miller, *Crisis in Freedom: The Alien and Sedition Acts* (Boston: Little, Brown and Company, 1951), 146–50.

[21] *Virginia Gazette and General Advertiser*, January 1, 1799; Albert J. Beveridge, *Life of John Marshall* (4 vols.; Boston: Houghton, Mifflin Company, 1916–1919), II, 389.

[22] "Journal of the North Carolina House of Commons," December 24, 1798, Jenkins, ed., *Records of the States of the United States* (Microfilm, University of California Library, Berkeley).

[23] Samuel Johnston to James Iredell, December 23, 1798, in Griffith J. McRee, ed., *Life and Correspondence of James Iredell* (2 vols.; New York: Peter Smith, 1947), II, 542.

more as a result of the Alien and Sedition Acts. In January, Thomas Sumter reported to Jefferson that "the republicans in S.C. has [sic] gained 50 per cent in numbers since [the state] election which was in the moment of the XYZ fever."[24] But the following December the friends of government in the South Carolina Senate were able to suppress a Republican attempt to introduce the Kentucky Resolutions for debate on the floor by a vote of 14 to 11, which reflected roughly the same proportion of party strength as the votes on preparedness in the lower house the year before.[25]

A modest public defense of the laws was evident even in Savannah, where the *Georgia Gazette* briefly resumed its partisanship by republishing Timothy Pickering's famous lengthy reply to the hostile address of the citizens of Prince Edward County, Virginia.[26]

The Alien and Sedition Acts received their stoutest and most uncompromising defense in Virginia, where they became the central issue in the state campaign, which raged from autumn, 1798, to the elections in April, 1799. The Republicans' successful crusade against the laws in the General Assembly of 1798–1799 provoked an immediate response from the friends of government. Fifty-eight of the sixty-three assemblymen who voted against the Virginia Resolutions in January signed an address to the people by the "Federal members" of the state legislature. Theodore Sedgewick, the New England Federalist, observed that the address, which he claimed was the work of John Marshall, one of the fifty-eight, was "able and elegant and eloquent."[27]

---

[24] Jefferson to Madison, from Philadelphia, January 30, 1799, Jefferson Papers, Vol. 105.

[25] "Journal of the Senate of South Carolina," December 24, 1799, Jenkins, ed., *Records of the States*. There were no significant party divisions in the South Carolina House of Representatives in 1799.

[26] Issues of October 25, November 1, 1798.

[27] Sedgewick to Hamilton, from Philadelphia, February 7, 1799, in Hamilton, ed., *Works of Hamilton*, VI, 392–93.

Actually the effort was labored, vituperative, repetitive, and short on logic.

The friends of government based their entire defense of the laws—and of the provisional army as well—upon the assumption that by 1798 "we had but to choose between submission to the will of a foreign nation, and the maintenance of our independence." The Alien Act was thus an obvious necessity and was constitutionally justifiable, since Congress already had acted upon this assumption and had assumed such warmaking powers as the granting of letters of marque and reprisal, the formation of rules regarding captures upon land and water, and the establishment of defenses to protect the states from invasion. The Federalists were unable to find justification for the Sedition Act in a strict reading of the main body of the Constitution. Undeterred, they blandly claimed that the general language of the preamble and the necessary and proper clause in Article I, Section 8, provided ample legal basis for the law. They asserted that in times of crisis the people had the right to prevent vile attacks against public figures and government officials. The friends of government did not mention the obvious fact that "the people" had little to do with the initiation or the passage of the legislation and nothing to do with its enforcement, which rested largely with partisan judges. None of these arguments were new; there was no hint of the imaginative political logic which had inspired the Virginia Resolutions. But although they were weak, they were presented with great force.[28]

A second pamphlet of note in refutation of the Virginia Resolutions was issued anonymously by Henry Lee the following month. Lee, too, was unable to serve his cause with

---

[28] "Address of the Fifty-Eight Federal Members of the Virginia Legislature to their Fellow Citizens in January, 1799," Augusta, Maine, Peter Edes (n.d.), in Henry E. Huntington Library, San Marino, Calif., especially 11, 17–18, 23–33.

notable intelligence and tried to make up for the loss through tedious repetition. Attempting to rebut Jefferson's theory of a federal compact, Lee merely reiterated the usual Federalist arguments that the national government was ever the superior and indivisibly sovereign body in the Union. He argued in crude style his belief that it was the duty of the central government to transcend and to protect the interests of the states wherever necessary.[29]

A third and somewhat earlier pamphlet apparently was written in defense of the Alien and Sedition Acts by Thomas Evans, the Federalist congressman from the Williamsburg district. Washington read it, and his correspondence indicates that he assumed others had as well.[30] Federalist sentiments on the controversial laws thus seem to have been given the widest possible exposure in Virginia.

It was not clear in the spring of 1799 that the remarkable adherence to party regularity shown by nearly all southern Federalists would redound to their political credit. The condemnation of the Alien and Sedition Acts by the North Carolina House of Representatives, the passage of the Virginia Resolutions, and the many indications of public apathy or outright opposition to the army, all seemed to indicate that the Federalists in the South had hastened their political oblivion by public adherence to party policy.[31] But the state

[29] "PLAIN TRUTH, Addressed to the people of Virginia by a Citizen of Westmoreland County, February 1799," in Henry E. Huntington Library, San Marino, Calif.
[30] Washington to Bushrod Washington, from Mount Vernon, December 31, 1798, in Fitzpatrick, ed., *Washington*, XXXVII, 81.
[31] Concerning the army, Washington reported to McHenry as early as October, 1798, that the "spirit and enthusiasm which were inspired by the Dispatches from our Envoys" was "evaporating fast." By the next February, Washington was near despair. Measures to build up the army, he reported, were "not only viewed with indifference, but deemed unnecessary by that class of people whose attentions [were] being turned to other matters." This being the case, "the officers, who in August and September, could, with ease, have enlisted whole companies of them, will find it difficult to recruit any." It was at this point also that Hamilton and the

elections in Virginia gave the Federalists another opportunity to appeal for public support and to prove that their influence in the South was not yet ended.

Virginia Federalists were not disheartened by recent events, but accepted them as a challenge to be met and overcome. Party members campaigned and organized on three distinct levels. At the highest level were the great figures of the party's past, who lent their prestige and talents to the cause in a limited degree. In the final year of his life Washington reappeared as a valuable, though unreflective, party leader. In addition to his complete identification with the army, he openly defended the Alien and Sedition Acts and demonstrated his unhesitating adherence to the worst Federalist shibboleths concerning the presence of "aliens . . . who acknowledge no allegiance to this Country, and in many instances are sent among us (as there is the best Circumstantial evidence to prove) for the express purpose of poisoning the minds of our people and to sow dissensions among them, in order to alienate their affections from the Government of their Choice."[32]

Washington's greatest influence, however, was over his own party and its relationship with the political opposition. The general's bitterness toward the Republicans was profound by this time. When imparted in correspondence to

---

high Federalists thought they saw in the Virginia militia a plot to resist the Alien and Sedition Acts by force. The Inspector General, in commenting on this plot, hinted darkly that "public opinion has not been ameliorated; sentiments dangerous to social happiness have not been diminished; on the contrary, there are symptoms which warrant the apprehension that among the most numerous class of citizens, errors of a very pernicious tendency have not only preserved, but extended their empire." Washington to McHenry, from Mount Vernon, October 14, 1798, in Steiner, *Life and Correspondence of McHenry*, 337; Washington to Hamilton, February 25, 1799, Hamilton to Jonathan Dayton, 1799, in Hamilton, ed., *Works of Hamilton*, VI, 383–84, 401.

[32] Washington to Alexander Spotswood, from Philadelphia, November 22, 1798, in Fitzpatrick, ed., *Washington*, XXXVII, 23–24.

fellow Federalists, it stirred their emotions, thus contributing to that atmosphere of implacable malevolence within which the party campaigns in Virginia were conducted.[33] Washington unleashed a typical outburst of anger when writing to William Vans Murray at the end of the year. "The Alien and Sedition Laws," he remarked, "are now the desiderata in the Opposition. But any thing else would have done; and something there will always be, for them to torture, and to disturb the public mind with their unfounded and ill favored forebodings."[34] When George Logan made the brave error of attempting to acquaint the general with the motives for and outcome of his private mission to the Directory, Washington coldly and deliberately ignored him, turning the meeting into an exercise in studied effrontery.[35]

Patrick Henry was another popular hero who became an asset to the Federalist cause. Upon Washington's solicitation he had agreed to run for the General Assembly from Charlotte and was successful.[36] But the once fiery orator indicated his growing sense of fatigue and age in his reply to Washington's request.[37] Although he wrote letters in support of Marshall's Congressional candidacy, Henry "hand-

[33] During the legislative session of 1798–1799, Jefferson remarked that he had never seen such party bitterness, and there is evidence that gentlemen from rival parties simply could not live or eat together—or even pass each other on the street—in Richmond. For example, at one point when Assemblyman James Cureton, a Federalist of Prince George County, entered a Republican tavern, a fight quickly broke out whose outcome remains unrecorded. "Party Violence, 1790–1800," *Virginia Magazine of History and Biography*, XXIX (1921), 174. See also the *Virginia Federalist*, May 14, 1800, for an example of the continuation of this trend through the presidential election year.

[34] Washington to Murray, December 26, 1798, in Fitzpatrick, ed., *Washington*, XXXVII, 72.

[35] "Memorandum of an Interview," November 13, 1798, *ibid.*, XXXVII, 18–20.

[36] Earl G. Swem and John W. Williams, *A Register of the General Assembly of Virginia, 1776–1918, and of the Constitutional Conventions* (Richmond: Davis Bottom, Supt. of Public Printing, 1918), 53.

[37] Fitzpatrick, ed., *Washington*, XXXVII, 90n.

somely" declined to add the luster of his name to the final three-man mission which in February Adams determined to send to France.[38] By June, Henry was dead, a fact sincerely lamented by the friends of government.[39]

On the second and far more intense level of party activity stood the tried and true members of the old Richmond faction, now reinforced by recruits from the state's Congressional delegation and from within the various counties. After February Lee and his friends abandoned the fight against the Virginia Resolutions and those who had sponsored them and turned their attentions to the Congressional and General Assembly campaigns. Yet the Virginia Resolutions and the defense of the army were not forgotten, for the Republicans had indelibly stamped these issues upon the campaigns. Neither side let the citizen of Virginia forget that when he cast his ballot he was granting a mandate not only to men but to measures as well.

Both interests professed optimism over the probable outcome of the April elections. In February, after observing the flood of public letters and pamphlets written to prove that the United States suffered more from Great Britain than from France, Jefferson professed serenity. "The materials now bearing on the public mind," he wrote, "will infallibly restore it to its republican soundness in the course of the present summer."[40] The Federalists were no less energetic and optimistic, but their optimism contained a vindictive tone. Referring once again to the Virginia Resolutions, one friend of government, writing in March, claimed that "the

[38] William Wirt Henry, *Patrick Henry: Life, Correspondence and Speeches* (2 vols.; New York: Charles Scribner's Sons, 1891), II, 591–94, 598; Adams to Pickering, from Quincy, May 8, 1799, Adams Papers, Reel 119.

[39] Washington to Marshall, from Mount Vernon, June 16, 1799, in Fitzpatrick, ed., *Washington*, XXXVII, 235–36; *Virginia Federalist*, December 18, 1799.

[40] Jefferson to Monroe, February 11, 1799, to David Stuart, February 13, 1799, Jefferson Papers, Vol. 105.

authors of this execrable work are sinking fast into contempt. There let them forever rest. To this end it is not sufficient that we content ourselves with the victory, it must be followed up until every germ of faction be destroyed."[41]

The Federalists had laid the groundwork the previous fall for their hoped-for war of extirpation against the Republicans when Charles Lee, working from Philadelphia, had drawn up a Federalist ticket of moderate size for the Congressional campaign. Individual members of this ticket apparently were given whatever aid was necessary from Philadelphia in the weeks preceding the election. Josiah Parker, for example, since he represented the Norfolk district, appeared personally vulnerable to Republican charges that the Federalists were far more interested in raising an army for the purpose of intimidation than in building a navy for honest defense. An anonymous partisan in Philadelphia wrote a long letter to Parker's hometown newspaper several weeks before the elections, pointing out Parker's record as a persistent and energetic advocate of adequate defenses for his city.[42]

Most Federalists in Virginia apparently campaigned actively for Congressional and Assembly seats. The *Norfolk Herald* reported in late March that political excitement was sweeping the state. Moreover, the Federalists were becoming less arrogant and less aloof in their relationships with the electorate. A spirit of liberal innovation began to take hold of the Federalists as the campaign progressed, and they even went so far in some instances as to recruit their local officeseekers from the ranks of the plain folk.[43]

[41] *Norfolk Herald*, March 19, 1799.
[42] *Ibid.*, January 26, March 12, 1799.
[43] "Great efforts are making in order to change the Membership at the next session of the Assembly," one Federalist correspondent observed, "so that an alteration of MEASURES may take place." The correspondent added, however, that "it is feared that whilst an opposition can be made to the word Government, error and political intemperance will remain in *status*

As the campaign built toward its climax and popular resentment of the army continued, both Marshall and Lee almost completely severed their connections with the recruiting program.[44] Firmly committed to the government in a time of peril, the Virginia Federalists willingly modified their elitist standards for the sake of immediate public support.

A willing liberalization of elitist values regarding the wishes of the electorate was only one surprising feature in the Federalists' campaign in Virginia in 1799. Anonymous friends of government also began publicly urging fellow party members to make a determined bid to wrest control of the upcoming General Assembly from the Republicans.[45] Such a proposal had never before been made by a reputable member of the Federalist interest, yet it apparently was carried out with marked success.

Party activity on both sides reached down to a third level in Virginia by 1798–1799. Mobism and vigilantism, directly attributable to party animosities, flourished on the popular level throughout the state. As early as July, 1798, the students at Republican-oriented William and Mary College paraded with a representation of the President receiving a "Royal Address" and searching through a bundle of ready-made answers for a reply. At the same time those excitable Federalists at Richmond and Petersburg who were possessed of more than modest means began raising private militia

---

quo. As a striking instance arising from this reflection, it is fit to mention the Federal County of Mathews. The principle of *equality* and *equal respectability* is there understood; but in order to innovate, some industrious persons lately proposed to START (as it is termed) the JAILOR, as their next representative in the House of Delegates; but he had no sooner set out on his canvass, than he was objected to, as a man TOO MUCH attached to GOVERNMENT." *Ibid.*, March 21, 1799.

[44] Washington to McHenry, June 6, 1799, in Fitzpatrick, ed., *Washington*, XXXVII, 224.

[45] *Norfolk Herald*, March 19, 1799.

Defense and Diversion, 1799 / 221

units for the express purpose of terrifying "the sans culottes." Somewhat later in the year rival political mobs were formed at Fredericksburg. The Federalist mob chained an effigy of Gallatin to the public stocks for two days. The Republicans acted a bit later when John Marshall came through town. Marshall was insulted publicly in the town theater by the Republican rabble, which declared that he should receive the same treatment accorded to Matthew Lyon by Federalist rowdies at Trenton and New Brunswick.[46]

Conflicts revolving around emotional commitments to rival party images and ideals did not abate as the year ended. The Republican legislature purchased large quantities of arms and established a state armory at Richmond for the ostensible purpose of protecting the state from an invasion by the federal army coming to enforce the Alien and Sedition laws and to expunge the Virginia Resolutions. The pronounced Federalist sympathies of regular army officers stationed in the Richmond-Manchester area and their veiled threats against the editor, Thomas Callender, gave the Republicans' hysteria some basis in fact. As the state elections drew near, the Federalists intensified their campaign of fear and uneasiness on the popular level. Reports once again were circulated widely that war with France was imminent, despite the President's recent decision to dispatch still another mission to the Directory.[47] However reprehensible such activities by local Federalist leaders and followers may have been, they indicate clearly the beginnings of local party cadre, as yet undisciplined, untrained, and irresponsible, but capable of becoming in time an able and respectable party force. If the friends of government in Virginia had at-

[46] "Party Violence," 171–76; Daniel Anderson to Duncan Cameron, from Petersburg, Virginia, July 23, 1798, Cameron Family Papers.
[47] Ebenezer Stolt to Richard Bennehan, from Petersburg, March 24, 1799, Cameron Family Papers.

tempted to lure these local partisans into responsible party activity, the Federalists might have become firmly entrenched in the politics of the state for years to come.

The outcome of the elections in Virginia shocked the Republicans. Jefferson reported in dismay that "the Virginia congressional elections have astounded everyone . . . how long we can hold our ground I do not know."[48] While there was little danger of a Federalist majority in the Congressional delegation, more outspoken friends of government had been sent to Philadelphia by the Virginia electorate than at any time since the emergence of the Republican party. Of the state's twenty-one representatives, eight eventually were identified as Federalists. Parker of Norfolk, Evans of Williamsburg and York, Marshall of Richmond and Henrico, Henry Lee from Westmoreland, and Leven Powell representing the Spotsylvania district and the town of Alexandria, were considered friends of government from the start. By late 1800, Robert Page of Frederick County, Edwin Gray of Southampton, and Samuel Goode of Chesterfield, also were denounced by the Virginia Republicans as Federalists. Yet the Federalists suffered a decided reverse as well when James Machir, representing the counties of the state's northwestern frontier, was overthrown by George Jackson, a firm Republican.[49]

One of the most significant advances in Federalist party activity in Virginia occurred soon after the spring elections of 1799. John Stewart of Accomac County apparently provided the decisive backing for the first overt Federalist party newspaper in Virginia, and during the last week in May

[48] Jefferson to Tench Coxe, from Monticello, May 21, 1799, Jefferson Papers, Vol. 105.
[49] *Norfolk Herald*, April 27, 1799; Washington to Marshall, from Mount Vernon, May 6, 1799, Marshall Papers; George Jackson to Madison, from Harrison County, May 14, 1799, Madison Papers, Vol. 21; *Virginia Argus*, December 19, 1800.

the *Virginia Federalist*—a biweekly—made its appearance in Richmond under the editorship of W. A. Rind.[50] Ten months later Rind, in a front page statement of editorial policy, laid down the reasons for the newspaper's establishment and some of its expected achievements. "It was to be regretted," Rind wrote,

that in the Metropolis of the important and extensive State of VIRGINIA, no Federal Printer had appeared, whose Press had been conducted in a manner which editorial consistency would seem to require on the one hand; and the Friends of Order and the General Government, certainly had a right to expect on the other.

The object of the VIRGINIA FEDERALIST is to remedy this evil— Professing our admiration of the manly measures pursued by the General Government; seeing the beneficial effects which have already been experienced, and considering them as an evidence of their wisdom, that speaks plainly to the understanding of us all, and happily disproves the gloomy predictions of those who advised a contrary policy;—professing a deep-rooted hostility to foreign influence of every kind, our efforts will be unceasing to maintain harmony among the States; and point the public mind to UNION, as the best means of securing individual happiness, and the only all-efficient Guardian of National Independence.[51]

Rind was as good as his word. Soon after the paper was started, the *Federalist* had entered into the mainstream of the party's growing nationwide system of newspapers. Rind boasted in the spring of 1800 that the paper enjoyed wide circulation both within and beyond Virginia; and from the beginning he reprinted much material from Federalist newspapers in the North and from the several regional headquarters of the provisional army, as well as partisan essays by Federalist writers within the state. He also quickly

[50] "Party Violence," 176; the first extant issue of the *Virginia Federalist* is of June 1, 1799.
[51] *Virginia Federalist*, May 7, 1800.

entered into a bitter war with James Thomas Callender, the psychotically partisan editor of the pro-Republican Richmond *Examiner,* and he urged the establishment of other Federalist newspapers in Virginia, notably at Petersburg.[52]

One of the first tasks which the editor set for himself was to promote in Virginia the ideology of patriotism first developed by Federalists in North Carolina two years before. Rind often prefaced partisan essays with lurid accounts of the murder of captured American seamen by French naval and privateer captains and with a reminder to the reader that the Republican party and its press constantly attempted to explain away such atrocities. The long essay which followed recalled unwarranted French meddling in American domestic affairs and with American rights, and concluded by stressing again the allegedly consistent attempt by the Republicans to rationalize these acts. One such essay dwelt upon the XYZ humiliation and the Republicans' "treasonable" reaction to it. American envoys went to Paris "clothed in the robes of peace," one essayist wrote.

> In both hands they presented the olive. And how were they treated? With derision and contempt. . . . Surely this was a time when every nerve of patriotism must have vibrated! Coldness would have been treason and moderation a veil for cowardice. National spirit, like a lion fresh from his slumbers, must have roused to vengeance. But what said our patriots the Jacobins[?] The leaders in Congress endeavored to suppress the dispatches. Did they hope to *annihilate* insult by *smothering* it, or to heal the wounds of national honor by keeping them concealed? . . . But the fortune of America prevailed; and the dispatches were published. With joy I declare it, they electrified our Country, America seemed to send forth a general shout; the shout of indignant freemen, resolved to continue *free.* But what said our patriots the Jacobins? Look into their prints. They first affected to doubt, then strove to palliate, and at last raised a clamor against their

[52] *Ibid.,* August 3, 14, 17, 24, September 11, October 5, 1799.

Defense and Diversion, 1799 / 225

own government to drown the reproaches which were bursting out against France. This, then, is patriotism! This is sensibility to national honor and sympathy in the insults of our Country! But the Jacobins have not stopped even here. So far from feeling *indignation* they give us *joy* for having "escaped so well." This, sir, is too much to be borne with patience. . . . We should have sacrificed every prejudice of party on the *altar of our Country.* We should have pardoned those errors which necessarily adhere to every human government. One great object, *our Country* should have filled our souls; one great sentiment, *patriotism* have absolved all the rancour of party.[53]

Having labeled all opposition to the government as unpatriotic and the Republican opposition, in particular, as traitorous, Rind continued to publish a flood of essays and addresses embellishing and expanding this theme. Included in this outpouring was Governor Trumbull's address to the Connecticut legislature which "harmonizes with our own political opinion in all its parts." Trumbull prefaced some lengthy remarks about the need to sustain a sense of patriotism in the face of continuing crisis with France by urging that "our general policy should be American, not European." There was a continuing need, he said, "to guard with vigilance against the arts and intrigues of the general enemies of the union whose insidious influence will be particularly extended to individual states, seeking to produce division and disunion, thereby to weaken and enervate our general exertions."[54]

The Federalists' cult of patriotism at this point was appealing and pertinent to current political conditions. But friends of government in Virginia could not long resist the temptation to expand their ideological offensive to include expressions of unabashed hostility to the doctrines of equality and democracy and to demand that a suitable patriotic temperament also include a stout defense of traditional elitist

[53] *Ibid.,* August 17, 1799.
[54] *Ibid.,* October 26, 1799.

political values and norms. One Federalist essayist, for example, tried to prove through "historical analysis" that "whenever the revolutionary *mania* has prevailed"—as with the French and, as friends of government alleged, among the Republican opposition in America as well—"confusion and conspiracy have been the symptoms of the disease and massacre its crisis." He wrote of "the fickle climate of democracy" which the Republicans embraced while pursuing an "implacable principle of opposition, which has hitherto directed the virulence of our leading demagogues against everything that is American, either in religion or laws."[55]

The determination of friends of government to identify their ideology of Americanism with the interests of the traditional ruling gentry in Virginia and in the nation was made explicit in a long editorial in the *Federalist* late in the summer of 1799. The elite of Richmond had formed an association to drive James Callender out of town, and one of Callender's inebriated supporters had boasted openly in a tavern that if the Federalists succeeded in their aim, he would raise an army of three thousand to tear down the fashionable part of the city brick by brick. Rind immediately leaped to the defense of the wealthy inhabitants of "brick row," who, he claimed, were "generally, if not without exception friends to the Constitution and government of our country." The Federalist editor claimed the opposition of brick row not only to the party of Jefferson, but also to all political movements which might encourage the rise of democracy and the ideal of equality at the expense of the gentry. Referring to the residents of brick row, he wrote, "It must, of course, be very galling to our modern Republicans who are all friends to *equality*, that men of this description should possess the very finest parts of the city. More-

[55] *Ibid.*, August 24, 1799.

over, they are no enthusiastic admirers of all the tyranny of the French Directory, and therefore this brick row will be too happy if, one day or other, it does not experience the fate of the city of Lyons."[56]

Virginia Federalists were thus highly active in the year preceding the presidential campaign of 1800. The founding of the *Virginia Federalist* under a vigorous and outspoken editor marked a significant advance toward a modern party organization. But whether such activity was effective in obtaining or retaining popular support for the federal administration is another matter. Rind and his fellow journalists projected a powerful and possibly erroneous image of a besieged, apprehensive Federalist gentry, grimly opposing the Jeffersonian Republicans because of their identification with liberal democratic change. Writers in the *Federalist* honestly defended the politics of conservatism and portrayed all change in prevailing political practices and values as tantamount to revolution and anarchy. Thus, Federalist journalists prepared the way for a stark conflict between profoundly divergent political philosophies in Virginia during the election of 1800.

Despite the emergence of an active, though still small, Federalist interest in Virginia during the latter half of 1799, the political composition of the General Assembly when it met in December was difficult to assess in terms of party preference. The spring elections had alarmed many Republicans, who were fearful of a growing Federalist influence in several electoral districts in the state. As a consequence, they pushed through the legislature a General Election Law providing that in future presidential elections the state's electoral vote would be cast in a bloc reflecting majority sentiment. This was as flagrant a piece of party legislation as Virginia had yet seen, and it passed by a scant five votes,

[56] *Ibid.,* August 14, 1799.

78 to 73.[57] It is tempting but doubtless erroneous to assume that all seventy-three who voted against the General Election Law were firm Federalists. To determine with any precision just how many who voted "anti-Republican" on this measure were Federalists, it would be necessary to answer the unanswerable: how extensive were partisan feelings, and how deep did party discipline extend into the Virginia legislature by December, 1799? Or, to put the question another way: had the increasingly violent party battles in Virginia over the past five years wholly driven the old ideal and sense of political independence forever from the minds of gentleman legislators? Even at this comparatively late date in party conflict, an affirmative answer to the latter question would be a bold supposition.

Nonetheless, it seems safe to say that the vote indicated a great deal of dissatisfaction with the Republicans' crude conduct, a dissatisfaction which might be capable of effective exploitation by an alert, energetic Federalist minority. The opponents of the General Election Law, who might be considered either Federalist or strongly open to Federalist persuasion, came from all geographic subdivisions of the state. They represented the yeoman farmer and the emerging planter classes below the James, the commercial agriculturalists of the upper valley, and the frontiersmen in the extreme northwestern and southwestern counties. They also represented, of course, the Tidewater and Potomac River planters and urban groups which had united to send Marshall, Parker, Evans, Lee, and Powell to Congress.[58]

Apparently the Federalist party in the South experienced mixed gains and losses rather than the decline that traditionally is suggested for the final year of the eighteenth

---
[57] "Virginia General Assembly, Journal of the House of Delegates," January 17, 1800, Jenkins, ed., *Records of the States.*
[58] See Appendix, Table 3.

century. In Virginia, where they were forced to seek a mandate from an aroused and often hostile populace, the Federalists expanded their influence into the countryside, the legislature, and the press, to an extent which alarmed their opponents. They also extended their organizational network over much of the state and broadened it to embrace an ever-wider segment of the voting public. On the eve of the 1800 election Virginia Federalists at last firmly grounded their organizational structure—as they had their earlier occasional appeals for support—in the grassroots.

For the friends of government in the Carolinas, however, 1799 was a year in which partisan political activity was neglected, explaining at least in part the corresponding decline of their influence. In North Carolina Federalism had experienced a sharp decline with the division in the House over the Alien and Sedition Acts, although the twenty-one assemblymen who publicly supported those laws did represent, in drastically reduced form, the same wide geographic and socioeconomic interests which had earlier supported the President's policies concerning the Directory.[59] The vote in the South Carolina Senate in December, 1799, to reject a Republican motion for consideration of the Kentucky Resolutions is not wholly traceable. The constituencies of five of the fourteen senators who voted for rejection do not appear in the Senate Journal. Yet at least one of the nine whose constituencies are ascertainable represented the backcountry district of Spartanburg.[60] On the other hand, a Republican representative from South Carolina told a North Carolina Federalist in February, 1800, that the lower house of his state legislature had taken on a "highly Republican" cast as a result of the state elections the previous autumn.[61]

[59] See Appendix, Table 5.
[60] See Appendix, Table 7.
[61] Robert Williams to Duncan Cameron, from Philadelphia, February 10, 1800, Cameron Family Papers.

The reverses which the friends of government suffered in North and South Carolina were not irredeemable when viewed within the broad context of contemporary party development. As late as January, 1800, Republican political organizations in the southern states did not differ markedly from those developed by the friends of government. Indeed, the Republicans often seemed content to duplicate existing Federalist organizational forms rather than to develop their own broader structures. In South Carolina, for example, neither side had formal party structures throughout the election year. The Republican leader, Charles Pinckney, grappled with Henry DeSaussure, not as the head of a popular party reflecting the will of the people, but as a rival political boss. The struggle for South Carolina in 1800 was not to be fought between two rival party organizations, but between two influential individuals and their personal followings, each representing one of the two national political parties.[62] Even in Virginia, as of January, 1800, "there was no formal [Republican] party machinery," according to Noble Cunningham. In fact, the Republican hierarchy had not even achieved the degree of cohesion attained by the Federalists' Richmond and Alexandria factions some years before. Republican "party organization was to be found in the informal cooperation of Jefferson, Madison, Monroe and other Republican leaders" who, to be sure, already had "given much system to the Republican efforts."[63]

Despite some setbacks, Federalists in Virginia and the Carolinas entered the election year of 1800 with organizations and influence roughly parallel to that of their opponents. The Republicans, however, were utterly determined

[62] Noble E. Cunningham, *The Jeffersonian Republicans: The Formation of Party Organization, 1789–1801* (Chapel Hill: University of North Carolina Press, 1957), 160–61.
[63] *Ibid.*, 149.

to seize presidential power in 1800, and with dramatic abruptness they expanded their organizational structures and their popular contacts to cover their commitment. The friends of government meanwhile became increasingly divided and embittered over the questions of party leadership and suitable candidates for the presidency. It is no exaggeration to say that the vote in the South defeated the Federalists in the election of 1800. But even as they slipped from power —or from their identification with power—the friends of government below the Potomac continued to make significant contributions to the growth of the first American party system.

VII. 'The Violent Spirit of Party': The Election of 1800

The election year opened with a series of somber developments for the Federalist party. First was the reemergence of sectional conflict within Federalist ranks in December, 1799, over the election of a Speaker of the House of Representatives, which the party then controlled by a fairly comfortable margin. The open rivalry between Theodore Sedgewick and John Rutledge, Jr., was also in part an implicit indication of the emerging struggle between the high Federalists and the President for dominance within the party. Sedgewick was wholly subservient to Hamilton; Rutledge had proven skillful in evading classification. While he clearly had been unhappy over Adams' decision to seek further negotiations with France, he retained his close friendship with the President's chief supporter in New England, Harrison Gray Otis, with whom he often vacationed in Newport during the later 1790's.[1] The fact that John Marshall handled Rutledge's campaign for House Speaker is also significant. Rutledge nonetheless saw the struggle in purely sectional terms.

> The election of a Speaker [has] puzzled & perplexed the federal party of the House more than any of the difficulties it has heretofore had to struggle with. The southern & middle States Delegates thought, that as the government was very much in eastern hands, & as there had been one Speaker from New England, & two from the Middle States, it would be wise & proper to elect a southern gentleman to the chair, & they nominated me.

'The Violent Spirit of Party': The Election of 1800 / 233

He indicated, however, that after three futile caucuses he and his supporters were at last forced to give in to the adamant New Englanders, and that having made the submission in good grace, sectional harmony returned for a time to the Federalists' Congressional phalanx.[2]

A second unhappy development, whose origins also went back to 1799, was the rapid emergence of ultimately irrepressible conflict within the party hierarchy between Hamilton supporters and the President. Hamilton's followers in Congress and the cabinet had delayed for months the dispatch of the President's latest—and as it turned out, final—mission to Paris. Only after insistent pressures from his own followers, including Attorney General Charles Lee of Virginia, had Adams left his Quincy home and his ailing wife to rush to Philadelphia and see personally to the departure of the embassy and the thwarting of the hopes of the militarists in and out of his cabinet.[3] Although the President had not yet determined to move against his enemies in the Executive Department, he knew fully who they were, and their intrigues left him deeply embittered. By the early winter of 1800 he had begun to speak openly of forming a third party composed of moderates recruited from both Federalist and Republican ranks.[4] At the same time Hamiltonian Federalists spoke with an equally deep bitterness, born of frustration, of deserting the President and of throwing their support behind either King or Ellsworth in the forthcoming campaign. Upon reaching Philadelphia and hearing that news,

[1] H. G. Otis to John Rutledge, Jr., from Boston, November 12, 1799, John Rutledge, Jr., Papers, Southern Historical Collection, University of North Carolina, Chapel Hill, N.C.

[2] John Rutledge, Jr., to Bishop Smith, from Philadelphia, December 3, 1799, ibid.

[3] John Spencer Bassett, *The Federalist System, 1789–1801* (New York: Harper and Brothers, 1906), 249–50.

[4] Stephen G. Kurtz, *The Presidency of John Adams: The Collapse of Federalism, 1795-1800* (New York: A. S. Barnes & Company, Inc., 1961), 393.

Marshall informed his brother sadly "that the situation of our affairs with respect to domestic quiet is much more critical than I had conjectured." Significantly, Marshall placed the source of opposition to Adams with "the eastern people," not the southerners.[5]

Prior to the President's abrupt dismissal of Pickering and McHenry in mid-May, however, both wings of the party worked in uneasy tandem. In January, Adams' chief agents in the House, John Marshall of Virginia and Harrison Gray Otis of Massachusetts, publicly defended the provisional army. And Marshall, who was lauded for his abilities, later voted against Republican attempts to reduce the size and power of the army. At the same time Josiah Parker of Norfolk initiated a correspondence campaign on Adams' behalf to reach southern political leaders of both parties. Parker's correspondence campaign deeply alarmed at least one prominent Congressional Republican.[6] Hamilton gave his blessing to efforts to preserve a united front in and out of Congress, indelicately but aptly summing up his sentiments on the matter only a week before the Secretaries of State and War were fired. Support of the President then and in the forthcoming campaign "is the only thing that can possibly save us from the fangs of *Jefferson*," he said.[7] The Inspector General's concern was justified, because another series of unpleasant events in the winter and early spring confirmed Federalism's declining prestige.

[5] Marshall to James Marshall, December 16, 1799, Marshall Papers.

[6] Elizur Goodrich to David Davenport, from Philadelphia, December 7, 1799, January 3, 1800, History Note Card File, Independence Hall National Park Office, Philadelphia; William H. Hill to Duncan Cameron, from Philadelphia, February 11, 1800, Cameron Family Papers; Nathaniel Macon to Andrew Jackson, from Philadelphia, February 13, 1800, in J. S. Bassett, ed., "Some Unpublished Letters of Nathaniel Macon," *Historical Society of Trinity College Publications*, VI (1906), 58.

[7] Hamilton to Theodore Sedgewick, May 4, 1800, in John C. Hamilton, ed., *The Works of Alexander Hamilton* (7 vols.; New York: John F. Trow, Printer, 1851), VI, 436.

In the South the party's already-thin network of influential leadership was weakened by the deaths of George Washington and Edward Rutledge within a month of each other at the turn of the year. In purely political terms neither loss could be measured. Washington's death was not only a deep blow to Federalist influence in Virginia and the South; it also meant the removal of the last symbol of unity from the party. Intraparty conflicts revolving about the formation of the army had indicated that a word from Mount Vernon still often carried decisive weight in party councils.[8] Now that no final decisions were to be forthcoming from Washington, the way was open for the free exercise of intrigue and the indulgence of personal and sectional animosities within the party hierarchy.

The death of Edward Rutledge marked the beginning of the decline of Federalist influence in South Carolina. The Charleston lawyer—governor of the state at the time of his death—might have eliminated by the sheer force of his influence the grave organizational weaknesses which inhibited the South Carolina Federalists. His death created a temporary vacuum in the state's party leadership, since both Pinckneys, young Rutledge, and Harper all were involved in national service. The Charleston financier Henry William DeSaussure stepped into the breach; but while he filled Rutledge's post with energy and ability, he could not match his predecessor in prominence and authority.

Adding to the Federalists' problems at this time was the sudden erosion of their former power in New York and in many key areas of the South. Rutledge's election to the governorship in South Carolina had been won despite firm

---

[8] Adams at one point in 1798 wrote to Washington in evident unease: "If the Constitution and your convenience would admit of my changing places with you, or of my taking my old Station as your Lieutenant Civil, I should have no doubts of the ultimate prosperity and Glory of the Country." June 25, 1798, Adams Papers, Reel 117.

Republican control of the lower house of the state's legislature.[9] Representative Robert Williams in his letter to Duncan Cameron had remarked that reports circulating in Philadelphia claimed Republican dominance of the legislatures of Georgia and the frontier states of Kentucky and Tennessee after the autumn elections of 1799. This was to be expected, but in Virginia the following spring many of the old corps of Federalist supporters were turned out of the General Assembly, despite some spirited campaigning by members of the Richmond Federalist faction, including James McClurg. Monroe reported that at least twenty-five Federalists had been replaced by staunch Republicans in the April elections for state office.[10] Only in North Carolina did the Federalists apparently retain some influence during the early months of the election year.[11]

The loss of the New York City elections and the successive Federalist defeats in the South filled party leaders with foreboding. Hamilton told Sedgewick that the city elections were a key to party strength throughout the state, and the marked partiality of the urbanites for Republicanism seemed to make it "too probable that the electors of President for

[9] Robert Williams to Duncan Cameron, from Philadelphia, February 10, 1800, Cameron Family Papers; *Aurora* (Philadelphia), January 30, 1800.

[10] Monroe to Jefferson, from Richmond, April 26, 1800, Stanislaus Murray Hamilton, ed., *Writings of James Monroe* (7 vols.; New York: G. P. Putnam's Sons, 1898–1903), III, 175–76; Abraham Baldwin to Joel Barlow, from Philadelphia, May 14, 1800, History Note Card File, Independence Hall National Park Office, Philadelphia (original in Baldwin Collection, Yale University Library).

[11] A correspondent writing to the *Gazette of the United States* in late January claimed that the North Carolina legislature "is truly Federal," as evinced by the gubernatorial election within that body and also by the appointments to fill the officer corps of the militia. On the latter point the correspondent remarked with evident relish that "all those" whom "the Jacobins . . . have offered for militia officers have failed." Obviously, North Carolina Federalists continued to pin their hopes of retaining power upon continued control of the military, including both state and national units. January 23, 1800.

this State will be anti-federal."[12] It was against this unhappy background that Hamilton issued his call for party harmony.

Even as Hamilton admonished his followers, a decided decline in Federalist strength in Congress was apparent, paralleling the deterioration of Federalist prestige in New York and the South. When Congress had convened in November, 1799, there had been forty-one new members in the lower house, all elected during the height of the XYZ fever the previous year. According to Jefferson, the Federalists confidently counted upon a House majority of twenty.[13] However, one of the new representatives, Robert Williams of North Carolina, assured a reader that in fact he and his colleagues originally were "in search of a middle way" and revealed "an indifference to party." Yet neither party by this late date was content to accept the old ideal of gentlemanly independence. Man is a social animal, Williams added philosophically, and as a result the new members were "at length forced into one or the other of those fashionable Climes, this tends to prove how short [is] the knowledge of even the best informed, not immediately within this political Circus, as to the extent of party at this place."[14]

The friends of government found themselves ill-prepared to campaign to retain the loyalties of this crucially important swing group in the House. First, they lacked a dominating floor leader. Marshall apparently came the closest to filling this role, but at least one of the new representatives felt that

[12] Hamilton to Sedgewick, May 4, 1800, in Hamilton, ed., *Works of Hamilton*, VI, 436.
[13] Jefferson to Madison, from Philadelphia, May 12, 1800, Madison Papers, Vol. 21.
[14] Williams to Duncan Cameron, from Philadelphia, February 10, 1800, Cameron Family Papers; Abraham Baldwin to Joel Barlow, from Philadelphia, March 6, 1800, History Note Card File, Independence Hall National Park Office, Philadelphia (original in Baldwin Collection, Yale University Library).

Gallatin overshadowed him.[15] Secondly, the Federalists in the House were as deeply divided over party policy as were those in the executive branch. "In our councils, there is no fixed plan," Hamilton wrote. "Some are for preserving and invigorating the navy and destroying the army. Some among the friends of government for diminishing both on pecuniary considerations."[16]

By the middle of May, Jefferson reported triumphantly that the Federalists clearly had lost the balance of power in the House. The "new & moderate men" quickly had seen through to "the true character of the party to which they had been well disposed while at a distance" and had abandoned it. The initial majority of about twenty counted by the friends of government had been erased, and "the federalists have not been able to carry a single strong measure in the lower house the whole session."[17] In the closing days of the session the Republicans took the offensive in Congress for the first time since the summer of 1796 and managed to abolish the hated provisional army.[18]

In early May the Federalist party at last collapsed from within, as Adams turned out the high Federalist obstructionists in his cabinet. Whether this action alone would have been sufficient to destroy politically the President and the image of the party which nominally he still led is open to question. The high Federalists have never been described as a popular group, but persistent sectional jealousy and mistrust among many southern Federalists subsequently gave Hamilton and his followers an influence over many friends of government which they normally would not have had. In 1798 the

[15] William H. Hill to Duncan Cameron, from Philadelphia, February 11, 1800, Cameron Family Papers.
[16] Hamilton to Rufus King, from New York, January 5, 1800, in Hamilton, ed., *Works of Hamilton*, VI, 417.
[17] Jefferson to Madison, May 12, 1800, Madison Papers, Vol. 21.
[18] *Annals of Congress*, VI, 403.

southern Federalists had been the President's bulwark against the emerging militaristic wing of the party. Two years later many of them, influenced by sectional suspicion in an election year, finally fell under Hamilton's sway, persuading themselves of the need to subvert New England and Adams to Hamilton and his southern ally, Charles Cotesworth Pinckney. This blending of sectional with personal rivalry within the Federalist party ensured its destruction as the ascendant political force in the nation.

Sectional harmony within the Federalist party was in constant jeopardy from December, 1799, onward. The specter of sectional conflict, apparently interred since 1797, had been raised once again in the struggle between Sedgewick and Rutledge for the post of Speaker of the House. It was inevitable with Adams in the presidency and Hamilton again politically active that the revived sectional jealousies would become crucial in the conflict between the two. In 1796, Adams electors in New England had thrown away some votes pledged to Thomas Pinckney to assure the ascendancy of their candidate. As the campaign of 1800 would indicate, southerners had never forgiven Adams for his apparent countenance of such a move. Hamilton and his men, on the other hand, had staunchly supported Pinckney; and by 1799 another and even more prominent member of that family was backing Hamilton. If Adams was to retain the significant support he had built up in the South in 1798 and had held substantially the following year, it was necessary for him to avoid an open break with Hamilton. For the President was powerless to prevent a recurrence of suspicion of his motives and a revived sense of betrayal among the southern electorate. The fact that he would accept, or even urge the necessity of, a southern running mate was no guarantee of his eventual faithfulness to southern interests. Only if the problem of sectional suspicion was subverted thoroughly by party harmony and clearcut agreement could the President hope to avoid disastrous loss of support in the South.

Adams preserved the image of party unity as long as possible. As late as April, 1800, southern Federalists confidently predicted his reelection, and while the choice of his southern running mate reflected the below-the-surface struggle between his followers and those of Hamilton, there was as yet no indication that Adams would not be supported for the presidency in the South.[19] The persistent intrigues of the high Federalists at last forced the President's hand, however, and with his dismissal of Pickering and McHenry in May, the party was shattered, not only on the national level, but at least in one crucially important southern state as well.

Reaction to the dismissals among most southern Federalists was reserved. William H. Hill's comments were typical. "You will have observed that great changes have been made in the administration by removal and resignation of several of the officers in the high departments," he wrote to a North Carolina correspondent. "The causes are not fully and clearly developed—a variety of conjectures are in circulation but from too uncertain a medium of information to trouble you with."[20] Hill's remarks seem to indicate either a lack of close contact between the Executive Department and a majority of southern Federalists in Congress or, more

[19] John Marshall to Reuben George, from Philadelphia, March 16, 1800, History Note Card File, Independence Hall National Park Office, Philadelphia (original in Virginia State Library, Richmond); Joseph Dickson to William Lenoir, March 28, April 20, 1800, Lenoir Papers, Southern Historical Collection, University of North Carolina, Chapel Hill, N.C. Both Marshall and Cotesworth Pinckney were widely talked of within Federalist ranks as vice presidential candidates as early as December, 1799. Jonathan Dawson to Madison, from Philadelphia, December 12, 1799, Madison Papers, Vol. 21. From Hamilton's statements in early May concerning Adams and Pinckney, it would appear that the Federalist caucus in Congress had agreed to this ticket by then.

[20] Hill to John Haywood, from Chester, May 15, 1800, Haywood Collection.

'The Violent Spirit of Party': The Election of 1800 / 241

likely, a deliberate determination by southerners to remain aloof from the schisms in the cabinet.

The Federalist press in the South could not afford to be detached. Obviously something had to be said about the open disruption of party harmony at the highest levels. From the beginning, however, southern Federalist editors simply followed the official party line on the dismissals as laid down at Philadelphia by John Fenno and his *Gazette of the United States*. Fenno initially admitted the existence of a sharp break between Pickering and the President "on political grounds." Sometime later a Federalist newspaper in Boston carried an embarrassingly candid account of the reasons behind Pickering's departure which also reached the progovernment press in the South. But by early June, Fenno had recovered his wits sufficiently to try to present the affair in the best possible light, and his highly imaginative, though totally false, portrait of restored party harmony duly appeared in the southern Federalist papers.

According to Fenno, "Mr. Pickering on hearing that general Marshall had accepted his late berth, expressed the highest satisfaction, and publicly declared, he did not think that the Department had ever been so well filled." Fenno followed this remarkable account of Pickering's unaccustomed outburst of modesty and magnanimity with another revelation which must have surprised—if it did not wryly amuse—the angry and estranged principals when they read it. "It is also much to the credit of both Mr. Adams and Mr. Pickering," Fenno wrote, "that they still speak in the handsomest terms of each other; by which those secret enemies who endeavored to widen the breach have completely missed their aim."[21]

One southern Federalist, however, who unequivocally had aligned himself with Hamilton, did not attempt to hide his

[21] Quoted in the *Virginia Federalist*, May 21, 31, June 7, 1800.

bitterness over the President's decision to banish the hawks within the cabinet. James Gunn enlightened the absent John Rutledge, Jr., on the affair and included in his summary the latest gossip concerning changes in the upcoming presidential race. As a result of the dismissals, Gunn claimed, "Mr. *Adams* and his Dear friend Mr. *Jefferson* have been *twice closeted* together, Since Saturday last, and it is generally understood to be agreed on between them that Genl Pinckney is not to be the President—A declares Mr. J the only man in America qualified to fill the appointment, Except himself—"[22]

Gunn was not the only serpent to whisper of certain sectional betrayal in young Rutledge's ear. Representative James A. Bayard of Delaware, another Hamilton supporter,[23] also hinted at it. "The point of understanding subsisting between him [Adams] and Mr. Jefferson it is scarcely possible to ascertain," Bayard told the young South Carolinian in June. Bayard added, however, "it is confidently stated, that if Mr. J. should be elected President and Mr. A. Vice President, that Mr. A. will serve under Mr. J. in his ancient capacity. But this condescension is not expected in case Mr. P. should be the successful candidate."[24] Rutledge was enjoying a brief and enforced vacation at home in South Carolina when he received both of these letters.[25] Their very contents

---

[22] James Gunn to John Rutledge, Jr., May 12, 1800, John Rutledge, Jr., Papers, Southern Historical Collection, University of North Carolina, Chapel Hill, N.C.

[23] Bayard to Hamilton, August 18, 1800, in Elizabeth Donnan, ed., "Papers of James A. Bayard, 1796–1815," *Annual Report of the American Historical Association*, 1913 (2 vols.; Washington, D.C.: Government Printing Office, 1914), I, 113.

[24] Bayard to Rutledge, June 8, 1800, from Wilmington, *ibid.*, 111.

[25] Rutledge nearly became one of the first victims of his own party's Sedition Law. He had acted as Bayard's second in a political duel with Congressman William Champlin of Connecticut in which Champlin was injured. Governor McKean of Pennsylvania and District Judge Coates, both staunch Republicans, threatened to arrest and try both Federalist congressmen on a charge of treason against a member of the United States Congress.

indicate that they must have enjoyed wide circulation among the young congressman's Federalist colleagues in the lowcountry. A deep suspicion of the President's motives and future moves was implanted in the minds of South Carolina Federalists by the poisonous insinuations of the Hamiltonians. The practical effect ultimately proved disastrous to party fortunes both in the state and in the nation.

As the Federalist party was being torn to pieces by its friends on the national level, party machinery and effective techniques of mass appeal continued to be perfected in all of the southern states except Georgia. The Federalist party in 1800 was in fact a paradoxical political movement. On the national level party leaders divided bitterly and struggled implacably for power in the face of a formidable political opposition; many friends of government on the local levels, where the hard tasks of vote-getting and office-seeking had to be performed, continued their quiet reception to progressive political change. It is this dichotomy between Federalist party activities on the national and local levels that has eluded historians of the period. Beginning with the revival of Federalist strength in 1797, a cadre of state and local party figures gradually had been recruited. These people were not concerned primarily with the making of high party policy nor embroiled in the personal rivalries between party leaders, but concentrated upon the advancement of the party on a state or local level. This was a new and distinct breed of political animal, composed of what might be called two species. The managers included such loyal workers on the county level as Duncan Cameron of North Carolina and Bushrod Washington of Virginia and

---

Both Bayard and Rutledge fled to their homes, though Rutledge had returned to Newport by July. John Rutledge, Jr., to Bishop Smith, from Poplar Grove Plantation, May 24, 1800, from Newport, July 25, 1800, John Rutledge, Jr., Papers, Southern Historical Collection, University of North Carolina, Chapel Hill, N. C.; *Virginia Federalist,* May 21, 1800.

such state political bosses as Henry William DeSaussure and Leven Powell. The expositors, the political editors, included such influential figures as Abraham Hodge in North Carolina and W. A. Rind in Richmond. As has been known and emphasized, the Republicans had an abundance of such men in 1800. The history of southern politics in the later 1790's shows that the Federalists had them too, and in many ways they reached a peak of activity and competence during the election year of 1800.

Federalist party activity in the South in 1800 took three forms, which actually varied little in content but often greatly in effectiveness from the Republican opposition. First, Federalists in the South continued to perfect and to extend their formal party organization—or their informal channels of communication where formal organization was lacking or deemed unnecessary, as in South Carolina. Second, the friends of government concentrated upon the development of a vigorous and articulate partisan press. Each of the three southern states where Federalist activity was evident in 1800 contained at least one newspaper committed to propagandizing the Federalist cause. The day of the political editor had arrived for both sides. Finally, the Federalists in many areas of the South carried their campaigns to the people with an intensity and an effectiveness never before shown. Unfortunately, they became increasingly burdened, and their efforts were increasingly compromised by the growing schisms within the national party leadership. Eventually, this burden became too great for many of them to bear and they fell into confusion and apathy allowing their more vigorous and united Republican opponents ultimately to win the southern states and national power. The chief blame for the failure of the southern Federalists rests to a great extent with the national hierarchy which served them so poorly. The essence of the Federalist collapse in 1800 was the overwhelming of the party's many progressive impulses by a reactionary national leadership.

Southern Federalists began to assemble for the coming state, Congressional, and presidential campaigns as early as January, 1800. In Virginia, the apparently well-organized friends of government were jolted into action by their Republican opponents, who met at Richmond early in the year to form a ticket and to establish committees of correspondence in each county. Soon after, the Federalist members of the legislature held a caucus and reorganized and expanded their party structure in the state to duplicate that of the Republicans. A general committee was formed at Richmond, and county committees were duly created, charged with meeting at certain intervals to formulate strategy.[26] The ease and rapidity with which the Federalists were able to match their opponents' elaborate organization demonstrates that the friends of government enjoyed wide and sympathetic contacts throughout Virginia before 1800. The subsequent rapid formation of a statewide electoral ticket reinforces this impression. "The American Republican Ticket," as it was called, unabashedly pleaded for the support of those who possessed "a sacred regard for the constitution and all those blessings of which it is the source."[27] A full slate of

---

[26] Noble E. Cunningham, *The Jeffersonian Republicans: The Formation of Party Organization, 1789–1801* (Chapel Hill: University of North Carolina Press, 1957), 152–53, quoting the *Virginia Argus*, March 28, 1800; *Virginia Federalist*, May 28, 1800. The Federalists apparently did not inform the people of the state of the establishment of a statewide network of party county committees in late March, but rather let the opposition press speak for them.

[27] A handbill copy of this ticket and its accompanying address to the people may be found in the Charles William Dabney Papers, Southern Historical Collection, University of North Carolina, Chapel Hill, N.C. The ticket and the address also were reprinted in each issue of the *Virginia Federalist* between May 28 and August 2. When he first printed the ticket, Rind urged "our federal typographical brethren throughout the state to give it a conspicuous place in their invaluable Gazettes; and to remember that they cannot republish it too *expeditiously*—nor continue it too *long*."

electors was prepared, most of them obscure political figures. The Federalists thus placed themselves in a position in terms of organization to battle their opponents across the state.

Formulation of statewide political machinery in North Carolina was a far more difficult task for the Federalists since, unlike in Virginia or South Carolina, friends of government in North Carolina had never established any central organization. And the unwillingness of the more prominent Federalist leaders to give their attention to party organization and the retention of popular support during the final year of the century proved a decisive factor in reshaping the Federalists' political practices in North Carolina in 1800. The neglect of practical political problems by the traditional leaders induced local party workers themselves to organize and campaign on a limited scale. Such grassroots activity in the absence of central direction proved to be a boon to Federalist fortunes in North Carolina. For whether planned or not, party activities were soon conducted along a more democratic course than southern Federalists had been willing to follow so far. In being forced to concentrate initially upon party activity on the county and local levels, the friends of government in North Carolina thus were brought into the mainstream of political change in America.

As early as January various "Federalist persons" in the state began to make plans for the coming campaign.[28] The Hillsboro merchant, planter, and lawyer, Duncan Cameron, for example, saw to it that various partisan publications, notably *Porcupine's Gazette*, and doubtless the *Virginia Federalist* as well, were given the widest possible dissemination through his section of the state. His sources of supply for these publications were the British merchants of Petersburg, which strongly indicates that Federalists in this Vir-

[28] Duncan Cameron to Charles Harris, from Hillsboro, January 21, 1800; John Maddell to Cameron, from Newfield, January 8, 1800, Cameron Family Papers.

ginia commercial center, at the head of the trade routes from central and western North Carolina, were involved deeply in the maintenance of Federalist influence on local levels in those regions.[29] Charles Harris, a Halifax lawyer, also became active in party matters. He and Cameron began to sound out the several "victorious & patriotic Gentlemen" in the various counties "who are exerting their best talents and using their most zealous endeavours to save our sinking Country by developing the views of the factious democrats."[30] Cameron already knew of "four persons in each of the Counties of Chatham, Wake & Orange whom I think you can rely on for firmness and zeal." He was unable to conceal from Harris his deep pessimism concerning the future of Federalism in North Carolina despite the state's apparent current partiality for the party. He was determined to campaign actively for Federalism to an end that he felt was sure to be bitter. "Nothing now remains for us," he wrote, "but to make a last exertion." Should that fail, "we shall find a rich consolation in having done the duties of citizens striving to promote the real interests of the Country."

These early efforts of Cameron, Harris, John Maddell, and others to construct a firm Federalist machine stretching across the state received encouragement from North Carolinians then at Philadelphia. In March, Congressman William Hill warned Cameron that "Mr. Adams reelection depends on the powerful exertion of the friends of government—and unless this is assiduous and well directed we have reason to fear the worst . . . from the unremitting & extensive application of the Jacobins . . . pervading every part of the Union."[31]

[29] R. Anderson to Cameron, January 14, 1799; Daniel Anderson to Cameron, August 11, 1800, James Anderson to Cameron, October 24, 1800, *ibid*.
[30] Cameron to Harris, from Hillsboro, January 21, 1800, *ibid*.
[31] Hill to Cameron, March 22, 1800, *ibid*.

By June a Federalist in Halifax reported that the "general attention as to public affairs is set upon the election of president and vice-president." By this time, too, both parties had almost completed the formation of statewide electoral tickets and had made rather firm assessments about the state of public opinion. Federalist hopes frankly were high.[32]

In South Carolina formal party organization, such as it was, existed already among the Federalists. DeSaussure, Harper, Thomas Pinckney, and young Rutledge all enjoyed a wide range of contacts throughout the state which could be activated for the cause. These gentlemen composed an informal, but nonetheless potent and reasonably cohesive, central committee. The presidential campaign in South Carolina was fought strictly between two sets of elitist-oriented political factions; the Federalists were led by Henry William DeSaussure and Thomas Pinckney, while Charles Pinckney and Pierce Butler directed the Republicans.[33]

Next to party organization, an energetic and outspoken partisan press proved to be an integral part of the Federalist compaigns. At Richmond the *Virginia Federalist* continued its active service throughout the early part of the year. In January, W. A. Rind expanded the size of the paper to allow "that our Fellow-Citizens should be accurately informed of the true situation of affairs of the United States." The following May the paper's front page for the first time was thrown open to the strident defenders of administration policies, a practice that broke with a hallowed tradition of Anglo-American journalism which dictated that local business and advertisements should take precedence over hard news and

[32] Dr. Charles W. Harris to Robert Harris, June 20, 1800, in Henry M. Wagstaff, ed., "The Harris Letters," *James Sprunt Historical Publications*, Vol. XIV, No. 1 (Durham, North Carolina: The Seeman Printery, 1916), 73–74; *Virginia Federalist*, May 31, 1800.

[33] Monroe to Madison, November 7, 1800, Hamilton, ed., *Writings of Monroe*, III, 219.

competitive politicking.³⁴ In an age when the press exerted an especially powerful influence over daily lives, this steady intensification of partisan political journalism obviously stimulated further the growing interest in public affairs among the electorate. It also placed a heavy burden of competence upon partisan writers.

In 1800, Federalists everywhere were faced with the problem of recasting party ideology after Adams' dispatch of the three-man mission to Paris the previous November. As members of the high Federalist faction were agonizingly aware, the President's action robbed the party's simplistic patriotic ideology of most, if not all, of its force. Too many friends of government allowed themselves the fatal luxury of blind hatred against the President as the result of his decision for peace, but many others went to work to shift the party's ideological appeal to what they considered a more durable base. This was especially true in Virginia, where Federalist journalists rather quickly reconstructed party philosophy around a stout and uncompromising defense of traditionally legitimate political and religious norms.

Virginia Federalists and their allies in North Carolina proudly labeled themselves "the friends of religion and of the present government."³⁵ Defenders of order and of established social institutions and practices, they stood opposed unalterably to "Gigantic discord, the foe of liberty, in the garb of Republicanism."³⁶ Federalist writers who urged the people to cleave to the teachings of the Bible, which specifically included piety and faithfulness, were given prominent space in Rind's paper. The right of a well-known Episcopalian priest to enter the political lists in Virginia in behalf of Federalism was upheld vigorously by friends of govern-

[34] *Virginia Federalist*, January 18, May 28, 1800.
[35] *Ibid.*, June 11, 1800, quoting the *North Carolina Minerva* (n.d.).
[36] *Ibid.*, May 7, 1800, quoting the *London Observer* (n.d.).

ment who saw themselves as the sole champions of established political and religious institutions.[37] Histories of the Washington and Adams administrations, structured and written in the Biblical style and presenting leading figures in government as Old Testament heroes, were conspicuously displayed in Rind's paper.[38]

Closely tied to the idolatry of contemporary government officials in the Federalist press of Virginia was the steady development of the cult of Washington. The general's death was exploited suitably for partisan ends, and a series of essays immediately appeared which recalled his many services for the country and his connection with the Federalist party.[39] In February, 1800, his birthday was celebrated ostentatiously by detachments of the provisional army; and various eulogies, which also included pleas for the continuation of orderly government, were spoken throughout the state.[40] The most striking attempt by the friends of government to capitalize upon Washington's towering reputation among the people was the publication of "WASHINGTONIANA: A Collection of Papers Relative to the DEATH AND CHARACTER OF GENERAL GEORGE WASHINGTON," that appeared in April and was ad-

[37] *Ibid.*, March 19, 1800, quoting the *Baltimore Federal Gazette* (n.d.), April 20, 1800.

[38] One such history, concerned with the decision to form a provisional army and to recall Washington to lead it, ran as follows:

"16. And they appealed unto ADAMS with one heart & with one voice, & said, 'well done thou good and faithful servant, thou hast merited well of thy country.'

"17. And the Rulers of the people said, we will now call forth the men of Valour, who fought for the liberty of Columbia, of old time, and the young warriors also.

"18. And they said unto Adams, appoint from amongst the mighty men of valour such as have approved themselves faithful and firm in the day of battle.

"19. And Adams wrote a letter unto Washington, and sent it by the hands of the Chief man of war. . . ."

Ibid., June 11, 1800.

[39] *Ibid.*, December 11, 1799–January 18, 1800.

[40] *Ibid.*, March 5, 19, 29, 1800.

vertised prominently in the *Virginia Federalist.* This collection seems to have included many previously unpublished private papers, including the general's last will and testament.[41] The tasteless American practice of displaying the private lives of recently deceased popular heroes before an overcurious public was thus begun by those who thought of themselves as the better, more sophisticated class in society.

Possibly the Federalists might have derived some tangible political benefit from their identification with Washington, if not from their outspoken conservative defense of entrenched religious and political institutions and practices. However, the Federalist spokesmen also were forced to defend the existing policies of the national administration; and worse still, they deliberately chose to couple their identification with entrenched interests to a virulent, unrelenting attack upon democracy and the principles of social and political equality.

Virginia Republicans had effectively attacked the Alien and Sedition Acts on several counts. They had revived the charge of Adams' tendencies toward monarchy, they claimed that Fries' Rebellion resulted solely from unwise military and taxation policies by the national administration, and they passed a general election law which threatened to limit the political influence which Federalists held in several portions of the state. The Federalist response to this onslaught was shrill, but largely unimaginative. According to one writer, "Fries and his adherents . . . merely attempted to execute what was planned in Philadelphia" by a subversive Republican cabal headed by the Vice President. Insofar as the Alien and Sedition Acts were concerned, the right of any government to punish abuses of freedom was energetically maintained: "The *freedom of citizens* consists in *their*

[41] *Ibid.,* April 19, 1800.

subjection to the Constitution and laws." As for the charge that Adams wanted to introduce monarchy into America through these acts, "the unreasonable discontents and opposition of the Jacobins have made more converts to monarchy in ten years than all the ambitions of our rulers." However, for the convenience and edification of the people, a Federalist partisan somewhat later synopsized Adams' *Defense of the American Constitutions* to prove that the President entertained no monarchist sentiments.[42]

Occasionally, an essay of superior quality appeared in Rind's newspaper. In late May, Alexander Addison presented a cogent argument against the Virginia Resolutions, asserting that the state legislature unwarrantably had arrogated to itself judicial power over the acts of the federal government. He warned of inevitable chaos if such usurpation was permitted to go unchallenged. Several weeks later "A Citizen of Halifax," in a forceful essay, pointed out that the people had had no direct influence over the legislature's passage of the Resolutions. Hence, he argued, the Resolutions represented a tyrannical attempt by the Republican majority in the Virginia legislature to obtain a stranglehold over both the politics of the state and the administration of the national government without consulting the people in any way or at any time.[43]

Very few of the essayists whose work appeared in the *Federalist* proved as adept as Addison and the "Citizen" in blending intelligent criticism with partisan attack—a fact appreciated by the editor, who, in recommending the "Citizen's" essay to his readers, commented, "five such men as the *Citizen of Halifax* would save our modern Sodom from sinking."

The image of a "sinking Sodom" as applied to current

---

[42] *Ibid.*, May 14, 1800, quoting the *Philadelphia Gazette* (n.d.), June 28, 1800.
[43] *Ibid.*, May 28, June 18, 1800.

politics reflected the openly expressed despair of Federalists throughout the nation about the tide of democracy which seemed to be rising about them. "The histories of all the Republics of the world are before us," wrote one typically disillusioned friend of order. "While they admonish—they teach us that in all of them LIBERTY has been destroyed and DESPOTISM established by discontented hot-heads, flattered and spurred on by artful and ambitious demagogues. A *deluded* and *fanatic* MOB have made an IDOL of their LEADER and he, in turn has made himself their TYRANT—Such are the Causes which have produced the JULIUS CEASARS, [sic] the CROMWELLS, and the BUONAPARTES of the REPUBLICS." "Have your employers," he concluded, addressing the Jeffersonian Republicans, "yet determined who shall subvert the LIBERTIES OF AMERICA?" In usual elitist fashion, Federalist writers expressed enraged astonishment that their opponents would seek through *"lies* and *slander"* to convince the electorate "that WASHINGTON and ADAMS and CONGRESS, have been either knaves or fools, and that wisdom and virtue had taken up their abode with the *minorities* in Congress."[44]

In essays and letters Federalist writers asserted that "infidelity and political innovation go hand in hand" and that "man remains unaltered, and will never yield to the *reforming* mould of sanguine imaginations."[45] They continued to reflect the philosophy of a numerically small, entrenched elite, deeply mistrustful of the political capabilities of the common man. At the same time, though, the Federalists tried to win a continued mandate to rule from the public. Whether such a mandate could be obtained depended greatly upon the degree to which a democratic temperament had taken hold among Americans living south of the Potomac.

In South Carolina the friends of government established

[44] "Letter from Litchfield, Connecticut to three Richmond Republicans," *ibid.*, May 28, 1800.
[45] *Ibid.*, June 11, 1800, quoting the *Baltimore Federal Gazette* (n.d.).

their own *Federal Carolina Gazette* at Charleston, which was issued from the office of the already established *South Carolina Gazette and Timothy's Daily Advertiser*. The paper, under the direction of Benjamin F. Timothy with aid from Thomas Shepard and later Andrew McFarlan, printed a steady stream of pro-Adams essays and editorials during its year or so of existence.[46] Federalists in these two critically important states also received notable support from other papers. Valentine Davis' *Virginia Gazette* was, in effect, the Federalists' informal party sheet in the Old Dominion and remained a zealous supporter for the government cause throughout the year.[47] Davis republished important speeches of Virginia congressmen at Philadelphia, whipped up anti-Republican and anti-French sentiment in general—especially after Gabriel's uprising in October, which was attributed to French democratic influence—and in the last days of the presidential campaign opened up his pages to Federalist essays.[48] In South Carolina by 1800 the Charleston *City Gazette* had slipped from moderate Federalism to neutrality, but throughout the year its pages were open to essayists and letterwriters of both persuasions.

In North Carolina the Federalist press was as vigorous as in Virginia in defending religion and the current administration. The arrival of Joseph Gales as Republican printer broke the Federalists' monopoly over North Caro-

[46] Clarence S. Brigham, *History and Bibliography of American Newspapers, 1690–1820* (2d ed.; 2 vols.; London: Archon Books, 1962), II, 1032; *Federal Carolina Gazette*, November 13, December 25, 1800.

[47] Davis in fact held a federal postmastership under Adams. Dice Robins Anderson, *William Branch Giles: A Study in the Politics of Virginia and the Nation from 1790 to 1830* (Menasha, Wisconsin: George Banta Publishing Company, 1914), 91.

[48] *Virginia Gazette and General Advertiser*, May 2, July 18, December 26, 1800. The *Virginia Gazette* for the autumn months of 1800 is no longer available, but the *Norfolk Herald* usually reprinted party essays and letters from the former. *Norfolk Herald*, October–November, 1800. See also John to Duncan Cameron, from Lunenberg, September 22, 1800, Cameron Family Papers.

lina's press, and an implacable newspaper war broke out early in the year and was carried on until the results of the presidential election were known in late November. The battle had grown intense as early as July, causing one weary reader to complain to Gales. "Having an opportunity of seeing a number of newspapers," wrote the correspondent, who signed himself "HERMIT," "I cannot but regret the violent spirit of Party which pervades many of them and which has so manifest a tendency to destroy domestic happiness and shake the foundation of public tranquility."[49] Later in the year allies of Gales and the Federalist editor William Boylan, respectively, entered into a public brawl which certainly did upset the public tranquility of the state and further focused popular attention upon the currently raging party battles.

The tone of the partisan essays which appeared in Abraham Hodge's *North Carolina Minerva* did not differ from those found in the *Virginia Federalist*. Defenders of the administration openly deplored the existence of "extreme party spirit" which divided the country and forced friends and opponents of the national administration alike to organize and proselytize. They asked rhetorically what caused such extreme party spirit and answered: "it is the consequence of extreme liberty, and a higher degree of liberty cannot exist without endangering the whole. The reason why it cannot exist is that the nature of man will not admit of it; his pride and ambition require very powerful restraints; therefore, all those who teach the doctrine of modern liberty and equality are false teachers; they are deceivers, or are deceived themselves." In spite of such openly expressed contempt for human nature, in general, and the political capacity of the common man, in particu-

[49] *Raleigh Register and North Carolina Weekly Advertiser,* July 22, 1800, hereinafter cited as *Raleigh Register.*

lar, the friends of government in North Carolina could no more refrain from publishing essays which were intended "to rouse the Federal party from this sleep, and when roused, to stimulate them to counteract the baneful plots of Jacobins" than could their colleagues in Virginia. Other Federalist essayists urged the citizens of North Carolina to cultivate an attachment to the national government "as necessary to our general happiness and as the best security against oppression," while portraying John Adams as the leading figure in the American impulse toward liberty in 1776 and Jefferson as "only a *secondhanded* varnished Deist."[50] However, the intensity of these latter essays could not obscure the fact that the friends of government presented the people with an ambiguous platform at best with respect to popular political and civil rights.

Federalists and Republicans in the South were both well organized for the partisan battles of 1800, but the crucible of sustained campaigning eventually exposed the weaknesses and disorders within Federalist ranks. For all of their flexibility and activity, friends of government in the South eventually allowed themselves to be outmaneuvered by their opponents in those areas and states where local victory for one side or the other held the key to the ultimate national victory. Southern Federalists were well aware in 1800 of the importance of the outcome of local campaigns, but their exclusivist ideals prevented them from matching fully the competence of their opponents in the game of democratic politics.

Southern Federalists ran their strongest and most successful campaign of 1800 in North Carolina. Throughout the summer, political excitement in the state was high. In early July, Charles W. Harris told his brother that the toasts drunk at various Fourth of July celebrations were viewed by the

[50] *North Carolina Minerva*, August 13, 1800.

'The Violent Spirit of Party': The Election of 1800 / 257

friends of government as "a kind of key to the political sentiments of the most reputable class of citizens." He added that "Federalism and its opponent become daily more distinctly divided by districts, counties, towns or neighborhoods," a sure indication of the profound effect which the activities of both parties were having on the common people. Rumors also swept the state, including one that Jefferson had died unexpectedly.[51]

Local Federalist cadre repeatedly indicated that they viewed the coming election in apocalyptic terms. John Osborn of New Bern complained of being assaulted

> by ranting Democrats who vapour for Jefferson & Liberty. I cannot but hope that before the election arrives some change may take place in the minds of our misguided fellow citizens, if not, we may sing a requiem over our liberty and Independence, & expect distractions and confusion, which may result in the disunion of the States if not worse—God of heaven avert such an event.[52]

Spurred on by such visions of the imminent dissolution of the social and political fabric, North Carolina Federalists in practice abandoned whatever restraints the elitist tradition might have imposed and tenaciously battled their opponents for public favor. In August Osborn once again wrote his friend, this time asking him to obtain a copy of Jefferson's "Notes on Virginia," as "they may be useful for some purpose. Our politics are as when you were here."[53] The next month Osborn used Simpson as an agent in the dissemination of party propaganda.

> I send you some copies of Sheppard's Circular Letter [Sheppard was the Federalist candidate for elector for New Bern] & will

---

[51] Charles W. Harris to Robert Harris, from Shockoe Springs, July 11, 1800, in Wagstaff, ed., "Harris Letters," 76–77.
[52] Osborn to Samuel Simpson, June 18, 1800, Simpson-Bryan Papers.
[53] Osborn to Simpson, August 7, 1800, *ibid.*

thank you to distribute them in the manner you shall think best calculated to secure the general cause—the advertisements you can dispose of in the manner you approve.—The period is now arrived, when it is important that the friends of the independence of our Country should exert themselves for its preservation. You will direct the Letters & send them to those persons in your Vicinity who you may suppose may make a beneficial use of them.[54]

Osborn's persistent fears for the future of American liberty if the Republicans should win revealed the extent to which Federalist leaders viewed the campaign of 1800 from the perspective of 1798. Any indications of the old ideal of political independence were viewed in the harshest terms. The determination of Judge John Haywood, Federalist candidate for elector from Halifax, to defend a leading Republican accused of land fraud angered Dr. Harris. "He is wavering and undetermined," the doctor grumbled, "and his conduct of late has not only ruined his own popularity but injured the cause which we expected he would promote."[55]

The circumstance which produced a special sense of excitement and measure of venom in the party battles in North Carolina was the rivalry between the Federalist editor, Abraham Hodge, and the recently arrived Republican printer, Joseph Gales. Prior to 1800, Hodge had enjoyed the undisturbed benefit of the public printing, despite the frequently Republican orientation of the North Carolina legislature. When Gales arrived in the state as the first outspoken Republican editor, however, Nathaniel Macon and Thomas Blount soon attempted to separate Hodge from his lucrative post. Thus, Hodge and his paper became the rallying point for Federalist activity in North Carolina during the late summer of 1800. Active lines of communica-

[54] Osborn to Simpson, September 20, 1800, *ibid*.
[55] Charles W. to Robert Harris, from Warrenton, July 29, 1800, in Wagstaff, ed., "Harris Letters," 78.

tion, information, and propaganda eventually flowed to Hodge who placed the *Minerva* and its press completely at the disposal of the party. In addition to publishing the paper, Hodge printed and distributed a number of tracts, essays, and addresses, some of which he wrote himself, and copies of Federalist newspapers from out of state, most notably *Porcupine's Gazette*.[56]

Despite the Federalists' strenuous efforts, however, the General Assembly elections in August went badly for them. Their fears that Gales would win the post of public printer, combined with humiliation at their setback, led one of them —William Boylan, Hodge's nephew and coeditor of the *Minerva*—to provoke a notorious brawl with Blake Baker. Baker was Attorney General of the state and the Republican candidate for United States Senator in the upcoming General Assembly. His beating at the hands of Boylan on a dusty Raleigh street salved the wounded feelings of some friends of government and apparently also ended his political career.[57]

It was in this setting of violence and excitement that the results of the state's Congressional elections became known. The Federalists suffered a decided loss of power. Two years before they had claimed seven members of the state's ten-man delegation as supporters of Adams. In 1800 it is doubtful if the friends of government could have counted on support from more than four members of the state's delegation—Grove, Henderson, Hill, and John Stanly. Two of those reelected, Hill and Henderson, represented the yeoman farmers of western North Carolina.

[56] The entire course of the Hodge-Gales rivalry and its impact on Federalist pol:tics in the summer and autumn of 1800 may be found in the letters of Charles W. to Robert Harris, August 3, 29, September 18, 1800, *ibid.*, 79-84.

[57] For further Federalist reaction to the Boylan-Baker match, see R. Bennehan to sister, from Chapel Hill, September 5, 1800, Cameron Family Papers.

After a brief pause in campaigning in September, Federalists and Republicans toward the end of the month resumed their battle for the state's electoral vote.[58] Some weeks later, with the election but a few days off, Boylan told Cameron that he expected "hot work here on the day of elections." Already Republican spokesmen were "spouting to every collection of Men" they could find "in street, store or grog shop."[59] Boylan's distaste for the crudest forms of politicking was shared by his colleagues. On election day they worked not to cajole and persuade, but rather to control, the populace. In Fayetteville, for example, "the Scotch" were sent "flocking in from all quarters—Several hundred came parading in town following the *bag pipes* and nothing but piping was heard in several parts of the town all the morning—this scene was truly mortifying to the Jacobins." Such intimidatory tactics were successful, but they were probably unnecessary in such a traditionally safe district as the upper Cape Fear. But in Wake County the "great exertions, indeed" made by six or seven friends of government proved unavailing as the party was defeated, though by a surprisingly narrow margin.[60]

The Federalists nonetheless were rewarded for the tenacity and flexibility which they had shown during the campaign. Voting for electors was in the hands of the people in the twelve districts of the state. In 1796 the Federalists had captured one of these districts; four years later they won four of them. Complete returns from five of the twelve districts and partial returns for a sixth were published in Gales' *Register*, and the *Virginia Argus* somewhat later published the party affiliations of the successful candidates. The Federalists carried two of the six districts in which

[58] P. Broune to Duncan Cameron, from Halifax, September 24, 1800, *ibid.*; *Raleigh Register*, September 30, October 21, 28, 1800.
[59] Boylan to Cameron, October 31, 1800, Cameron Family Papers.
[60] Boylan to Cameron, from Raleigh, November 5, 1800, *ibid.*

partial or complete returns are available, and their overall strength in these six districts amounted to 43 percent of the popular vote. Of the four out of twelve districts in which Federalism predominated, two were in the eastern coastal area, Wilmington and Edgecombe, one was in the upper Cape Fear, Fayetteville, and one surrounded the western commercial center of Salisbury. Available statistics also indicate that the Federalists had not lost completely their hold over the yeomen of the far west. In Morgan district Archibald Henderson won a decided majority in Lincoln County. In addition, the Federalists barely lost in New Bern district, as the Federalist candidate Sheppard actually won four of six counties, but was so badly beaten in one that he lost the district by less than two hundred votes.[61]

Federalist activity in Virginia seems to have been at first nearly as intense as in North Carolina, and the friends of government had the added advantage of an established central organization.

The elections for state offices were held in the spring, and the friends of government made the recently passed General Ticket Law the focus of their attack. The law would handicap the people in November, forcing them to vote for at least nineteen or twenty strangers, rather than choosing from among several candidates in their local electoral district, all of whom they were likely to know well. The formation of party tickets by Federalists and Republicans was designed to provide the confused voter with some partisan focus. It also would hasten the polarization of political attitudes and loyalties around the two well-defined national party organizations in the state. The Federalists, however, were convinced that the General Ticket Law had generated much ill-will which they determined to exploit.

[61] *Raleigh Register,* November 11, 18, 1800; *Virginia Argus,* November 25, 1800.

During the spring elections and throughout the year the Federalists hammered at the iniquity of the general ticket plan and attempted to turn popular opinion against it. The law was presented to the voting public as part of a plot to "attempt to influence your votes" which "upon the truest interests of republicanism" the friends of government wished to see "remain free and unbiased." The fact that the Republican majority in the Assembly had "compelled you to vote for twenty one Electors, dispersed through every district of the state, all of whom, except the resident in your own district must be generally unknown to you" also was emphasized, and again as part of a broad plot by the Republicans to "direct your choice" in matters political. On this latter point Congressman Thomas Evans, near the end of the presidential campaign, noted that one of the effects of the plan was to stimulate broad, sophisticated party organizations. Evans added that the law was

> an experiment perfectly in the Jacobinical style, rendering laws, when passed, perfectly inefficacious, if not aided by a central committee, who create and direct the affiliated committees in a manner concealed from public view throughout the Country. Govt., if such measures may so be called, thus becomes the property of a few, daring characters, whilst ancient forms, for a while, remain, tho's they cannot possibly be more than forms.[62]

The tone of Evans' remarks suggests strongly that while the Federalists themselves had established a hierarchical party structure, including a central committee and local committees of correspondence, in their hearts they knew such organizations to be wrong in terms of traditional political practices.

[62] "AN ADDRESS to the Voters for Electors of President and Vice President of the United States, in the State of Virginia," broadside in Dabney Papers; *Virginia Federalist*, March 5, 19, July 9, 1800; Thomas Evans to Leven Powell, from Accomac, October 30, 1800, in William E. Dodd, ed., "Correspondence of Leven Powell," *The John P. Branch Historical Papers of Randolph-Macon College* (Richmond: Everett Wadding Co., 1901), 54–55.

The Federalists thus projected a strong and clear image of themselves in the spring elections. They stood solidly for the traditional rights of the individual gentleman freeholder, the strongest of which were his independent character and his vote. They deplored the machinations of well-organized political parties which sought to control or manipulate for purely partisan ends the "hitherto unlimited freedom of election" enjoyed by the individual citizen. They spoke out strongly against "innovation" and turned sharply away from "the eager desire for change" in political customs.

At the same time, however, the friends of government—as they implied in their address to the people—were forced into broad organization, ticket formulation, and wide appeals for support to make their influence and ideology known. The Republicans, in passing the General Ticket Law, had forced the Virginia Federalists into a corner, and the friends of government either could bend with the prevailing political wind and fight the campaign battles the way their opponents had dictated, or they could simply retire in frustrated impotence.

Madison reported determined Federalist politicking on the eve of the state elections. "Considerable exertion is used to raise prejudices agst the measures of the last Session of Assembly," he wrote, "especially the . . . mode of appointing Electors." Federalist leaders seemed aware of the need to tighten discipline within the party during the campaign. Leven Powell, for example, complained of the stubborn determination of two Federalists who were still personal enemies to run against each other for an Assembly seat. The retiring Alexandria congressman also urged his followers to choose an acceptable Federalist candidate to take over his seat at Philadelphia before "some antifederal candidate will get the start."[63]

[63] Madison to Jefferson, April 20, 1800, Madison Papers, Vol. 21; Leven Powell to anonymous, April 6, 1800, Personal Miscellany File, LC.

The Republicans had maintained from the beginning that the General Ticket Law was generally popular,[64] and the results of the spring elections bore them out. The Federalist decline, once begun, could not be stopped. When John Marshall vacated his Congressional seat to become the Secretary of State after Pickering's dismissal, the Republicans filled it in a special election in August, despite a strong campaign by the Federalist candidate, Colonel John Mayo. "With Candour" Mayo informed the people of his determination to support the political *status quo,* including the current administration. His heavy defeat, therefore, was a clear indication that the great majority of the electorate in his district welcomed the profound change in the character and conduct of state and national politics. Mayo's setback caused the leader of the Richmond Federalist faction to lament that there was "a tide in the affairs of nations, of parties & of individuals. I fear that of real Americanism is on the ebb."[65] At about the same time Henry Lee's close friend in Congress, James A. Bayard, wrote to Hamilton that "Virginia is sold and past all salvation." Evidently, most friends of government outside the state shared this view from the beginning of the year. Three separate predictions on the outcome of the presidential race appeared in the *Virginia Federalist;* all gave the state to Jefferson without comment.[66]

In Virginia the palpable decline of Federalist influence with the electorate during the spring and summer quite naturally led to deterioration of morale and activity within the party. In late June, W. A. Rind placed on the front page of the *Federalist* an address from Russell's *Commercial Gazette* in which "the supineness of the great body of the

[64] J. Barbour to Jefferson, from Richmond, January 20, 1800, Jefferson Papers, Vol. 106.
[65] *Virginia Federalist,* July 9, 1800; Marshall to Harrison Gray Otis, from Washington, August 8, 1800, Marshall Papers.
[66] Bayard to Hamilton, August 18, 1800, in Donnan, ed., "James A. Bayard," 113; *Virginia Federalist,* May 28, June 7, July 9, 1800.

friends of government in the United States" was noted and mourned, and alarm was expressed over "the unceasing machinations of the jacobins." In the same issue Rind attempted to arouse his colleagues into action in the forthcoming city election to maintain the Federalists' control of Richmond. The editor had tickets struck off "which we beg our Federal Friends to send or call for."[67]

Within a month, however, Rind had become completely discouraged. The apathy of the friends of government during Colonel Mayo's campaign was more than the editor could understand or tolerate. On August 2 he published the final issue of the *Virginia Federalist* and prepared to move to the new city of Washington where his partisan talents could be employed on behalf of the friends of government in Maryland, who were waging a spirited campaign to win that key state for Adams. "The Antis were successful in the last election," Rind sadly observed in farewell.

Report says Mr. Tazewell was elected by a large majority. We had vainly endeavored to excite the activity of the Federalists in this important election, by appeals both to their interest and their honor—the intense heat, or something constitutional [an allusion to the Federalists' depression over the apparent popularity of the General Ticket Law] counteracted the well-meant effort by keeping them at home.

As the presidential elections approached and Federalist strength in Virginia continued to decline, the "Government Men" who remained active were faced with the added burden of supporting a highly unpopular candidate. John Adams had been portrayed throughout Virginia as a monarchist since 1789 when his campaign to introduce titles fell flat in Congress. In their formal address to the people, which accompanied the American Republican ticket, the Virginia

[67] *Virginia Federalist*, June 28, 1800.

Federalists tried to solve the Adams problem by evading it. Thus, they lauded the "unvarying course of prosperity" enjoyed by the country and chided their readers for possibly forgetting that they had but recently been preserved "from two impending wars" and "a close alliance" with either France or England. But Adams' name never appeared in the lines. "Our Government" had been the agent of national preservation and protection, not the President. The singularity of Adams' exclusion from conspicuous mention in the address was emphasized by the prominence given to Washington's deeds. "To the adoption of our Constitution, to the sage maxims of administration established by the immortal WASHINGTON, and steadily pursued by his virtuous successor, may fairly be ascribed our present prosperous situation."[68]

Despite an unpopular candidate, plus the abrupt appearance of a slave uprising and a yellow fever epidemic,[69] both of which sharply curtailed political campaigning in the eastern sections of the state on the eve of the election, some friends of government remained active to the end. A Philadelphia correspondent reported in mid-September that "party spirit and animosity rage in North Carolina and Virginia to a degree that must excite the regret of every real friend of our country." Several political duels were reportedly fought in Virginia, and brother literally turned against brother.[70] The extent to which Federalist candidates and their friends actually campaigned is unclear, though the President himself made several partisan speeches at Alexandria soon after the federal government moved to Washington.[71] Party presses were also active, and the party ticket and address were printed up as handbills and spread throughout the state.

[68] "ADDRESS . . . to the People of Virginia," Dabney Papers.
[69] *Norfolk Herald,* October 24, 1800; Monroe to Jefferson, September 9, 22, 1800, to Thomas Newton, October 5, 1800, in Hamilton, ed., *Writings of Monroe,* III, 205, 209–10, 213.
[70] Reprinted in *Augusta Chronicle,* October 4, 1800.
[71] Kurtz, *Presidency of John Adams,* 398.

Remaining Federalist editors also were busy, even occasionally following the Republicans' lead late in the campaign by publishing sample party ballots for the electorate, as well as republishing the ticket in all issues of their papers immediately preceding the election.[72]

The Federalists' efforts in Virginia produced no tangible results, however, as the party suffered a shattering loss in November. According to the most complete returns, Jefferson carried eighty of the eighty-nine counties and boroughs in the state which reported results. Jefferson likewise outpolled Adams in the popular vote, 21,311 to 6,024, giving him 77.9 percent of the total vote to 22.1 percent for Adams. In some counties, notably Amelia and Nottoway, Adams did not receive a single vote. In others, such as Caroline, Dinwiddie, and Prince Edward, the President's supporters numbered only a handful, no more than four or five in each county out of a total of approximately three hundred fifty votes cast.[73]

Important as were the events in Virginia, and especially in North Carolina, in 1800, South Carolina more than any other state—including New York—held the key to the presidential election that year. Both the friends and opponents of the current administration realized this.[74] Virginia's complete defection to Republicanism had been expected; North Carolina's partial conversion to Federalism was rewarding, but in the end was not decisive. But South Carolina had generally been Federalist. Only the temporary estrangement of the dominant Rutledge-Pinckney faction in 1795–1796 had given Jefferson eight important electoral votes that year, and

[72] *Norfolk Herald*, October 9, 11ff., 1800.
[73] *Virginia Argus*, December 2, 1800.
[74] William R. Davie to John Steele, from Catawba, North Carolina, September 20, 1800, in Kemp P. Battle, ed., "Letters of William R. Davie," *James Sprunt Historical Monograph*, No. 7 (Chapel Hill: North Carolina Historical Society Publications, 1907), 42; Charles Pinckney to Thomas Jefferson, November 22, 1800, in Hamilton, ed., *Writings of Monroe*, III, 245n.

the Federalist candidate, Thomas Pinckney, had received equal support. In 1800, with Jefferson generally discredited in those Federalist circles where he had been embraced four years before, it was hoped by some partisans that South Carolina would assure the retention of the presidency by the Federalists.[75]

In contrast to the Virginia campaign, the Federalist campaign in South Carolina was carried on with effectiveness, despite the death of Edward Rutledge. Party leaders worked diligently—though often not directly—to conduct a campaign of greater depth and scope than ever before. They sought to obtain as much support as possible in every county, parish, and river fork in the state. This necessitated an extensive knowledge of South Carolina's political geography, which DeSaussure and Thomas Pinckney both possessed. Even Robert Goodloe Harper in distant Maryland was able to exert strong influence over events in the backcountry through consistent contact during the campaign with political leaders there.

The letters of these three gentleman-politicians were filled with information about which individuals dominated in which narrow areas, who might be counted on for support in both sections of the state, and the areas in which the populace decidedly favored one or the other of the parties. Federalist correspondence also indicates that each party leader in South Carolina had constructed his own private network of correspondence, which was used during the campaign for partisan political purposes. Usually these lines of communication were used either to implore prominent friends of government to stand for the state legislature, if only for the year, to insure the nomination of electors favorable to Federalism, or to urge party lieutenants out in the

[75] *Virginia Federalist*, June 7, 1800.

counties and parishes to establish closer contact and greater influence with the electorate.[76]

In addition to the work of influential leaders, Federalist essayists and letterwriters in and out of the state's press matched their opponents in output and scurrility.[77] DeSaussure himself wrote and publicly acknowledged his authorship of an "Address to the Citizens of South Carolina. . . ." In this partisan effort the Charleston financier branded the Republicans as old Antifederalists, claimed that Virginia, the headquarters of that faction, sought to dominate the southern states, and in general condemned Jefferson as an abolitionist and a tool of French democratic interests, while carefully defending both Adams and Pinckney as men who had spent years in devoted public service to the nation. The pamphlet was circulated widely in John Rutledge, Jr.'s district of Orangeburg, where it attracted much public interest, inspiring intense protest from the Republicans and triumphant rebuttals from the Federalists.[78]

Perhaps the greatest break with the past which the Charleston oligarchs made in 1800 was their decision to engage in the dirtier side of popular politicking. The gentleman-politicians lost their aloofness and even, it would seem, their reserve, as they cajoled and pandered to the common

[76] Henry William DeSaussure to Rutledge, from Charleston, August 14, 1800; Robert Goodloe Harper to Rutledge, from Baltimore, September 20, 1800; Thomas Pinckney to Rutledge, from Moultrieville, September 23, 1800, John Rutledge, Jr., Papers, Southern Historical Collection, University of North Carolina, Chapel Hill, N.C.

[77] An avowed Republican of St. Bartholomew's parish bitterly complained some days before the election of being "beset with and run down by Federalists, Federal-Republicans and their pamphlets." Charleston *City Gazette*, October 3, 1800.

[78] Henry William DeSaussure, "Address to the Citizens of South Carolina on the Approaching Election of PRESIDENT AND VICE-PRESIDENT of the UNITED STATES, by a Federal-Republican," Charleston, W. P. Young, 1800, in Henry E. Huntington Library, San Marino, Calif.; Charleston *City Gazette*, October 17, 1800.

people and shepherded voters to the polling places. Charles Pinckney, reporting on the city elections in October, expressed a horror, which may or may not have been genuine, at the underhanded tricks of his opponents.

> As much as I have been accustomed to Politics and to Study mankind, this Election in Charleston has opened to me a new view of things. Never certainly was such an election in America. We mean to contest it for 8 or 9 of the 15. It is said several Hundred more Voted than paid Taxes. *The Lame, Crippled, diseased and blind were either led, lifted or brought in Carriages to the Poll.*

The friends of government took a further step to insure their continued domination of the city. Pinckney added:

> ... the sacred right of Ballot was struck at, for at a late hour, when too late to counteract it, in order to know how men, who were supposed to be under the influence of Banks and federal officers and English Merchants, Voted, and that they might be Watched to know Whether they Voted as they were directed, the Novel and Unwarrantable measure was used of Voting with tickets printed *on Green and blue and yellow paper* and Men stationed to watch the Votes.[79]

A comparison of the efforts and achievements of the Virginia Republican party machine and the South Carolina Federalist oligarchy during the presidential campaign of 1800 reveals a striking fact. Party organization developed by the elites where energetically directed, skillfully employed, and not threatened by legislation which placed the full weight of political power and party activity on the state rather than the local level, was not yet anachronistic in an age of emerging democratic party politics. Exclusivist be-

[79] Pinckney to Jefferson, October 16, 1800, "South Carolina in the Presidential Election of 1800," *American Historical Review*, IV (October, 1898), 115.

'The Violent Spirit of Party': The Election of 1800 / 271

liefs did not yet preclude the exercise of power and influence. Quite the contrary: the gentleman-politician with his numerically small private faction, if dispersed over a wide geographic area for maximum effect, still remained a powerful political force.

There were, however, other less benign aspects of elitist politics which gravely hindered the Federalists' chances in South Carolina in 1800. One was simple carelessness where interpretations of party loyalty and responsibility were concerned. Robert Goodloe Harper's decision in the summer of 1799 to remove himself to Maryland,[80] for example, threatened South Carolina Federalism with an immediate collapse of influence in the crucial backcountry regions. Harper finished his term as congressman from Ninety-Six district before retiring for many years from active public life; and during the election of 1800, as has been noted, he attempted by correspondence to reconfirm his constituents in the Federalist faith. The main focus of his efforts on behalf of the party, however, was limited to Maryland and adjoining states.[81] Not once did he visit his constituents, and, as a result William Butler, a firm Republican, captured Harper's district in the autumn elections.

Similar in effect to Harper's conspicuous absence from South Carolina during the critical months of the campaign was the refusal of young John Rutledge to foresake newfound friends and pleasures at Newport to return home to help the party. Rutledge, in fact, had good reasons to remain in the North so long as he could be assured of the firm Federalism of his native state. DeSaussure and Pinckney, however, made him aware early enough that despite their exertions Federalism was in a precarious position in South

[80] James McHenry to Harper, from Philadelphia, August 1, 1799, Harper Papers, LC.
[81] George Cabot to Hamilton, from Brookline, August 21, 1800, in Hamilton, ed., *Works of Hamilton*, VI, 459.

Carolina. Rutledge undoubtedly could have given greater support to his party—and better advanced his own developing intrigues—from Charleston than from Rhode Island, but he contented himself with drafting a long, arrogant defense of the Adams administration and of himself, which he sent to his constituents in July. Thereafter he seems to have done nothing to advance party prospects in his native state, and for this he suffered some gentle criticism from Harper.[82]

A stubbornly independent attitude and a disdain for the increasing demands for party discipline and loyalty also marked the conduct of members of Senator Jacob Read's faction before and during the campaign. Read's supporters continued to exhibit a bitter hostility toward the members of the old Rutledge-Pinckney faction, and when David Ramsay was chosen to deliver the public eulogy of Washington early in 1800, William Read reacted with surprise and chagrin.[83] During the campaign itself there is no evidence that either Jacob or William Read rendered material aid, publicly or privately, to the Federalist cause.

Age and an overall appearance of timidity at critical moments also hampered Federalist efforts in South Carolina in 1800, despite the party's brief involvement in overt political skullduggery at the time of the Charleston elections. By this time it had become abundantly clear that, the absent Messrs. Harper and Rutledge notwithstanding, the friends of government in the state no longer were young men. The elitist vice of exclusivism had restrained the Federalists from actively recruiting able and energetic young politicians. In 1800 the party projected an image of elderly patricians instinctively resisting the changes being brought into South

[82] John Rutledge, Jr., to Bishop Smith, from Newport, July 25, 1800, Harper to Rutledge, September 20, 1800, John Rutledge, Jr., Papers, Southern Historical Collection, University of North Carolina, Chapel Hill, N.C.
[83] William to Jacob Read, from Charleston, January 7, 1800, Read Papers, Duke University Library, Durham, N.C.

'The Violent Spirit of Party': The Election of 1800 / 273

Carolina's public life by a younger generation oriented toward the Republican party. DeSaussure illuminated the Federalist dilemma in an unintentionally revealing remark. He assured Rutledge that "all the elderly men, of high Character, whose health will allow them . . . will come out efficiently at the election [for the state legislature] & many of them will be candidates. Mr. Russell, Mr. Jones, Mr. Corbett & others of that stamp will offer to go."[84]

In this same letter DeSaussure alluded to the comparative timidity—or was it simple courtliness?—of the older Federalist gentlemen. After pledging to "converse freely and write fully" on behalf of the party, he added primly, "but you know they use some weapons which we cannot condescend to do." At the same time Thomas Pinckney complained of the increasing loss of taste and decorum in political debate and of the corresponding increase in overt party rancor.[85] When the time arrived for the battle in the legislature, Charles Pinckney's comparative youth and enthusiasm proved to be potent political weapons.

But the prime factor which destroyed the Federalist party in South Carolina in 1800, and thus destroyed the party's national power, was the intrusion of the Hamilton-Adams conflict into the politics of the state. The irrevocable division of the party hierarchy into two bitterly opposing camps and Hamilton's announced determination to support Pinckney for the presidency[86] put the friends of government in South Carolina in a cruel dilemma. If they resisted the temptation to support Pinckney ahead of Adams, they were in no way assured of reciprocal loyalty for Pinckney from the harassed followers of the President. The problem would

[84] DeSaussure to Rutledge, August 14, 1800, John Rutledge, Jr., Papers, Southern Historical Collection, University of North Carolina, Chapel Hill, N.C.
[85] Thomas Pinckney to Rutledge, September 23, 1800, *ibid.*
[86] Hamilton to Sedgewick, from New York, May 10, 1800, to Wolcott, from New York, July 1, 1800, Hamilton Papers, Vols. 75, 77.

have caused sufficient anguish in any case, but with memory of the betrayal of 1796 still fresh in the minds of many and constantly being refreshed during that spring and summer by the friends of Hamilton, the temptation to work for a juggled ticket became irresistible.

Cotesworth Pinckney himself was of no help. In a private letter to McHenry on June 10, the general, then at a provisional army encampment at Shepherdstown, Virginia, expressed anger at the "very unworthy and indecorous treatment Mr. Pickering & you have received" at Adams' hands. Pinckney made the pious statement that "if the Federalists will act with decision, energy & union I have no doubt but they will gain a complete victory at the ensuing Election over the Jacobinical party." Soon, however, Pinckney coyly reverted to a line of argument which rendered such prospects impossible to fulfill. His caution was admirable, his sense of intrigue refined. He wrote:

With regard to the conduct of the Southern States at the ensuing Election, I think they are bound fairly and candidly to act up to their agreement entered into by the federal party at Philadelphia, with out the Eastern States should be convinced of Mr. A's abandonment of federal principles, his attempt to form a party with Jefferson, and his unfitness to be President, and on these accounts or some of them, should consent to substitute another Candidate in his stead. This event I do not think impossible, & his [Adams'] conduct & the critical situation of our Country may require it. But to preserve the Union, this must originate to the Eastward, the Middle States can then take it up, & the Southern ones with propriety follow.[87]

Pinckney's determination to move toward the presidency slowly and subtly decided the issue for most South Carolina Federalists. By midsummer Harper and Rutledge had joined Hamilton and became part of a quartet of ardent southern

[87] Quoted in Steiner, *Life and Correspondence of McHenry*, 460.

and New England Hamiltonians who talked openly of reversing the previously-agreed-upon Federalist ticket.[88] In South Carolina itself party leaders and cadre also fell into line behind Pinckney. DeSaussure, when telling Rutledge of the vigorous attempts being made to insure the success of Federalism in South Carolina, spoke only of Pinckney. Later Harper remarked ominously that "Mr. Adams is expected, by all my letters as being very doubtful. I am glad however that all my friends there exert themselves fairly in his support."[89]

The friends of government, then, were forced to conduct their campaign and to solicit public favor contrary to the expressed will of the party caucus and thus emphasized to supporters and the uncommitted alike the deep schism which afflicted the Federalist interest. In September, Thomas Pinckney committed a blunder which further accentuated tensions within the party. William Duane of the *Aurora* somewhat earlier had been indicted under the Sedition Law for publishing a letter supposedly written by John Adams in 1792 in which the then Vice President had written privately that Thomas Pinckney had secured his recent appointment to the Court of St. James through family intrigue and flagrant British influence. Duane, however, had not been able to produce the original of the letter, and after some "legal Pantomime," as he called it, the trial had been postponed. Pinckney, however, could not resist the temptation to reply, and on September 15 he dispatched a curious letter to the Charleston *City Gazette*, claiming that the letter which Duane had reproduced was either a Republican "forgery calculated for electioneering purposes, or *if genuine*, must have been founded on a misapprehension of persons." Pinck-

[88] Harper to Hamilton, June 5, 1800, *ibid.*, 457; Elizabeth Cometti, "John Rutledge, Jr., Federalist," *Journal of Southern History*, XIII (April, 1947), 195–96.
[89] DeSaussure to Rutledge, August 14, 1800, Harper to Rutledge, September 20, 1800, John Rutledge, Jr., Papers, Southern Historical Collection, University of North Carolina, Chapel Hill, N.C.

ney's resurrection of the incident was bad enough, but his refusal to reject completely the Republican inferences of profound conflict between Adams and him was worse. In his letter Pinckney begged the people to delay judgment "until the event of an investigation, which I shall immediately commence." The following day he wrote to Adams directly, enclosing a copy of the Baltimore paper in which the original Adams letter had appeared and the issue of the *City Gazette* containing his public reply. The tone of this letter was frigid and left a strong impression that Pinckney did believe the 1792 letter to be genuine, and more importantly, that the letter still was capable of creating antagonism in his mind. Pinckney closed with a peremptory demand that Adams explain himself satisfactorily. He next apparently traveled to Washington to confront the President personally. According to the October 3 issue of the *Aurora,* Pinckney recently had gone to Duane, examined a letter which Duane now claimed to be the original, and then, with John Rutledge, Jr., in tow, had "waited on Mr. Adams expressly in consequence of this letter." Duane "was informed that Mr. *Adams* did not deny the authenticity of the letter," but stated that his allusion was to Charles, not Thomas or Cotesworth Pinckney.

The entire account of the affair, especially Pinckney's trip north, is suspect on two counts—first, because it came from the pen of a zealous Republican editor, and secondly, because Pinckney had been in poor health for several years. But the fact remains that all the materials, including the public letter in the *City Gazette* and the somewhat sour private note to Adams, are found in Box 10 of the Pinckney Family Papers in the Library of Congress. Even if the account of the trip north and the confrontation was a fabrication, Pinckney's letter to his fellow citizens, which appeared in the *City Gazette,* was sufficiently damaging to Federalist fortunes, since Pinckney obviously was ready to take Republican

'The Violent Spirit of Party': The Election of 1800

campaign charges against Adams at face value. If the entire story is true, as it possibly is, then Pinckney's meeting with Adams emphasized dramatically the continuing dislike and distrust of John Adams among South Carolina Federalists.

With party leaders themselves bitter and mistrustful toward the President, it must have seemed to many of South Carolina's political leaders that loyalty to Federalism was risky. New England Federalists might yet sacrifice southern interests for the sake of preserving their own, while the disciplined and united Republicans, also led by a prominent southerner, seemed to demonstrate political constancy. The Federalists had retained the right to rule in the state from 1789 onward by preaching stability and order in government, but by 1800 their leading representatives could no longer claim to exemplify these values. Rather, they were victimized by internal intrigue, jealousy, and ambition. In 1800 only the Republican party in South Carolina honestly could appeal to those who sought the preservation of well-regulated government, as well as to others who yearned for an extension of political democracy and the promise of the Declaration of Independence.

Such considerations, however, did not initially influence South Carolina's politics in 1800. The relative efficiency and skill of the Federalist leaders, the popularity of Cotesworth Pinckney, and the previous traditions of political allegiance all helped to sustain the apparent Federalist ascendancy in the state during the elections. The local oligarchs had worked ably on behalf of the ticket, and the results of the Charleston legislative election[90] dismayed the

[90] Charles Pinckney reported that only four of the fifteen-man city delegation to the lower house of the state legislature were Republicans. However, an examination of the partisan tickets put forth by both sides indicates that apparently no less than fourteen were either moderate or high Federalists. Charles Pinckney to Jefferson, from Charleston, October 16, 1800, in "South Carolina in the Presidential Election of 1800," 114; Charleston *City Gazette*, October 13, 18, 1800.

Republicans and gave the Federalists perhaps a fatal dose of confidence.[91] Though it is not clearly documented whether the friends of government went to Columbia with a working majority or not, it is certain that prior to Charleston's decision Federalist and Republican leaders alike had confidently predicted or conceded South Carolina's loss to the Jeffersonians.[92] Now the issue again was in doubt.

It was at this point, however, that the endemic weaknesses of sectional jealousy and suspicion within the South Carolina Federalist faction first began to hinder fatally its political effectiveness. The letters of Charles Pinckney and Peter Freneau describing the critical legislative session are filled with news of Republican caucuses and passionate pledges by the membership to cleave to party orthodoxy. Pinckney was never still. Agonizingly aware of South Carolina's central importance in the election of a Republican President, he had come to Columbia after the Charleston election to rally his initially dispirited forces and to assault the apparent Federalist majority. He eventually was successful in doing both. The Federalists, however, were not indolent, and young Pinckney spoke of "how hard and strongly contested" the election at Columbia was. Cotesworth Pinckney himself was present to lend force and prestige to the Federalist interest, led by William Washington.[93] What destroyed Federalist cohesion and effectiveness at Columbia in Decem-

[91] Charles Pinckney wrote to Thomas Jefferson of "the federal Interest connected with the British" and aided by "the Banks and the federal Treasury," which created a "Weight of Talent, Wealth and Personal and family influence" of formidable proportions. Indeed, Pinckney remarked in retrospect that the 1800 South Carolina legislature was at least initially "the most federal I ever knew." October 16, December, 1800, January 24, 1801, in "South Carolina in the Presidential Election of 1800," 115, 122, 128.

[92] Madison to Jefferson, September, November 10, 1800, Madison Papers, Vol. 21; William Boylan to Duncan Cameron, from Raleigh, October 31, 1800, Cameron Family Papers.

[93] Pinckney to Jefferson, October 12–December 6, 1800; Peter Freneau to Jefferson, December 2, 1800, in "South Carolina in the Presidential Election of 1800," 114–23.

ber, 1800, was the reemergence of the Hamilton-Adams split.

According to reports circulated in Columbia, certain anonymous Republicans, apparently believing it impossible to carry their electoral slate through the legislature, approached their opponents and offered to abandon party strife and settle on a compromise Jefferson-Pinckney ticket. Charles Pinckney, for the Republicans, and Christopher Gadsden, for the Federalists, both hotly denied the existence of such a proposed deal.[94] Of course, both had obvious partisan reasons for doing so. Whether or not such a proposition actually had been advanced, a rumor to that effect swept through the taverns and boarding houses of Columbia. John Harold Wolfe, after a most thorough examination of the controversy, has concluded that an agreement to form a Jefferson-Pinckney ticket probably could have been arranged except that no one on either side dared to initiate it. However, available evidence strongly supports the contention that at least some high ranking South Carolina Federalists did actively contemplate, if not overtly seek, a deal with the Republicans at Columbia. On December 3, 1800, the day after the balloting for electors in Columbia, George Washington's young cousin, Bushrod, then in Raleigh, North Carolina, received a letter from DeSaussure in which the latter stated with apparent calmness that "it is more than probable that Genl. Pinckney will have the whole [of South Carolina's] eight votes with Mr. Jefferson."[95] DeSaussure no doubt wrote from Columbia, and whether his remarks may be taken as sufficient evidence of an overt

---

[94] Charles Pinckney to Jefferson, from Charleston, January 24, 1801, *ibid.*, 127–28; Gadsden to John Adams, from Charleston, March 11, 1801, in Charles Francis Adams, *The Works of John Adams* (10 vols.; Boston: Little, Brown and Company, 1850–1856), IX, 579.

[95] John Harold Wolfe, *Jeffersonian Democracy in South Carolina, The James Sprunt Studies in History and Political Science*, Vol. XXIV, No. 1 (Chapel Hill: University of North Carolina Press, 1940), 158–62n.; William Polk to John Steele, December 5, 1800, in Wagstaff, *John Steele*, I, 193.

willingness among the Federalists to deal with the Republicans, they certainly indicate a singular drift in the thinking of many friends of government at Columbia. At a moment when unquestioned fidelity to party discipline might well have kept South Carolina in support of Federalism and John Adams, DeSaussure and his allies could not seem to bring themselves wholly to trust the President. As a result, they exposed to public view the weaknesses which continually had plagued the Federalist interest after the Hamilton-Adams schism. The firmness of the Republican interest under. Charles Pinckney likely attracted many waverers away from an initial Federalist commitment, thus giving the state to Jefferson and Burr. The friends of government in South Carolina had made some notable strides toward construction of a crude local party organization and the development of several effective techniques of mass appeal since 1795, but the meaning of and the necessity for party unity on a national scale continued to elude many of them, even as late as 1800. Hamilton and his friends had worked effectively, to emphasize sectional and personal interests at the expense of party loyalty in the minds of many influential lowcountrymen, and the Federalist cause suffered disastrously from Hamilton's success.

Balloting for electors took place on December 2, and South Carolina fell to the Republicans by an eighteen-vote margin. Individuals on the Federalist ticket, headed by General William Washington, received from 63 to 69 votes, while members of the Republican ticket received from 82 to as many as 87 votes. In short, the South Carolina legislature was Republican by a not too comfortable 8.5 to 6.5 ratio.[96]

Since the balloting was secret, it is impossible to ascertain the geographic and socioeconomic configuration of the vote.

[96] Charleston *City Gazette,* December 6, 1800.

The only determinant of relative party strength in South Carolina emerges from the results of the Congressional elections and from remarks in private correspondence. Writers on both sides agreed on one point: that the city of Charleston remained under firm Federalist domination. So thorough was the Federalist hold, in fact, that DeSaussure told Rutledge in August that the Republicans were having difficulty in finding anyone willing to challenge Thomas Lowndes in the Congressional race. Lowndes, who replaced retiring Thomas Pinckney, subsequently was sent to Philadelphia, though the margin of his victory was not reported.[97] Federalism still predominated in the rest of the lowcountry, with Benjamin Huger sweeping all of the counties in the Georgetown-Cheraw district, and John Rutledge, Jr., retaining his seat from the Orangeburg-Beaufort area, although the Saxe-Gotha region went heavily Republican. In the backcountry, however, the results were different. William Butler captured three of the four electoral areas in Ninety-Six district; the fourth, Abbeville, remained Federalist by a 2 to 1 margin. Thomas Sumter continued his domination of Camden district in all but the Fairfield area, defeating Richard Winn, whose politics probably leaned toward moderate Federalism. Thomas Moore, who represented the Washington-Pinckney region, was also a Jeffersonian supporter.[98] Thus, for a brief period around 1800 the political configuration of South Carolina, with a few exceptions, took on a classic sectional cast, with the Republicans holding a

[97] Charles Pinckney to Jefferson, from Charleston, October 12, 1800, in "South Carolina in the Presidential Election of 1800," 114; DeSaussure to Rutledge, August 14, 1800, John Rutledge, Jr., Papers, Southern Historical Collection, University of North Carolina, Chapel Hill, N.C.

[98] Charleston *City Gazette*, October 15, 21, 22, 25, 27, 31, 1800. The only assessment of Winn's political character which I have run across is in a letter from William Loughton Smith to Alexander Hamilton, from Winnsborough, April 24, 1793, Hamilton Papers, Vol. 19. Manning J. Dauer, *The Adams Federalists* (Baltimore: Johns Hopkins Press, 1953), 331, 342.

tight control over most of the backcountry area and the Federalists still controlling the coast.

A final humiliation awaited the South Carolina Federalists in the legislative session of 1800. Jacob Read failed to be elected to the United States Senate by a narrow margin of 75 to 73. His successor, John E. Calhoun, was as staunch a friend of Jefferson as Charles Pinckney, the other South Carolina senator. The event marked the beginning of the Republican ascendancy in the state.[99]

[99] *North Carolina Minerva*, December 23, 1800; Charles Pinckney to Jefferson, from Columbia, December 6, 1800, in "South Carolina in the Presidential Election of 1800," 123.

VIII. *Southern Federalists and the Party System, 1789-1800*

The establishment of the first American party system was accomplished substantially by the close of the elections of 1800. The development of this novel system, which in terms of practical politics represented the United States' greatest contribution to the eighteenth-century western world, was the work of many men of both political parties in every section of the country. Between 1789 and 1800 no single interest or party, no individual or group of individuals could hold a monopoly upon political innovation. The changes which led to the emergence of a national party system, a more open political climate and electoral process, and an ever greater participation by the common people in political decision making, were as often instigated by elitist-minded friends of government seeking to perpetuate their entrenched hold upon national power, as by those who sought equal access to political power. From the perspective of southern politics, the Federalists' indispensable contributions to the building of the first national party system are clear.

It was the friends of government who first organized into active, constant, and well-defined partisan interest groups in nearly every state as early as George Washington's first administration. This basic contribution to the making of a party system was not often matched by the Jeffersonian Republicans until the eve of the 1800 elections. It was the friends of government, moreover, who, despite a deep and enduring commitment to elitist values, nonetheless pioneered in the development of techniques of mass appeal and of mass participation in the political decision-making process. The *ad hoc* public meetings, which the Federalists first arranged in Virginia and in the North in the autumn of 1793 and again in the spring of 1796, were called with authoritarian purposes in mind, to be sure. They were planned to obtain popular ratification for existing policy rather than to suggest new lines of action. Yet the taste of power, influence, and political experience which the public gained from these meetings could not help but have further stimulated its already strong desire for an even greater participation in the affairs of state. Finally, the friends of government from both the North and the South showed for the first time in 1798 how a united, disciplined partisan political interest could shape the national legislative process for its own ends. Obviously, the activities of the Federalists in the South from as early as 1791 onward—and certainly from 1798—belie the traditional conclusion recently reemphasized that "the Federalists entertained a deep and abiding hostility to the whole notion of permanent political associations."[1]

From 1797 to 1800 the elitist-minded southern Federalists moved even closer to party status as a result of the crisis with France and the persistence of a powerful opposition interest. During this time the friends of government formed broad coalitions of support in Virginia and the Carolinas and perfected various forms of party machinery in an attempt to maintain the gains they had made.[2] In the normal course

[1] J. R. Pole, "Jeffersonian Democracy and the Federalist Dilemma in New Jersey, 1798–1812," *New Jersey Historical Society Proceedings*, LXXIV (October, 1956), 264.

[2] Georgia's persistent resistance to Federalism in the 1790's carried over into the election of 1800. From all available evidence there seems to have been but a single letter in Adams' behalf in the Georgia press in 1800. At the same time members of James Jackson's Republican machine were equally quiet, indicating confidence rather than apathy. When the legisla-

of events the state, Congressional, and presidential elections of 1800 would have served as a test of the durability of these coalitions and of the practicability and efficiency of the organizations established to maintain them. But this was not to be.

Partially as a result of the General Ticket Law, which demanded the immediate creation of an active, powerful political force throughout Virginia, and partially because of the burden of carrying Adams' candidacy in Jefferson's own state, Federalists in the Old Dominion carried only eight scattered counties in 1800, all but one of which had voted consistently Federalist since 1795.[3]

In South Carolina the Federalists ultimately saw their impressive successes in obtaining popular support fatally compromised by the bitter divisions within the Federalist party leadership on the national level. The schism between the friends of Adams and those of Hamilton had become so deep by the autumn of 1800 that long-standing sectional animosities and fears were revived among South Carolina Federalists, causing them to lose faith in their northern colleagues and in the legitimacy of the ticket. Thereafter, the party was doomed to defeat in South Carolina and in the presidency as well. Even so, Federalists in both North and South Carolina in 1800 apparently retained some influence within all of the socioeconomic groups which they first had attracted two years before.[4]

---

ture met in November to cast its four votes for Jefferson, the event was noted in the most perfunctory terms, while the state's Congressional elections were not even discussed. *Augusta Chronicle,* June 28, 1800; *Georgia Gazette,* October 16, November 27, 1800.

[3] The eight counties were Accomac, Augusta, Greenbrier, Hampshire, Hardy, Loudoun, Northampton, and Westmoreland. *Virginia Argus,* December 2, 1800.

[4] In North Carolina, it will be recalled, the Federalist candidate for elector in Morgan district—in the western section—did win one county. Federalist candidates in other unreported western districts may have

But while southern Federalists contributed materially to the making of the first American party system, most of them stoutly resisted to the end the basic spirit and purpose of the new system. From the beginning southern Federalists were interested not in the politics of persuasion, but solely in the politics of control. All partisan activity, all techniques of mass appeal, and all efforts to create correspondence and campaign networks were employed to insure that the party as a whole would retain its authoritarian grasp upon power.

Philosophically, the beginnings of a consistent Federalist ideology in the South began in 1797 with an effective appeal to the "patriotic sensibility" of the electorate, a sensibility which one foreign observer of American institutions has claimed is as deep and enduring an ingredient of public conscience as is the impulse to liberty.[5] When Adams' determination to maintain peace with France forced practical abandonment of this philosophy, however, friends of government below the Potomac joined Federalists elsewhere in increasing praise of the *status quo*. During the great ideological confrontation of 1800 between eighteenth-century American social and political traditionalism and Jeffersonian liberalism, southern Federalists staunchly upheld their party's commitment to the defense of elitist rule and of entrenched religious and political institutions and practices, to the

captured one or two counties. In South Carolina a residue of Federalist strength could be found in the backcountry settlements of Abbeville and Fairfield. There also appears to have been a significant yeoman farmer element in the lowcountry parishes which also voted Federalist. Any assumption that these lowcountry yeomen were controlled by the planters and thus may be discounted as a distinct political force must take into account the incident in 1786 when the yeomen of St. James Goose Creek openly defied the expressed will of Ralph Izard and voted for their favorite, Thomas Tudor Tucker, against Izard's son. George C. Rogers, Jr., *William Loughton Smith of Charleston; Evolution of a Federalist, 1758–1812* (Columbia, S.C.: University of South Carolina Press, 1962), 128.

[5] M. Ostrogorski, *Democracy and the Organization of Political Parties*, Vol. II: *U.S.A.* (New York: Anchor Books, 1964), 302–306.

maintenance of a privileged social status for the wealthy few, and to the broadest possible restriction upon social mobility and popular participation in the political decision-making process. While a surprisingly large number of electors within all social and occupational classes in the Carolinas remained sufficiently conservative to support such a stand, they ultimately proved too few to retain these states for Federalism. In Virginia, the home of Republican theory, the Federalists' incessant articulation of the philosophy of elitism must be recognized, even more than the General Ticket Law or the burden of the Adams candidacy, as the major cause of Federalism's downfall. Surely one of the great ironies of the Federalist defeat in the South in 1800 is that the more effective the friends of government became in spreading their archaic, unpopular gospel of elitist politics through the various agencies of current party organization, the more certainly they paved the way for their own collapse.

Even in the realm of party ideology, however, the Federalists made a substantial contribution to the shaping of the first American party system. Federalists and Republicans in 1800 fashioned a climate of competing opinion from which an already aroused electorate could develop a sense of partisan commitment. In 1800 for the first time both parties consistently attempted to enlist the support of the common folk in determining the broad outlines of the future course of American political, economic, and social development. The Federalists unabashedly championed the closed society of the past in which individual opportunities for marked economic gain and social advancement were limited to the entrenched elite and only the most ambitious and most fortunate few from among the lower orders. The Republicans with their broad doctrines of equality and democracy encouraged the further breakup of static socio-economic relationships and encouraged the growth of an open, mobile society. A significant number of southerners chose to cleave to tradition and to the Federalist party in 1800, demonstrating the extent to which political conservatism remained rooted within southern thinking. The gradual erosion of this conservatism by a more liberal democratic order became the most significant theme of southern political history after 1800.[6]

With the party, its vision, and many of its values at last driven from national power, many Federalists in Virginia and the Carolinas soon abandoned their political positions and either joined with the Republicans or withdrew from public life. Accustomed to occupying a minority political position in all states except South Carolina, the main impetus which southern Federalists had to political activity—a pride of identification with the national administration—was abruptly removed. Even before the results of the presidential election were fully known, a North Carolina politician wrote scornfully that "the strongest Adamites that were in the habit [of ab]using Mr. Jefferson with the greatest scurrility now begin to say that they believes [sic] that Mr. J is as good as Mr. A and if he should gain his Election, they will be as happy as if Mr. Adams had, all place hunters and trimmers."[7] The following spring such party stalwarts as Henry Lee, Thomas Evans, Josiah Parker, and Leven Powell, vanished from the Virginia Congressional delegation, never to reappear. Two years later William Barry Grove, William H. Hill, and Archibald Henderson left national life forever.[8]

[6] Fletcher M. Green, "Democracy in the Old South," *Journal of Southern History*, XXII (June, 1946), 3–23; and Dewey W. Grantham, *The Democratic South* (Athens: University of Georgia Press, 1963), provide valuable insights into the persistent conflict between conservatism and democracy in the old and new South.

[7] Pugh Williams to John Haywood, November 7, 1800, Haywood Collection.

[8] The departure of these North Carolina Federalist congressmen in 1803 was hastened by their ostentatious refusal to be instructed by the Republi-

Some former friends of government persevered for a time, no doubt heartened by the claims of at least one partisan newspaper that the great progress made by the infant union during its first dozen years must be protected by those who constantly had adhered to the cause of orderly government and elitist rule.[9]

Benjamin Huger, John Rutledge, Jr., and Thomas Lowndes of South Carolina remained in office until they were defeated in the great Republican tide of 1804, which South Carolina Federalists apparently found useless to resist even though Cotesworth Pinckney had become the party's presidential candidate.[10] Federalism's complete collapse in South Carolina after 1804 was symbolically ratified by Hamilton's former supporter, William Loughton Smith, who by 1808 had "evolved" his political sentiments sufficiently to run unsuccessfully for Congress on the Republican ticket.[11] After 1804 the South was thoroughly Republican.[12]

The passing of Federalist power in the nation was greeted by its older friends in the South with occasional expressions of relief, but more often with bitterness, despair, and

---

can-dominated General Assembly. Davie also stood on this issue in his Congressional campaign, was defeated, and promptly went into retirement. Henry M. Wagstaff, "Federalism in North Carolina," *The James Sprunt Historical Studies*, Vol. IX, No. 2 (Chapel Hill: University of North Carolina Publications, 1910), 140.

[9] "Sketch of Parties," *Federal Carolina Gazette*, n.d., reprinted in the *North Carolina Minerva*, December 23, 1800.

[10] DeSaussure, in writing to an acquaintance in late August of 1804, made no mention of political affairs whatsoever, which was an unusual omission for the political boss. To Ezekial Pickens, from Charleston, August 22, 1804, Henry William DeSaussure Papers, South Caroliniana Library, Charleston, S.C.

[11] Rogers, *William Loughton Smith*, 380–82.

[12] John Harold Wolfe, *Jeffersonian Democracy in South Carolina, The James Sprunt Studies in History and Political Science*, Vol. XXIV, No. 1 (Chapel Hill: University of North Carolina Press, 1940), 195; Delbert H. Gilpatrick, *Jeffersonian Democracy in North Carolina* (New York: Columbia University Press, 1931), 128–31.

melancholy.[13] A few members of the old guard remained active; William Boylan and the *Minerva* became a center of Federalist activity in North Carolina largely because of the editor's unsuccessful but untiring efforts to reclaim the position of public printer.[14] In South Carolina, Jacob Read and Henry William DeSaussure showed deep interest in party affairs in 1808, and Cotesworth Pinckney, of course, was again the party's standard bearer in that year with young John Rutledge serving as his campaign manager.[15] For the most part, however, the old guard in the South, as in the North, slipped away during the early years of the Jeffersonian era, frequently entrenching themselves in a self-conscious manner—as in South Carolina—in several exclusive social "establishments."[16] They left partisan politics to younger men, who completed the transformation of Federalist political practices from elitist to egalitarian during the age of Jefferson.

Yet the time which the older Federalist leaders in the

[13] In 1802, speaking of the "increasing acrimony of Party Spirits," Richard Bland Lee complained that "social intercourse has been too much embittered," before going on to make overtures of renewed friendship to his old ally, James Madison. The attitude of Bushrod Washington to the Federalists' loss of national power was more uncompromising. In November, 1801, he wrote Hamilton of the "system of intolerance and proscription which seems to be the order of the day, from the General to many of the State Governments." Richard Bland Lee to James Madison, from Sully, Loudoun, March 27, 1802, R. B. Lee Papers; Bushrod Washington to Hamilton, November 21, 1801, in John C. Hamilton, ed., *The Works of Alexander Hamilton* (7 vols.; New York: John F. Trow, Printer, 1851), VI, 526. In 1805 the recently defeated John Rutledge, Jr., observed to Harper that Philadelphia "I suspect I shall find . . . sadly changed since the prosperous days of the Republic which we passed there so happily." August 3, 1805, from Charleston, Harper Papers, LC.

[14] Gilpatrick, *Jeffersonian Democracy in North Carolina*, 136–40.

[15] Jacob Read to Cotesworth Pinckney, from Charleston, June 10, 1807, Charles Cotesworth Pinckney Papers, South Caroliniana Library, Columbia, S.C.; DeSaussure to Ezekial Pickens, September 12, 1808, DeSaussure Papers; Rogers, *William Loughton Smith*, 379–80.

[16] Rogers cogently discusses this movement of South Carolina's "declining aristocracy," *William Loughton Smith*, 382–92.

South had spent in public life during the 1790's was by no means devoid of lasting influence upon the development of the American political tradition. Even as Jefferson came into office, Fisher Ames, the keeper of Federalism's darker conscience, already was beginning to note in bitter terms the "trust" which many of his colleagues had come to have "in the *sinless* perfection . . . of democracy."[17] Doubtless many retiring or soon-to-be retiring southern Federalists shared his views, despite all they had done to prepare the way for a major shift in the climate of political practice and principle in the young republic. Their epitaph as reluctant harbingers of great change in the style, scope, and scale of American politics unwittingly was written for them long years after by their arch foe, Thomas Jefferson, who, in remarking upon the slow growth of democratic traditions everywhere, observed that "the generation which commences a revolution rarely completes it."[18]

[17] Ames to Theodore Dwight, from Dedham, March 19, 1801, in Seth Ames, ed., *Works of Fisher Ames* (2 vols.; Boston: Little, Brown and Company, 1854), I, 292–93.
[18] Jefferson to Adams, 1823, quoted in Saul K. Padover, *Thomas Jefferson on Democracy* (New York: D. Appleton-Century Company, Inc., 1939), 21.

Appendix. Federalist Voting Strength in Three Southern States, 1795–1800

TABLE ONE: *Virginia: Vote on resolutions regarding Washington's conduct in connection with the Jay Treaty, House of Delegates, November, 1795.*[1]

Section	County	Representatives Supporting Washington	Total Representatives
Eastern Shore	Accomac	1	2
	Northampton	1	2
Piedmont: North of the James	Amherst	1	2
	Hanover	1	2
	Henrico	1	2
	Madison	2	2
Piedmont: South of the James	Pittsylvania	1	2
Northern Neck	Fairfax	1	2
	King George	2	2
	Loudoun	1	2
	Prince William	1	2
Tidewater	Elizabeth City	2	2
	Gloucester	2	2
	James City	2	2
	King and Queen	1	2
	King William	1	2
	Lancaster	1	2
	Princess Anne	1	2
	Richmond	3	3
	Warwick	1	2
	Westmoreland	1	2
	York	2	2
Shenandoah Valley	Augusta	1	2
	Bath	1	2
	Berkeley	1	2
	Botetourt	1	2
	Frederick	1	2
	Hampshire	2	2
	Hardy	2	2

TABLE ONE (*continued*)

Section	County	Representatives Supporting Washington	Total Representatives
Shenandoah Valley (*cont.*)	Pendleton	2	2
	Rockingham	1	2
Northwestern Frontier	Harrison	2	2
	Kanawha	1	2
	Monongalia	1	2
	Randolph	2	2
Southwestern Frontier	Bedford	2	2
	Greenbrier	2	2
	Montgomery	1	2
	Russell	1	2
	Washington	1	2
	Wythe	1	2
Boroughs	Richmond	1	1
	Williamsburg	1	1
TOTALS		58	85

[1] Source: *Virginia Gazette and General Advertiser,* November 25, 1795; Earl G. Swem and John W. Williams, *A Register of the General Assembly of Virginia, 1776–1918, and of the Constitutional Conventions* (Richmond: Davis Bottom, Supt. of Public Printing, 1918), 43–45.

TABLE TWO: *Virginia: Vote on the resolution declaring the Alien and Sedition Acts unconstitutional, House of Delegates, December, 1798.*[1]

Section	County	Representatives Opposing Resolutions	Total Representatives
Eastern Shore	Accomac	1	2
	Northampton	2	2
Piedmont: North of the James	Amherst	1	2
Piedmont: South of the James	Campbell	1	2
	Charlotte	2	2
	Greenville	2	2
	Halifax	1	2
	Isle of Wight	1	2
	Lunenberg	1	2

Appendix

TABLE TWO (continued)

Section	County	Representatives Opposing Resolutions	Total Representatives
Piedmont: South of the James (cont.)	Mecklenburg	1	2
	Pittsylvania	2	2
	Prince George	2	2
	Southampton	1	2
	Sussex	1	2
Northern Neck	Fairfax	1	2
	King George	2	2
	Loudoun	2	2
	Prince William	1	2
Tidewater	King William	1	2
	New Kent	1	2
	Princess Anne	2	2
	Westmoreland	1	2
	York	1	2
Shenandoah Valley	Augusta	2	2
	Bath	2	2
	Berkeley	2	2
	Botetourt	1	2
	Frederick	1	2
	Hampshire	2	2
	Hardy	2	2
	Pendleton	2	2
	Rockbridge	2	2
	Rockingham	2	2
Northwestern Frontier	Brooke	1	2
	Kanawha	1	2
	Monongalia	1	2
	Randolph	1	2
Southwestern Frontier	Bedford	2	2
	Greenbrier	2	2
	Montgomery	2	2
	Washington	1	2
	Wythe	2	2
Boroughs	Williamsburg	1	1
TOTALS		63	85

[1] Source: "Virginia General Assembly, Journal of the House of Delegates," December 21, 1798, William S. Jenkins, ed., *Records of the States of the United States* (Microfilm, University of California Library, Berkeley); *Virginia Gazette and General Advertiser,* January 1, 1799; Swem and Williams, *Register of the Virginia General Assembly,* 50–52.

TABLE THREE: *Virginia: Vote on the General Ticket Law, House of Delegates, January, 1800.*[1]

Section	County	Representatives Opposing Law	Total Representatives
Eastern Shore	Accomac	2	2
	Northampton	2	2
Piedmont: North of the James	Culpeper	2	2
	Fauquier	2	2
	Madison	1	2
Piedmont: South of the James	Campbell	2	2
	Charlotte	2	2
	Greenville	2	2
	Isle of Wight	1	2
	Lunenberg	1	2
	Mecklenburg	1	2
	Nansemond	2	2
	Nottoway	1	2
	Pittsylvania	1	2
	Prince Edward	1	2
	Prince George	2	2
	Southampton	2	2
Northern Neck	Fairfax	1	2
	King George	2	2
	Loudoun	2	2
Tidewater	Charles City	1	2
	Gloucester	1	2
	King and Queen	1	2
	King William	2	2
	New Kent	2	2
	Norfolk	1	2
	Princess Anne	2	2
	Westmoreland	2	2
	York	1	2
Shenandoah Valley	Augusta	2	2
	Bath	2	2
	Berkeley	2	2
	Botetourt	2	2
	Frederick	2	2
	Hardy	2	2
	Pendleton	2	2

Appendix / 297

TABLE THREE (continued)

Section	County	Representatives Opposing Law	Total Representatives
Northwestern Frontier	Kanawha	2	2
	Monongalia	2	2
Southwestern Frontier	Bedford	2	2
	Grayson	1	2
	Greenbrier	2	2
	Montgomery	1	2
	Wythe	2	2
Boroughs	Norfolk	1	1
	Richmond	1	1
TOTALS		73	88

[1] Source: "Virginia General Assembly, Journal of the House of Delegates," January 17, 1800, Jenkins, ed., *Records of the States;* Swem and Williams, *Register of the Virginia General Assembly,* 52–54.

TABLE FOUR: North Carolina: Vote on the Laudatory Address to John Adams, House of Commons, December, 1798.[1]

Section	County	Representatives Favoring Address	Total Representatives
Albemarle-Pamlico Sound and Northeast	Beaufort	1	2
	Chowan	1	2
	Currituck	1	2
	Halifax	1	2
	Hertford	1	2
	Northampton	1	2
	Pasquatank	1	2
East Central Region	Nash	1	2
	Onslow	1	1
	Pitt	1	2

TABLE FOUR (*continued*)

Section	County	Representatives Favoring Address	Total Representatives
Upper Cape Fear	Bladen	1	2
	Cumberland	1	2
	Duplin	2	2
Piedmont	Chatham	1	2
	Franklin	2	2
	Granville	1	2
	Johnston	1	2
	Moore	1	2
	Orange	1	2
	Person	2	2
	Robeson	2	2
	Wake	1	2
Western Counties	Anson	2	2
	Cabarrus	2	2
	Glasgow	1	2
	Guilford	1	2
	Iredell	1	2
	Lincoln	2	2
	Mecklenburg	1	2
	Richmond	2	2
	Rockingham	1	2
	Rowan	1	2
	Rutherford	2	2
	Stokes	2	2
	Surry	1	2
Mountain Counties	Buncombe	1	2
	Burke	2	2
	Wilkes	1	2
Boroughs	Fayetteville	1	1
	Salisbury	1	1
TOTALS		51	77

[1] Source: "Journal of the North Carolina House of Commons," December 24, 1798, Jenkins, ed., *Records of the States*.

Appendix

TABLE FIVE: *North Carolina: Vote on resolution condemning the Alien and Sedition Acts, House of Commons, December, 1798.*[1]

Section	County	Representatives Favoring Resolution	Total Representatives
Albemarle-Pamlico Sound and Northeast	Chowan	1	2
	Halifax	1	2
	Pasquatank	1	2
Central Region	Onslow	1	1
Upper Cape Fear	None		
Piedmont	Chatham	1	2
	Franklin	2	2
	Granville	1	2
	Wake	1	2
Western Counties	Anson	2	2
	Glasgow	1	2
	Iredell	1	2
	Lincoln	2	2
	Mecklenburg	1	2
	Montgomery	1	2
	Rowan	1	2
Mountain Counties	Burke	2	2
Boroughs	Salisbury	1	1
TOTALS		21	32

[1] Source: "Journal of the North Carolina House of Commons," December 24, 1798, Jenkins, ed., *Records of the States.*

TABLE SIX: *South Carolina: Vote on the report recommending the procurement of a stand of 5,000 more arms to be resold to the "privates in the respective Regiments of this State," House of Representatives, December, 1798.*[1]

Section	County, Parish or Settlement	Votes Favoring Report
Lowcountry	All Saints	0
	Charleston (St. Michael's) (St. Philip's)	11
	Christ Church	1
	Prince Frederick	0
	Prince George	3
	Prince William	1
	St. Andrews	1
	St. Bartholomew's	0
	St. George	2
	St. Helena's	3
	St. James Goose Creek	2
	St. James Santee	1
	St. John's Berkeley	3
	St. John's Colleton	2
	St. Luke's	3
	St. Paul's	4
	St. Peter's	0
	St. Stephen's	3
	St. Thomas & St. Denis	1
	Saxe-Gotha	1
	Williamsburg	2
	Winton	2
Backcountry	Abbeville	1
	Chester	1
	Darlington	1
	Fairfield	1
	Kershaw	1
	Kingston	1
	Newberry	1
	Pendleton	1
	Spartanburg	1
TOTAL		55

[1] Source: "Journal of the South Carolina House of Representatives," December 17, 1798, Jenkins, ed., *Records of the States.*

TABLE SEVEN: *South Carolina: Ascertainable vote on motion to consider the Kentucky Resolutions, Senate, December, 1799.*[1]

Section	County, Parish or Settlement	Federalist	Republican
Lowcountry	Charleston	X	
	Christ Church		X
	St. John's Bartholomew	X	
	St. John's Colleton	X	
	St. Luke's	X	
	St. Stephen's	X	
	Saxe-Gotha		X
	Winyaw-Williamsburg	X	
Backcountry	Abbeville		X
	Chester and Richland	X	
	Edgefield		X
	Fairfield	X	
	Greenville		X
	Kingston and Liberty	X	
	Laurens		X
	Newberry		X
	Pendleton		X
	Spartanburg	X	
	Winton		X
	York		X

[1] Source: "Journal of the South Carolina Senate," December 24, 1799, Jenkins, ed., *Records of the States*.

TABLE EIGHT: *North Carolina: Ascertainable results of the Presidential Election of 1800.*[1]

Section	District	County	Federalist	Republican
Eastern	Edgecombe	Beaufort	No count[2]	
		Edgecombe	303	202
		Greene	249	43
		Hyde	No count[2]	
		Pitt	388	209
	New Bern	Carteret	147	14
		Craven	331	301
		Johnston	168	92
		Jones	142	87
		Lenoir	122	227
		Wayne	22	413
			932	1,134
	Warren (Halifax)	Franklin	68	224
		Halifax	209	466
		Nash	47	101
		Warren	14	549
			338	1,340
Piedmont	Raleigh	Chatham	232	397
		Granville	187	379
		Person	62	241
		Wake	266	302
			747	1,319
Western	Morgan	Ashe	0	62
		Buncombe	26	155
		Burke	122	427
		Lincoln	240	11
		Rutherford	60	361
		Wilkes	36	357
			484	1,373
	Salisbury	Cabarrus	139	101
		Mecklenburg	274	292
		Montgomery	277	54
		Rowan	643	563
			1,333	1,010
TOTALS			4,774	6,630

[1] Source: *Raleigh Register*, November 11, 18, 25, 1800.
[2] Reported as strongly Federalist. *Ibid.*, November 18, 1800.

TABLE NINE: *South Carolina: Ascertainable Results of the Congressional Election of 1800.*[1]

Section	District	County, Parish or Town	Federalist	Republican
Lowcountry	Georgetown-Cheraw	Cheraw } Georgetown	603	401
		Williamsburg	167	110
			770	511
	Orangeburg-Beaufort	Orange	174	74
		Prince William	63	23
		St. Helena's	68	6
		St. Luke's	43	29
		St. Mathew's	95	28
		St. Peter's	98	1
		Saxe-Gotha	27	227
		Winton	206	192
			774	580
Backcountry	Camden	Claremont	9	157
		Clarendon	0	150
		Fairfield	510	132
		Kershaw	47	189
		Lancaster	No count[2]	
		Richland	37	233
		Salem	0	153
	Ninety-Six (Partial)	Abbeville	405	223
		Edgefield	69	563
		Newberry	173	414
TOTALS			2,794	3,305

[1] Source: Charleston *City Gazette*, October 21, 22, 27, 31, November 5, 17, 1800.
[2] Reported three to one Republican. *Ibid.*, October 21, 1800.

A Note on Sources

As I have indicated in the introduction, southern state politics during the Federalist era have received comparatively little serious and sustained scholarly attention in recent years. Much published and unpublished primary source material is available, however, for the use of historians and biographers. This book was written mainly from unpublished sources, including manuscript collections, newspapers, state legislative journals, and contemporary political pamphlets.

Unpublished manuscripts were of prime importance, and approximately sixty collections in libraries across the country were consulted. In the Library of Congress, the papers of Thomas Jefferson, Alexander Hamilton, James Madison, John Adams, and especially those of George Washington and the Pinckney family, were of indispensable aid in tracing both the contours and the details of growing Federalist partisanship and strength in the southern states after 1790.

A number of smaller collections in the Library of Congress also contained information on the structure of southern state politics and the attitudes and activities of influential southern Federalists in this period. Among the most notable of these were the Richard Bland Lee, Ralph Izard, John Marshall, Campbell-Preston, and William Loughton Smith papers. The Diary of William Heth covering the years 1792-1793 proved equally valuable. An examination of the Personal Miscellany File uncovered some important single pieces of

A Note on Sources / 305

correspondence concerning southern Federalists and southern politics in general at the close of the eighteenth century.

Duke University Library and the Southern Historical Collection at Chapel Hill have the next largest and most important collections of private papers of southern politicians during the administrations of Washington and John Adams. At Duke, the papers of Seaborn Jones, Edward Telfair, and James Jackson include much information pertaining to Georgia politics between 1789 and 1801. The Charles Cotesworth Pinckney, Jacob Read, and John Rutledge, Jr., papers trace the frequently vacillating and conflicting activities of the various South Carolina Federalist factions before and after 1794, while political developments in Virginia, and especially in North Carolina, prior to 1799 are documented in the papers and correspondence of James Iredell. The Southern Historical Collection at Chapel Hill also has an important collection of the papers of John Rutledge, Jr. In addition, the correspondence of William R. Davie, Ernest Haywood, and the Cameron and Lenoir family papers provide highly important insights into the Federalist role in Virginia and North Carolina politics throughout the 1790's.

Important correspondence and private papers of various southern Federalists also are available at the Historical Society of Pennsylvania in Philadelphia. The Dreer Collection contains important correspondence of the Rutledge family during 1796 and 1797. Southern Federalists' observations on state and national politics in the 1780's and 1790's may also be found in the Pierce Butler papers, the Gratz collection, the Anthony Wayne papers, and the Charles Francis Jenkins collection.

Important source material on South Carolina Federalism in this period may be found in the papers of Jacob Read, Edward Rutledge, John Rutledge, Jr., Charles Cotesworth Pinckney, Henry William DeSaussure, and Robert Goodloe

Harper at the South Caroliniana Library in Columbia. Recently discovered correspondence between William Loughton Smith and Edward Rutledge spanning the years 1789-1794 is now in the South Carolina Historical Society in Charleston. This correspondence details the course of early national political history with such thoroughness and candor as to demand skillful editing and immediate publication.

The University of Virginia Library at Charlottesville contains letters and papers in the Marshall Family and Wilson Cary Nicholas collections on the origins and development of the Federalist interest in the Old Dominion during and after 1793. The Anthony Wayne papers at the Clements Library in Ann Arbor are an important source of information concerning the genesis and often unsavory activities of the Federalist faction in Georgia in the early 1790's. The William Loughton Smith, Abraham Baldwin, and Lee Family papers in the Brock Collection at the Henry E. Huntington Library in San Marino, California, include important single pieces of correspondence.

Twenty-four newspapers fairly evenly distributed among the four South Atlantic states were consulted during this study. They proved invaluable guides to the day-by-day political history of their time and place and also often provided running accounts and commentaries on various election campaigns from which an assessment of the relative growth of party spirit and organization in various areas could be made. The names of these newspapers and the locations of extant copies may be found in Clarence S. Brigham, *History and Bibliography of American Newspapers, 1690–1820* (2 vols.; 2d ed.; London: Archon Books, 1962).

State legislative journals were valuable chiefly in providing detailed information on the results of key partisan legislative proposals that appeared in nearly all states with increasing

A Note on Sources / 307

frequency after 1795. In particular, these divisions permit the historian to make at least a tentative evaluation of the geographic and social sources of partisan allegiance as party activity and organization grew and expanded over ever wider areas of the South during the Presidency of John Adams.

Contemporary political pamphlets contain factual material and partisan interpretations of specific events and developments throughout the decade. The Huntington Library has a large collection of these pamphlets.

Published correspondence of various Federalist and Republican partisans was the final source of primary information consulted in the preparation of this study. In addition to the readily available and invaluable collected works of Washington, Jefferson, Madison, Hamilton, Monroe, John Adams, Fisher Ames, Rufus King, and Patrick Henry, there exists a sizable number of fragmentary collections of the writings of leading southern political figures of the Federalist era. Among the most important of these for North Carolina are Griffith J. McRee, ed., *The Life and Correspondence of James Iredell* (2 vols.; New York: Peter Smith, 1949); Alice Barnwell Keith, ed., *The John Gray Blount Papers*, Vols. I and II (Raleigh: State Department of Archives and History, 1952, 1959); William Henry Masterson, ed., *The John Gray Blount Papers*, Vol. III (Raleigh: State Department of Archives and History, 1965); and Henry M. Wagstaff, ed., *The Papers of John Steele* (2 vols.; Raleigh: North Carolina Historical Publications, 1924). In addition, Wagstaff and Kemp P. Battle collected and edited important political correspondence of William Barry Grove, Charles Harris, William R. Davie, and John Steele, which may be found in Numbers 3 and 7 and Volumes IX and XIV of the *James Sprunt Historical Studies*.

Much important data on the rise and decline of South Carolina Federalism between 1789 and 1800 may be found in Ulrich B. Phillips, ed., "South Carolina Federalist Correspondence," *American Historical Review,* XIV (July, 1909); Worthington C. Ford, ed., "Letters of Ralph Izard," *South Carolina Historical and Genealogical Magazine,* II (July, 1909); and the anonymously edited, "South Carolina in the Presidential Election of 1800," *American Historical Review,* IV (October, 1898).

Important aspects of Federalist activity in Georgia at the close of the eighteenth century may be found in Harriet Milledge Salley, ed., *Correspondence of Governor John Milledge* (Columbia, S.C.: State Commercial Printing Co., 1949); and in "Letterbook of James Jackson, 1788–1796," *Georgia Historical Quarterly,* XXXVII (March-December, 1953); "Papers of Lachlan McIntosh, 1774–1799," *ibid.,* XL (June, 1956); and "Papers of Lachlan McIntosh," *Collections of the Georgia Historical Society,* XII (Savannah, 1957), all edited by Lilla M. Hawes.

Index

Abbeville, S. C., 185, 281, 286n
Abolitionism, 7-11 *passim*, 105
Accomac County, Va., 222, 285n
Adams, Abigail, 168, 233
Adams, John: and elections of 1792, 35, 123; presidency of, 81, 159; and elections of 1796, 123-24, 126-27, 130-37 *passim*, 138n, 140, 141, 239; relations with Jefferson, 144-45, 146; support for, 145, 234; relations with Hamilton, 145; cabinet of, 145, 200, 203, 233-34, 238, 240-42, 274; relations with southern Federalists, 146, 148, 153-54, 201-202, 275-77; special message to Congress, 147, 149, 151; and XYZ mission, 150, 153, 167, 168-72 *passim*, 186, 197; patronage policies of, 153-54; address of North Carolina legislature to, 176, 297-98; relations with France, 188, 189, 194-95, 212, 229, 232, 286; relations with high Federalists, 200-204 *passim*, 232-34, 238-43 *passim*, 249, 273, 274-75, 279-80, 285; dispatches final peace mission to France, 203n, 218, 221, 233, 249; and provisional army, 206-208; and elections of 1800, 233-80 *passim*, 284n, 285, 287, 288; influence of George Washington on, 235n; attacked by Republicans, 251; Federalist defense of, 252, 254, 256, 269, 272; and elections of 1798, 259; and aristocratic titles, 265; mentioned, 8, 9, 176, 196, 199, 220, 250, 253. *See also* Elections; Franco-American relations; XYZ mission

Addison, Alexander, 252
Albemarle County, Va., 76, 210
Alexandria, Va.: and Bank of the United States, 39n; Federalists in, 157, 197, 230; and XYZ mission, 169; mentioned, 5, 119, 130, 188, 222, 266
Alien and Sedition Acts: origins of, 154-55, 156-57, 158; reaction to, 190-91, 193, 229, 251, 294-95, 299; and southern Federalists, 202, 211-15, 216; and Virginia militia, 216n; mentioned, 187, 199, 221, 242n, 275
Allston, Willis, 175, 178, 179n
Amelia County, Va., 267
American party system, development of, 4-5, 50, 231, 283-92 *passim*
American Revolution, 2-3, 49, 53, 56, 106
Ames, Fisher, 131, 291
Amherst County, Va., 10
Annapolis Convention, 19
Anglo-French war (1793), 74, 90, 99
Antifederalists: in South Carolina, 7-8, 54-55, 107; in Virginia, 7n, 10, 69-70, 130; in Georgia, 8, 16; in North Carolina, 14, 77, 84, 176; mentioned, 46
Army, U.S. *See* Provisional army
Assumption, Hamilton's plan of: and South Carolina, 30-32; and Edward Carrington, 40; opposed by James Jackson, 60. *See also* Funding, Hamilton's plan of
Augusta, Ga.: Federalists in, 98, 171, 186-87; and XYZ mission, 170; mentioned, 64, 93, 98
Augusta Chronicle, 62, 186
Augusta County, Va., 285n

Backcountry, southern, 52-53, 193-95
Baker, Blake, 259
Baldwin, Abraham, 34, 45
Ball, Burgess, 120
Bank of the United States: and Hamilton's patronage policy, 36, 37; membership of, 38-39; mentioned, 10, 32n, 42n, 43, 44. *See also* Hamilton, Alexander
Barnwell, Robert, 51, 138n, 185
Bayard, James A., 179n, 242, 264
Beard, Charles, 115
Beaufort, S. C., 180
Becker, Carl, 2
Beckley, John, 35n, 67-68
Berkeley County, Va., 129
Bertie County, N. C., 178
Beverly, Robert, 188
Blair, John, 22, 24
Bloodworth, Timothy, 84
Blount, John Gray, 13-14, 18, 106
Blount, Thomas: supports Constitution, 18; and sectionalism in North Carolina, 78-79; attitude toward Britain, 106; and Jay Treaty, 114, 128; Congressional resolutions of, 128, 140n, 141; accused of land fraud, 175n, 178; and elections of 1798, 178; supports Gales, 258; mentioned, 149
Blount, William: and northern speculators, 14; supports Constitution, 18; appointment as territorial governor, 23, 24; and federal patronage, 24; and Yazoo sale of 1789, 62; Republicanism of, 160; filibustering expedition of, 160; mentioned, 158n
Blount family: reaction to Hamilton's financial policies, 13-14; economic interests of, 18; Republicanism of, 113, 158; and Tennessee, 158n; mentioned, 105, 175n
Boston, Mass., 114-15
Botetourt County, Va., 168
Boylan, William, 255, 259, 260, 290

British merchants: of Charleston, 51, 106-12 *passim*, 116; in northern ports, 106, 112; in southern ports, 106n, 112; in Virginia, 120, 129; and elections of 1800, 270; mentioned, 105, 115, 246-47
British West Indies, southern trade with, 17, 18, 105-106, 112, 116, 120
Burke, Aedanus, 30, 54-55, 60n, 107, 116
Burke, Edmund, 56
Burke County, Ga., 118n
Burr, Aaron, 280
Butler, Pierce: in Constitutional Convention, 7; and federal patronage, 24, 25; social status of, 51; and Yazoo sale of 1789, 62n; Republicanism of, 102, 103; and South Carolina Federalists, 102, 181; and national elections, 143, 248; mentioned, 111
Butler, William, 271, 281

Cabell, Samuel J., 158
Cabinet, U.S.: appointments to, 23; and Creek Indians, 86, 88, 89; and filibustering expedition of Clark, 89; conflicts with Adams, 233-34, 238, 240-42, 274. *See also* Adams, John; Washington, George
Cabot, George, 82n
Calhoun, John E., 282
Callender, James Thomas, 221, 224, 226
Camden, S. C., 183
Camden district, S. C., 281
Cameron, Duncan, 236, 243, 246-47, 260
Capital, U.S., residence of, 6, 38
Carnes, Thomas P., 91, 95-96, 98, 118
Caroline County, Va., 76, 267
Carrington, Edward: and Hamilton's financial policies, 11, 12, 37, 40; and Society of the Cincinnati, 22-23; and federal patronage, 22-23, 40, 41; and Federalist organization in Virginia, 25; and Fairfax

Index / 311

Carrington, Edward (*continued*): purchase, 41-42; political career of, 72; social status of, 72, 73*n*; elitist political values of, 73*n*; and Genêt mission, 75; and Jay Treaty, 120, 128; and elections of 1796, 128, 130; and sectionalism within Virginia, 192; and provisional army, 206, 210; mentioned, 100, 101, 129

"Casca" essays, 68

Cassius essays, 42*n*

Champlin, William, 242*n*

Charles, Joseph, 33

Charleston, S. C.: and U.S. Constitution, 8; Federalists in, 37-38; and Bank of the United States, 38-39; British merchants in, 106-112 *passim*; and national elections, 143, 184, 269-70, 272, 277-78, 281; slave conspiracy in, 163-64, 182; and XYZ mission, 170

Charleston *City Gazette*, 183, 254, 275, 276

Charlotte, Va., 217

Chatham County, Ga., 63, 65, 93, 96, 247

Cheraw district, S. C., 116

Cherokee Indians, 17*n*, 18

Chester, S. C., 185

Chesterfield County, Va., 222

Christ Church Parish, S. C., 116

Cincinnati, Society of the: membership of, 19, 19*n*, 22-23, 24, 26, 39-40, 42, 50, 59, 68; and federal patronage, 19-20, 29; in South Carolina, 58, 170; mentioned, 28

Clark, Elijah, 86, 89-90

Clinton, George, 35, 123, 135, 136

Columbia, S. C., 59, 102, 116, 137, 185, 278, 279, 280

Columbia County, Ga., 93

Commercial Gazette, 264

Confederation, U.S., 1, 7*n*, 16*n*, 17, 21, 54

Congress, U.S.: and residence of national capital, 6; sectional fears expressed in, 8-9; relations with Hamilton, 28-29, 33-35, 36, 44;

Congress (*continued*): Federalists in, 32-35, 67-68, 147-54 *passim*, 197-200, 232-33, 237-38, 239, 240*n*; partisan activities of Madison in, 33; Republicans in, 34, 44, 99, 113, 129, 147-52 *passim*, 180, 198, 199, 238; and Jackson-Wayne election, 66, 67-68; and Creek Indians, 86, 88; and Jay Treaty, 93, 103*n*, 117, 118, 127, 128, 129, 139-40, 141; Jefferson's observations on, 147, 237, 238; Adams' special message to, 147, 149, 151; growth of party spirit in, 149-50, 237; and XYZ mission, 197; and provisional army, 208, 209; mentioned, 1, 27, 96, 214, 253. See also Federalists; Hamilton, Alexander; Republicans

Connecticut, 16*n*, 35*n*, 36

Constitution, U.S.: ratification of, 7-8, 30, 54-55, 107; support for, 16, 17-19

Constitutional Convention, 6-19 *passim*, 38, 56, 70*n*, 72, 73*n*

Continental Army, 19, 26, 49

Continental Congress, 2, 18, 21, 54

Continentalist VI, 1

"Correspondent" essays, 68

Crawford, William H., 93

Creek Indians: and Georgia, 15, 16, 59, 61, 64, 66, 68, 85-90, 91, 97, 133-34, 164, 195; and Spain, 16; and Yazoo sale of 1795, 92, 95-96; mentioned, 25*n*, 45. See also Georgia; Treaty of New York

Creek Treaty of 1790. See Treaty of New York

Culpeper County, Va., 12, 76, 188

Cunningham, Noble E., 230

Cureton, James, 217*n*

Dallas, Alexander James, 91, 110

Darlington, S. C., 185

Davie, William R.: and U.S. Constitution, 7, 18; and Hamilton's financial policies, 13, 15; repre-

Davie, W. R. (*continued*): sents British creditors, 18; and federal judiciary, 23; retirement of, 78, 157-58, 289n; and national elections, 79-80, 130; and Jay Treaty, 118, 129; attitude toward France of, 158; opposes freedom of speech, 158; political activities of, 174; and provisional army, 174, 210, 211; accuses Thomas Blount of land fraud, 175n; and XYZ mission, 176; mentioned, 80n, 178

Davis, Valentine, 42n, 81n, 254

Declaration of Independence, 277

Defense of the American Constitutions, 252

Democratic-Republican Societies (S. C.), 59

Democratic spirit, development of, 3, 4, 283-91 *passim*

DeSaussure, Henry William: social status of, 52; elitist political values of, 57; and Jay Treaty, 117; and Alien and Sedition Acts, 211-12n; and elections of 1800, 230, 248, 268, 269, 271, 273, 279-80, 281; leads South Carolina Federalists, 235; and high Federalists, 275; and elections of 1804, 289n; mentioned, 39, 185, 244

Dickson, Joseph, 175

Dinwiddie County, Va., 267

Directory, French. *See* France, Directory of

Duane, William, 275, 276

Edenton, N. C., 177

Edenton district, N. C., 178

Edgecombe district, N. C., 261

Election of 1796: in the South, 123-38 *passim*, 140-43 *passim*; in Virginia, 127-33, 142, 192, 193; in North Carolina, 127-30 *passim*, 142, 260; in Georgia, 133-34, 170; in South Carolina, 134-38, 143, 274; in Pennsylvania, 142; mentioned, 85, 146, 239

Election of 1798: in the South, 139, 172; in North Carolina, 174-75, 177-78, 179, 259; in South Carolina, 179-85; in Georgia, 186

Election of 1800: in Georgia, 187, 284-85n; in the South, 230-31; and sectional division among Federalists, 239; in South Carolina, 243, 248, 267-82, 285, 286n, 287, 303; in North Carolina, 246-48, 256-61, 285n, 287, 302; in Virginia, 245-46, 248-53, 261-67, 285, 287; party spirit in, 255-56, 258-59, 266; mentioned, 159, 197, 205, 227, 229, 283, 285, 286, 288. *See also* Adams, John; Hamilton, Alexander; High Federalists

Elections: of 1792, 35, 123; of 1797, 155-56; of 1799, 157, 187-89, 216-22 *passim*; of 1804, 289; of 1808, 290

Elitist political values: of Federalists, 3n, 4, 47, 48-60 *passim*, 72-74, 94-95, 113, 142, 179, 220, 225-27, 248, 252-53, 256, 263, 269-71, 272-73, 283-90 *passim*; of Republicans, 142

Ellsworth, Oliver, 233

England. *See* Great Britain

Ethnic politics, 193-94

Evans, Thomas: Federalism of, 147, 148, 152, 156, 222; and Lyon-Griswold affair, 198; and Alien and Sedition Acts, 215; and elections of 1799, 222, 228; and General Election Law of 1800, 262; retirement of, 288

Eveleigh, Nicholas, 23

Excise Tax (1791), 10, 12, 15, 32n

Fairfax County, Va., 76, 129, 131

Fairfax purchase, 42, 44, 157

Fairfield, S. C., 116, 281, 286n

Fauchet affair, 19n, 71, 155

Fauquier County, Va., 76, 129, 130

Fayetteville, N. C.: and national elections, 130, 142, 260; and XYZ mission, 168, 169; mentioned, 14, 79, 80, 177

Index / 313

Fayetteville district, N. C., 261
Federal Carolina Gazette, 254
Federalist party: emergence as permanent national political organization, 139-66; sectionalism within, 146, 200-204 *passim*, 232-34, 235, 238-40, 242-43, 244-45, 273-74
Federalists: develop partisan organizations in the South, 1-2, 46, 80-84 *passim*, 122, 132, 138-39, 154-57 *passim*, 165, 167, 169, 196-97, 205, 229, 243-49, 270-71, 280, 283-85; elitist political values of, 3n, 4, 47, 48-60 *passim*, 72-74, 81, 84, 94-95, 113, 142, 179, 220, 225-27, 248, 252-53, 256, 263, 269-73 *passim*, 283-90 *passim*; in New England, 3n; and development of American party system, 4-5, 50, 231, 283-92 *passim*; in Virginia, 7n, 25, 37, 39-45, 69-77, 100-101, 119-25 *passim*, 127, 130-33, 153-57, 168-69, 187-93 *passim*, 197, 198, 216-27, 230, 236, 245-46, 248-53, 261-67; and Society of the Cincinnati, 20; in South Carolina, 25, 37-39, 45, 51-59, 100-12, 115-18 *passim*, 134-38, 148-53 *passim*, 163-64, 170, 179-86, 229, 243, 248, 267-82; in Georgia, 26. 45, 59-69, 98, 133-34, 164-65, 170-71, 186-87; newspapers in the South, 26, 80, 94-95, 129-30, 131, 159-62, 165-66, 172-74, 178, 179, 186, 195, 196. 213, 222-27, 229, 244, 248-56 *passim*, 258-59, 266-67; in Congress, 32-35, 147-54 *passim*, 197-200, 232-33, 237-39; in North Carolina, 45, 77-80 *passim*, 112-14, 118, 127, 130, 157-62, 169-70, 173-79, 229, 236, 246-48, 256-61; social status of, 48-59 *passim*, 70-74 *passim*, 80; contacts with national party structure, 74-75, 95-96, 100-101, 123-27 *passim*, 128-30, 135-37, 145, 155, 157, 167-71, 189, 192, 197, 215, 219, 288; achievements of, 81-84,

Federalists (*continued*):
165-66, 174, 193-97, 203-204, 219, 228-31, 283-85, 290-91; of the "Old School," 82n; failures of, 83-84, 101-12, 138, 177-80 *passim*, 186, 197, 205, 229-30, 231, 285; and Washington's neutrality policy, 99-100; attitudes toward Britain, 105-19 *passim*, 120-21, 160-62, 165; attitudes toward France, 108-10, 144, 147-48, 150-51, 158-65, 167-73, 176-77, 180, 181-83, 198-99, 201, 208, 232, 254, 269, 297-98; petition campaign of (1796), 128-30; develop conservative political philosophy, 159-62, 167, 172, 173-74, 179, 181-83, 195-96, 202, 214-15, 216, 223-27, 249-56 *passim*, 257, 263, 280, 286-88; and provisional army, 202, 205-11, 214, 215, 218; historical attitudes toward, 284
—sources of strength: in Georgia, 80, 98, 171, 186-87, 194; in Virginia, 80-81, 121-22, 190-93, 222, 227-28, 229, 285, 293-97; in southern backcountry, 193-95; in North Carolina, 80-81, 176, 229, 236, 260-61, 267, 297-99, 302; in South Carolina, 80, 185-86, 229, 281-82, 300-301, 303
—decline of strength: in Georgia, 98-99; in South Carolina, 101-12, 137-38, 235, 273-82 *passim*, 280, 288-90; in Virginia, 100-101, 133, 236, 264-67 *passim*, 288, 289-90; in North Carolina, 133, 259, 260, 288
—revival of strength: in South Carolina, 143, 165, 243-44; in Virginia, 143, 165, 243-44; in North Carolina, 143, 165-66, 174, 179, 243-44, 246
—political activities of: in the South, 46-47, 50, 139, 205, 244, 256-80 *passim*, 287; in Georgia, 59-69 *passim*; in Virginia, 74-77, 127-33 *passim*, 188-89, 196. 205, 216-27 *passim*, 261-67, 284; in South

Federalists (*continued*):
Carolina, 136, 183-84, 268-80; in North Carolina, 246-48, 257-60
—in elections: of 1792, 123; of 1796, 123-38 *passim*, 140, 142-43; of 1797, 155-56; of 1798, 139, 172-86 *passim;* of 1799, 157, 187-89, 216-22 *passim;* of 1800, 230-31, 234-82 *passim;* of 1804, 289; of 1808, 290
—and Yazoo sale: of 1789, 61-64; of 1795, 85, 90-99 *passim*
—reaction of southern members to: Jay Treaty, 114-21 *passim*, 139, 140, 143, 293-94; Alien and Sedition Acts, 154-55, 156-57, 158, 202, 211-15, 251-52, 294-95, 299; XYZ mission, 167-72; dismissals from cabinet, 240-42; Hamilton, 238-43 *passim*, 273-74, 280
—*See also* Election of 1796; Election of 1798; Election of 1800; Georgia; High Federalists; North Carolina; South Carolina; Virginia
Fenno, John, 241
Few, William, 45, 59, 92
Fischer, David Hackett, 82*n*
Foushee, William, 42-43
France: Federalist attitudes toward, 108-10, 144, 147-48, 150-51, 158-65, 169-73, 176-77, 180, 181-83, 198-99, 201, 208, 232, 254, 269; and Jay Treaty, 143-44; commercial depredations of, 144, 151, 159, 160, 163, 224; Republican attitudes toward, 147, 151, 152, 162, 202; mentioned, 155. *See also* Franco-American relations; XYZ mission
France, Directory of: humiliates C. C. Pinckney, 143-44, 147, 150, 151, 159, 179, 181, 208; friendship for Monroe, 144; Logan's mission to, 173; mentioned, 152, 167, 201, 203*n*, 217, 221, 227, 229
Franco-American relations, 84, 143-53 *passim*, 158, 159-64, 167-72, 176, 179, 188, 194-95, 196, 199,

Franco-American relations (*cont.*): 200-201, 206, 212, 221, 224, 225, 266, 284. *See also* XYZ mission
Franco-American Treaty (1778), 144, 164
Frederick County, Va., 76, 122, 129, 222
Fredericksburg, Va., 76, 169, 221
French Revolution, 108
Freneau, Peter, 278
"FRIEND TO MERIT, A," essay of, 100-101
Fries' Rebellion, 251
Funding, Hamilton's plan of, 31, 40, 60-61, 124. *See also* Assumption, Hamilton's plan of

Gabriel's uprising, 254, 266
Gadsden, Christopher, 116, 279
Gales, Joseph, 174, 254-60 *passim*
Gallatin, Albert, 91, 150, 151, 155, 160, 221, 238
Galphia, Creek chief, 86
Gazette of the United States, 241
General Election Law (Virginia, 1800), 227-28, 251, 261-64, 265, 285, 287, 296-97
Genêt, Edmond, mission of, 74-77, 108, 110
Georgetown, S. C., 116, 183, 184
Georgetown-Cheraw district, S. C., 281
Georgia: Antifederalists in, 8, 16; and Creek Indians, 15, 16, 59, 61, 64, 66, 68, 85-90, 91, 97, 133-34, 164, 195; relations with federal government, 15-16, 59, 63-64, 85-91 *passim*, 133-34, 164, 170; support for Constitution in, 16; and federal patronage, 25-26; Federalists in, 26, 45, 59-69, 133-34, 164-65, 170-71, 186-87; Federalist press in, 26, 80, 94-95, 186, 213; social status of Federalists in, 59; political and social structure of, 59, 64-65; legislature of, 61-63, 91-94, 97-98, 186-87; sectionalism within, 64; and Treaty of New York, 64; Re-

Index / 315

Georgia (*continued*):
  publicans in, 64, 98, 116, 119, 133-34, 171, 186-87, 236; constitutional convention of 1795, 96; attitudes toward Britain in, 118-19, 165; attitudes toward France in, 165, 170-71; and provisional army, 211; mentioned, 53, 136
—Federalist strength in: sources of, 80, 98, 171, 186-87, 194; decline of, 98-99
—and Yazoo sale: of 1789, 61-64; of 1795, 85, 90-99 *passim*
—in elections: of 1792, 123; of 1796, 133, 134, 170; of 1798, 172, 186; of 1800, 187
—reaction to: Jay Treaty, 98, 118-19, 165; XYZ mission, 170; Alien and Sedition Acts, 213
Georgia Gazette, 26, 64, 68, 94-95, 186, 213
Gerry, Elbridge, 145, 154, 199, 201
Gibbons, Thomas, 66
Gibbons, William, Sr., 59
Giles, William Branch: Congressional resolutions of, 33, 34-35, 101; and Jackson-Wayne election, 67; political career of, 70; social status of, 70-71; mentioned, 27, 110, 160
Gillon, Alexander, uprising of, 3, 107
Glynn County, Ga., 170
Goode, Samuel, 222
Gray, Edwin, 222
Great Britain: proposed commercial discrimination laws against, 88, 99, 106, 107, 110, 113; commercial depredations of, 99, 100, 106, 108-109, 111-12, 114; activities in the Ohio Valley of, 99; Federalist attitudes toward, 105-19 *passim*, 120-21, 160-62, 165; mentioned, 144. See also British merchants; Jay Treaty
Greenbrier County, Va., 285n
Griffin, Samuel, 34
Griswold, Roger, 198, 199

Grove, William Barry: supports Hamilton, 34; and national elections, 84, 142, 175, 259; attitude toward Britain, 113; elitist political values of, 113; Federalism of, 113-14; and Lyon-Griswold affair, 198; and provisional army, 210; retirement of, 288; mentioned, 118, 130, 149, 152, 174
Gunn, James: and federal patronage, 26, 153; Federalism of, 26; and Society of the Cincinnati, 26, 68; social status of, 59; and Yazoo sale of 1789, 64; and Creek Indians, 64, 95-96; leads Georgia Federalists, 68-69; and Yazoo sale of 1795, 91-98 *passim;* and Jay Treaty, 93, 96; loss of political influence, 98; political inactivity of, 165; and XYZ mission, 171; and provisional army, 208-209; and elections of 1800, 242

Habersham, John, 59
Habersham, Joseph, 59, 64, 165
Halifax, N. C., 177, 247
Hall, Allamand, 159, 161, 162, 172-73
Hamilton, Alexander: on formation of partisan factions, 1-2, 4-5, 7n; financial policies of, 10, 28-29, 32, 36-39, 124; reaction to financial policies of, 10-15, 29-35, 78; and Society of the Cincinnati, 19, 29; patronage policies of 20, 28-29, 36-45, 53; and Congress, 28-29, 33-35, 44; and southern Federalists, 31, 33, 34, 36-37, 39n, 40, 43, 50, 123-24, 125-27, 131, 135, 145, 146, 238-43 *passim*, 273-74, 280; and Genêt mission, 75; and Creek Indians, 88; resignation as Treasury Secretary, 100; and elections of 1796, 123-27, 131, 135, 146, 239; and petition campaign of 1796, 128-30, 141; and Jay Treaty, 128-30, 135, 141; influence upon McHenry, 145; relations with Adams, 145, 233, 234, 239, 240,

Hamilton, Alexander (*continued*): 273, 274-75, 279-80, 285; and provisional army, 175, 190, 202-203, 206-208; high Federalism of, 200; and Alien and Sedition Acts, 215-16n; and elections of 1800, 234, 236-37, 273-75, 279-80. *See also* High Federalists

Hampshire County, Va., 285n

Hanover County, Va., 122, 191

Hardy County, Va., 285n

Harper, Robert Goodloe: political career of, 58n; and Yazoo sale of 1795, 93; and sectionalism within South Carolina, 104; and national elections, 135, 136, 137, 143, 180, 182, 185, 248, 268, 271, 272; and Jay Treaty, 140n; develops conservative political philosophy, 182-83; and XYZ mission, 183; attitude toward France, 183, 198; and Lyon-Griswold affair, 198; and high Federalists, 203n, 274-75; and provisional army, 209; and Alien and Sedition Acts, 211; mentioned, 148, 150-53 *passim*, 179n, 193, 235, 290n

Harrington, Henry William, 177

Harris, Charles, 247, 248, 256-57, 258

Harrison County, Va., 169

Harvie, John, 42-43

Hawkins, Benjamin, 13

Haywood, John, 113, 258

Henderson, Archibald, 175, 177, 193, 259, 261, 288

Henrico County, Va., 122, 188, 191, 222

Henry, Patrick: and Virginia legislature, 7n, 12, 188, 217; and Hamilton's financial policies, 12; and Yazoo sale of 1789, 62, 124; political career of, 70, 71, 72; social status of, 72; and national elections, 123-26, 130-32, 217; and Madison, 124-25; and Jefferson, 124-25; Federalism of, 124, 125; political influence of, 192; and Adams' final peace mission to

Henry, Patrick (*continued*): France, 217-18; death of, 218; mentioned, 46, 157, 193. *See also* Election of 1796; Virginia

Heth, William, 39-40, 43, 72, 73n, 75, 192, 210

High Federalists: emergence of, 197; and XYZ mission, 199; and John Marshall, 200-202; relations with Adams, 200-204, 232-34, 238-43 *passim*, 249, 273, 274-75, 279-80, 285; and provisional army, 207-208; and Alien and Sedition Acts, 216n; and elections of 1800, 232-80 *passim*. *See also* Election of 1800; Hamilton, Alexander

Hill, William H., 175, 240, 247, 259, 288

Hillsboro district, N. C., 175, 177, 246

Hodge, Abraham: on Hamilton's financial policies, 13; Federalism of, 80-81n, 159; develops conservative political philosophy, 159, 255-56; influence of in North Carolina, 162; and national elections, 178, 255-56, 258-59; opposes Gales for printing patronage, 258, 259; mentioned, 130, 179n, 244

Hopkins, Jonathan, 155-56

Huger, Benjamin, 184, 281, 289

Huger, Daniel, 39n, 51

Huger, Isaac, 23, 61

Humphreys, David, 25n, 28

Iredell, James: represents British creditors, 18; supports Constitution, 18; appointment to Supreme Court, 23, 24, 25, 78; opposes freedom of speech, 158; mentioned, 12-13, 80n, 132, 174, 188

Izard, Ralph: dislike of Adams, 8, 9n; Jefferson's dislike of, 24; and federal patronage, 24; and funding and assumption plans, 30-31, 25n; Federalism of, 46; social status of, 51, 52; elitist political

Index / 317

Izard, Ralph (continued):
values of, 56-57; and Yazoo sale of 1789, 62; and Butler, 102; retirement of, 104; opposes Edward Rutledge and C. C. Pinckney, 105, 110-11; attitude toward France, 109-10, 164; and Jay Treaty, 117; and elections of 1796, 135-36, 136-37; mentioned, 8-9, 103, 286n

Izard, Ralph, Jr., 211, 286n

Jackson, George, 222

Jackson, James: and Hamilton's financial policies, 34, 60-61; social status of, 59; supports Madison, 60; opposes Wayne (1791), 60-68 passim, 84; and Yazoo sale of 1789, 64; and "Old" Georgians, 65; and Creek Indians, 64, 87, 89, 134; and Yazoo sale of 1795, 91, 94, 96-98; and Jay Treaty, 98, 119; and Georgia legislature, 96-98, 186-87; and elections of 1800, 284n; mentioned, 170, 171

Jay, John, 75, 146

Jay Treaty: reaction to, 85, 112, 114-21, 128-30, 293-94; and Congress, 93, 103n, 117, 118, 127, 128, 129, 139-40, 141; and Georgia, 98, 165; and Republicans, 125, 159; and elections of 1796, 134, 135; and southern Federalists, 143; and France, 143-44; mentioned, 50-193 passim. See also Great Britain

Jefferson, Thomas: reaction to Shays' rebellion, 3; appointment as Secretary of State, 23; relations with southern Federalists, 24, 124-25, 148-51 passim, 198-99; political career of, 70; social status of, 70-71; and Jay Treaty, 120-21, 139-40; and elections of 1796, 131-38 passim, 140, 141, 267; relations with Adams, 144-45, 146; and Congress, 147, 148, 198-99, 237, 238; and North Carolina press, 174; Virginia Resolutions

Jefferson, Thomas (continued):
of, 190-91, 193, 213-21 passim; on party bitterness in Virginia, 217n; and elections of 1799, 218, 222; and elections of 1800, 234, 242, 264, 267, 268, 274, 279, 285n, 288; attacked by Federalists, 256, 269; on democracy, 291. See also Republicans

Johnston, Samuel: supports Constitution, 18; represents British creditors, 18; and federal patronage, 24-25; retirement of, 25, 45, 157-58; and Hamilton's financial policies, 35n, 38; and national elections, 77-78, 130; and Jay Treaty, 129; attitude toward France, 158; opposes freedom of speech, 158; political activities of, 174, 176

Jones, James, 187

Jones, Seaborn, 64, 91, 98, 118, 171

Judiciary, federal: Washington's appointments to, 22-23

Kentucky, 34, 140n, 236
Kentucky Resolutions, 212, 213, 229, 301
Kershaw County, S. C., 170
King, Rufus, 75, 123-24, 126, 233
King William County, Va., 129
Knox, Henry, 4, 19n, 61, 87-88, 89, 146, 207
Kurtz, Stephen G., 142, 192

Lafayette, Marquis de, 202n
Lanier, Clement, 94
La Rochefoucauld-Liancourt, le Duc de, 40n, 51n, 74
Laurens, Henry, 39
Lee, Charles, 41-42, 153-54, 157, 188, 203, 219, 233
Lee, Henry: reaction to Shays' rebellion, 4; on Hamilton's financial policies, 11, 12; and Fairfax purchase, 41-42, 157; and Society of the Cincinnati, 42; political career of, 42, 72; and Madison, 42n;

Lee, Henry (*continued*):
  Federalism of, 42n, 100, 222; social status of, 72; elitist political values of, 72; and Genêt mission, 75; and national elections, 119, 218, 222, 228; and Henry, 124, 125; and Gunn, 153; and sectionalism within Virginia, 192; and provisional army, 206, 210, 220; and Alien and Sedition Acts, 214-15; retirement of, 288; mentioned, 50n, 264
Lee, Richard Bland, 7n, 10, 34-35, 57, 290n
Lee, Richard Henry, 8-9
Liberty County, Ga., 63, 86
Lincoln County, N. C., 261
Livingston, Edward: Congressional resolutions of, 140n, 141, 199; mentioned, 127, 150, 201
Lloyd, James, 211
Logan, George, 173, 217
Longstreet, William, 94, 97
Loudoun County, Va., 130, 285n
Louisa County, Va., 156
Louisbourg, N. C., 168
Lowndes, Thomas, 281, 289
Lyon, Matthew, 198, 199, 221

McAllister, Matthew, 22, 26, 64, 67, 93
McClurg, James, 38, 42, 236
McFarlan, Andrew, 254
McGillivray, Alexander, 85-86, 87
McHenry, James: and Society of the Cincinnati, 19n; agent of Hamilton, 145; and provisional army, 209, 210; dismissal from cabinet, 234, 240; mentioned, 200, 203n, 215n, 274
Machir, James: Federalism of, 148, 152, 156, 222; and Fairfax purchase, 157n; and Lyon-Griswold affair, 198; and elections of 1799, 222
McIntosh, Lachlan: and federal patronage, 26; Federalism of, 26; and Society of the Cincinnati, 26, 59; social status of, 59; and Yazoo

McIntosh, Lachlan (*continued*):
  sale of 1789, 63, 64; and Creek Indians, 64; and Yazoo sale of 1795, 93; and Jay Treaty, 118; political activities of, 165; mentioned, 26n, 66, 171
McIntosh County, Ga., 170
Maclaine, Archibald, 12-13, 18, 78, 80n
Maclay, William, 8-9
McNeil, James, 62
Macon, Nathaniel, 258
Maddell, John, 247
Madison, James: reaction to Shays' rebellion, 3-4; fear of northern domination of the Union, 5-6; and Potomac River project, 5-6, 18-19; and residence of national capital, 6, 38; and Virginia politics, 7n, 119; and federal patronage, 24; partisan activities in Congress, 33; and funding plan, 40; and Richmond Federalist faction, 40-43 *passim;* and Jackson-Wayne election, 67; political career of, 70; social status of, 70-71; commercial discrimination plans of, 88, 99, 106, 107, 110, 113; and Yazoo sale of 1795, 94; and Henry, 124-25; and Jay Treaty, 141; and elections of 1800, 263; mentioned *passim*
Manchester, Va., 221
Manigault, Gabriel, 31-32, 52
Manigault, Louis, 52
Manufactures, Hamilton's report on, 36-37
Marshall, John: and federal judiciary, 22; and Federalist organization in Virginia, 25; and Fairfax purchase, 41-42, 157; and banking in Richmond, 42; and Hamilton, 43; political activities of, 70, 71, 72, 75-76, 77, 155-56; social status of, 71-72, 74; elitist political values of, 73n, 74; and Genêt mission, 75-76; and Yazoo sale of 1795, 95; and elections of 1796, 123-24, 128, 130, 132; and Jay

Index / 319

Marshall, John (*continued*):
Treaty, 128; and XYZ mission, 153-54; and Adams, 154, 201-202; unites with Alexandria (Va.) Federalists, 157; and elections of 1799, 188, 217, 222, 228; and sectionalism within Virginia, 192; and high Federalists, 200-202; attitude toward France, 201; and provisional army, 210, 220, 234; and Alien and Sedition Acts, 211-12, 213; Federalism of, 222; leadership in Congress, 232, 237-38; and elections of 1800, 233-34, 240n; appointed Secretary of State, 241, 264; mentioned, 44, 221

Marshall, Thomas, 73n
Martin, Alexander, 14, 79-80, 118, 160, 162, 173-74
Maryland, 18-19, 34, 35n, 55, 265, 271
Massachusetts, 3, 4, 9, 16n, 35n
Mathews County, Va., 147
Matthews, George, 69, 88, 89, 92, 93, 94
Mayo, John, 264, 265
Merrens, Harry Roy, 194
Milledge, John, 64, 98, 186
Mobs, political, 2, 220-21
Monroe, James: political career of, 70; social status of, 70-71; and French Directory, 144; mentioned, 40, 77, 110, 150, 151, 230, 236
Moore, Thomas, 281
Morgan, Daniel: social status of, 72; political career of, 72; elitist political values of, 73n; and national elections, 119, 142; and Jay Treaty, 129; Federalism of, 148, 152, 156; and Lyon-Griswold affair, 198; and provisional army, 206, 210
Morgan district, N. C., 261, 285n
Morris, Gouverneur, 7
Moultrie, Alexander, 61
Mount Vernon, conference of (1785), 19
Murray, William Vans, 217

Neutrality Proclamation, 42n, 69, 74, 75, 93, 99
New Bern, N. C., 79, 129, 177, 257
New Bern district, N. C., 261
New Brunswick, N. J., 221
New England, 3n, 34, 35n, 126, 152
"New" Georgians, 65
New Hampshire, 35n
New Jersey, 34, 35n, 36
New Jersey plan, 16n
New Kent County, Va., 191
Newport, R. I., 271, 272
New York, 2, 34, 35n, 123, 152, 235
New York City, 114-15, 128n, 236
Nicholas, John, 150, 160, 210
Nicholas, Wilson Cary, 41-42, 43, 44, 70, 71, 100
Ninety-Six district, S. C., 143, 185, 271, 281
Norfolk, Va., 39n, 76, 120, 169, 198, 203n, 219, 222
Norfolk Herald, 219
Norfolk-Princess Anne district, Va., 132
Northampton County, Va., 285n
North Carolina: and U.S. Constitution, 8, 17-18; Antifederalists in, 14, 77, 84, 176; northern speculators in, 14; legislature of, 14-15, 78-80, 176-77, 212, 236, 289n, 297-99; trade with British West Indies, 18; and federal patronage, 24-25; Federalists in, 45, 77-80 *passim*, 112-14, 118, 127, 130, 157-62, 169-70, 173-79, 229, 236, 246-48, 256-61; political structure of, 77-80 *passim;* sectionalism within, 78-80; Federalist press in, 80, 130, 159-62, 165-66, 172-74, 179, 195, 224, 249, 254-56, 258-59; Republicans in, 113, 114, 116, 133, 176, 258, 259, 260, 288-89n; attitudes toward Britain in, 118, 160-62; House delegation of, 152; attitudes toward France in, 158-62, 168, 169-70, 172-73, 176-77, 297-98; Republican press in, 174,

North Carolina (*continued*):
254-55, 258; and provisional army, 210-11, 236; and Federalist relations with national party structure, 247; development of Federalist partisan organizations in, 246-48, 284-85; mentioned, 7, 39*n*, 105, 136
—Federalist strength in: sources of, 80-81, 176, 229, 236, 260-61, 267, 297-99, 302; decline of, 133, 259, 260, 288; revival of, 143, 165-66, 174, 179, 243-44, 246
—in elections: of 1791, 77-78, 84; of 1792, 79-80, 123; of 1796, 128-30 *passim*, 133, 142, 260; of 1798, 172-79 *passim*, 259; of 1800, 246-48, 256-61, 285*n*, 287, 302
—reaction to: Hamilton's financial policies, 12-15, 34, 35; Jay Treaty, 118, 128-30 *passim*; XYZ mission, 168, 169-70, 297-98; Alien and Sedition Acts, 212, 215, 299
North Carolina Gazette, 118, 160
North Carolina Minerva, 159, 255-56, 259, 290
Nott, Abraham, 185
Nottoway County, Va., 267

"Old" Georgians, 65
Orangeburg-Beaufort district, S. C., 184, 269, 281
Orange County, N. C., 247
Orange County, Va., 156
Osborn, John, 257-58
Otis, Harrison Gray, 184, 232, 234

Page, Robert, 222
Parker, Josiah: Federalism of, 198, 222; and Lyon-Griswold affair, 198; and high Federalists, 203*n*; and national elections, 219, 222, 228, 234; retirement of, 288
Partisan ticket making: in South Carolina, 137-38, 183-84; in Virginia, 188-89, 219, 245-46, 261-67 *passim*; in North Carolina, 248

Party organization and growth of democracy, 5, 283-91
Patronage policies: of Washington, 20-27, 28, 35, 36, 44-45, 51, 53, 58*n*, 102-103, 125; of Hamilton, 20, 28-29, 36-45, 53; of Adams, 153-54
Pendleton, Edmund, 22
Pendleton, Nathaniel, 22, 26, 69, 93, 94, 97, 98
Pendleton, S. C., 185
Pennsylvania, 16*n*, 34, 35*n*, 36, 38, 100, 123, 142
Petersburg, Va., 76, 129, 169, 220-21, 246-47
Philadelphia, Pa. See Capital, U.S.
Philadelphia *Aurora*, 275, 276
Philadelphia Convention. See Constitutional Convention
"Phocion" essays, 137
Pickens, Andrew, 86, 138*n*
Pickering, Timothy: and Society of the Cincinnati, 19*n*; and Creek Indians, 96; and southern Federalists, 146, 153, 200-201; sectional jealousies of, 146, 200; high Federalism of, 200; and Alien and Sedition Acts, 211-12*n*, 213; dismissal from cabinet, 234, 240-41, 264, 274; mentioned, 180, 206
Pinckney, Charles: in Constitutional Convention, 7; and Treaty of New York, 32; and assumption plan, 32; social status of, 51; Republicanism of, 102-103; and national elections, 184, 230, 248, 270, 273, 277*n*, 278, 279, 280; mentioned, 45-46, 104-105, 111, 276, 282
Pinckney, Charles Cotesworth: in Constitutional Convention, 6-7; and Society of the Cincinnati, 24; and federal patronage, 24, 58*n*; and Hamilton, 37-38, 239; Federalism of, 46; social status of, 51; military service of during Revolution, 53; elitist political values of, 56; and Butler, 102; opposes

Index / 321

Pinckney, C. C. (*continued*):
Read, 104-105; estrangement from Federalism, 105, 111; opposes Izard and Smith, 105, 107, 110-11; attitude toward Britain, 106-12 *passim*; attitude toward France, 108, 208; and Jay Treaty, 116; ambassador to France, 135; humiliation by French Directory, 143-44, 147, 150, 151, 159, 179, 181, 208; described by Pickering, 146; and XYZ mission, 146, 150, 153; and provisional army, 175, 206-208, 209, 211; and Alien and Sedition Acts, 211-12*n*; and national elections, 239, 240*n*, 242, 269, 273-79 *passim*, 289, 290; mentioned, 103, 152, 154, 235, 276. See also Election of 1800; Franco-American relations

Pinckney, Thomas: and federal patronage, 22; and Society of the Cincinnati, 22; and funding plan, 32; social status of, 51; military service of during Revolution, 53; and Butler, 102; and elections of 1796, 126-27, 130, 135-36, 239, 268; relations with Adams, 146, 275-77; in Congress, 152, 198-99; and elections of 1798, 184; attitude toward France, 198-99; and elections of 1800, 248, 268, 271, 273, 275-77; retirement of, 281; mentioned, 145, 235. See also Election of 1796; Election of 1800

Pinckney Treaty, 120, 127
Pittsylvania County, Va., 11
Pleasants, Thomas, 13
"POLITICKS and VIEWS of a certain PARTY DISPLAYED, The," 38
Porcupine, Peter, 159
Porcupine's Gazette, 246, 259
Portsmouth, Va., 169
Potomac River project, 5-6, 18-19
Powell, Burr, 157
Powell, Leven: and national elections, 130-32, 157, 188, 222, 228, 263; unites with Richmond Federalists, 157; Federalism of, 222;

Powell, Leven (*continued*):
retirement of, 288; mentioned, 244
Prince Edward County, Va., 213, 267
Prince George County, Va., 217*n*
Prince William County, Va., 131
Provisional army: officer corps of, 173-74, 174-75, 208-11, 220, 236*n*; enlistments in, 174; as political issue, 185, 187, 189-90, 215, 234, 300; creation of, 199, 205-11; and southern Federalists, 202, 205-11, 214, 215, 218, 236*n*; mentioned, 147, 201, 221, 223, 235, 238, 250, 274
Public Credit, Hamilton's report on, 32

Quakers, abolitionist petitions of, 9, 10-11
"Querist" essay, 86-87

Raleigh, N. C., 168, 169, 174
Raleigh Register, 260
Ramsay, David, 104-105, 138*n*, 272
Randolph, Edmund: on Hamilton's financial policies, 11; and Fauchet affair, 19*n*, 155; and Society of the Cincinnati, 19*n*; and federal patronage, 23, 24; political career of, 70, 71, 72; social status of, 71-72; elitist political values of, 72; discusses Virginia politics, 155; mentioned, 12, 43
Read, Jacob: social status of, 51; and Jay Treaty, 93, 103*n*, 117; Federalism of, 103; opposes Smith, 103-104; opposed by Edward Rutledge and C. C. Pinckney, 104-105; and national elections, 184, 272, 282; political career after 1800, 290; mentioned, 105, 110, 163, 180
Read, William, 117, 272
Republicans: develop partisan organizations, 5, 82, 156, 230-31, 245; in Congress, 34, 44, 99, 113, 129, 147-52 *passim*, 180, 198,

Republicans (*continued*):
199, 238; in South Carolina, 45-46, 102-103, 111, 116-17, 134-38, 180, 184, 185, 230, 236, 248, 267-82 *passim*; in Georgia, 64, 98, 116, 119, 133-34, 171, 186-87, 236, 284*n*; in Virginia, 70-77 *passim*, 100-101, 122, 129, 132, 133, 188, 191, 192, 230, 236, 245, 287; and neutrality, 99; in North Carolina, 113, 114, 116, 133, 176, 258, 259, 260; develop as political opposition, 139, 140-42; elitist political values of, 142; newspapers of, 174, 254-55, 258; attitudes toward France of, 147, 151, 152, 162, 202; political activities of, 189-90, 244, 256, 257, 260; and Virginia General Election Law, 227, 228, 251, 262-64; and provisional army, 234; and Virginia Resolutions, 252; and development of American party system, 283; develop liberal political philosophy, 286, 287-88
—in elections: of 1796, 126, 132-38 *passim*, 140-42; of 1797, 155-56; of 1799, 218-22 *passim*; of 1800, 230-31, 244-45, 248, 251, 260, 261-82 *passim*, 284*n*
—reaction to: Yazoo sale of 1795, 91; Anglo-French war, 99; Jay Treaty, 114-21 *passim*, 125, 140, 141, 159; XYZ mission, 150, 153, 198; Alien and Sedition Acts, 211-12*n*, 213, 242*n*, 251. *See also* Georgia; North Carolina; South Carolina; Virginia
Revolution, American, 2-3, 49, 53, 56, 106
Revolution, French, 108
Richmond, Va.: Federalists in, 37, 75-77, 122, 127, 129, 130, 155-57, 168, 169, 197, 218, 220-21, 226-27, 230, 236, 264; and Bank of the United States, 39*n*; banking in, 42-43; and Jay Treaty, 129; and national elections, 131, 188, 265; and XYZ mission, 168,

Richmond, Va. (*continued*):
169; and Virginia Resolutions, 191; mentioned *passim*
Richmond County, Ga., 94, 118
Richmond County, N. C., 177
Rind, W. A.: edits *Virginia Federalist*, 223-27, 245*n*, 248-53, 264-65; develops conservative political philosophy, 223-27, 249-53; and elections of 1800, 245*n*, 248-53, 264-65; mentioned, 244
Rochefoucauld-Liancourt, le Duc de la, 40, 51*n*, 74
Rockingham, N. C., 168
Rutherford, Robert, 119
Rutledge, Edward: and federal patronage, 24, 39, 58*n*; Federalism of, 46, 163, 164; social status of, 51; military service of during Revolution, 53; and Smith, 103-104, 110; opposes Read, 104-105; estrangement from Federalism, 105, 111, 134-38 *passim*; opposes Izard and Smith, 105, 110-11; attitude toward Britain, 106-12 *passim*, 116; attitude toward France, 108, 163-64, 181-82; and Jay Treaty, 115, 116, 117, 135; and national elections, 134-38 *passim*, 180-82, 267; expresses sectional fears, 135; political influence of in South Carolina, 137; and Jefferson, 149, 163; and Adams, 163; develops conservative political philosophy, 181-82; and Alien and Sedition Acts, 211; as governor of South Carolina, 235, 236; death of, 235, 268; mentioned, 22, 150, 153, 170
Rutledge, Eliza, 148
Rutledge, John: and federal patronage, 22, 24; and Hamilton, 37-38; social status of, 51; in American Revolution, 53; estrangement from Federalism, 105, 111; attitude toward France, 108; attitude toward Britain, 106-12 *passim*, 116; and Jay Treaty, 115, 116

Index / 323

Rutledge, John, Jr.: social status of, 51; estrangement from Federalism, 105, 111; opposes Smith, 110, 149; and Jay Treaty, 116, 117; and national elections, 138n, 180, 184, 242, 248, 271-72, 273, 281; relations with Adams, 148, 153, 232; Federalism of, 148-53 *passim;* and Jefferson, 148, 150, 151, 163; attitude toward France, 151, 181; character described, 181; on politics in South Carolina, 184; and Lyon-Griswold affair, 198; and high Federalists, 203n, 274-75; and Alien and Sedition Acts, 211, 242-43n; and House Speakership, 232-33, 239; retirement of, 289; political career of after 1800, 290; mentioned, 164, 188, 235, 269, 276, 281, 290n

St. George Parish, S. C., 116
St. James Goose Creek Parish, S. C., 52, 56, 116, 286n
St. John's Parish, S. C., 116
St. Luke's Parish, S. C., 170
St. Mary's County, Ga., 170
Salisbury, N. C., 175, 176, 177, 261
Savannah, Ga., 27, 64, 65, 66, 93, 96, 114, 118, 134, 163, 213
Saxe-Gotha (S. C.), 281
Seagrove, James, 88, 89, 90
Sectional fears: in the South, 5-8, 10-11, 23, 135, 285; expressed in New York ratifying convention, 7n; expressed in Congress, 8-9
Sectionalism: within South Carolina, 52, 56-59, 104-105, 117, 281-82; within Georgia, 64; within North Carolina, 78-80; within Federalist party, 146, 200-204 *passim,* 232-34, 235, 244-45, 273-74, 278-80; within Virginia, 192-93
Sedgewick, Theodore, 213, 232, 236, 239
Shays' Rebellion, 3-4, 73n
Shenandoah County, Va., 76
Shepard, Thomas, 254
Shippen, Thomas Lee, Jr., 148

Simms, Charles, 131, 132
Simpson, Samuel, 257
Slavery: in South Carolina, 58n, 163-64, 182, 194; in Virginia, 254, 266
Smith, Major William, 150
Smith, William Loughton: expresses sectional fears, 9; and federal patronage, 24, 38-39; in Congress, 30, 149-50; and funding and assumption plans, 30, 31-32; and Hamilton, 31, 33, 35n, 37-38, 145; and Jefferson, 38; Federalism of, 46; social status of, 51; opposes James Jackson, 60; and Jackson-Wayne election, 67-68; opposes Read, 103-104; and Edward Rutledge, 103-104, 105, 107, 110-11; and British merchants, 107-108; attitude toward France, 109, 110; opposed by John Rutledge, Jr., 110-11, 149; and Jay Treaty, 117, 140n; and elections of 1796, 135-36, 136-37, 143; ambassador to Portugal, 152; and Adams, 153; Republicanism of, 289; mentioned, 113, 129, 148
Society of the Cincinnati. See Cincinnati, Society of the
Southampton County, Va., 222
South Carolina: Gillon's uprising in, 3; Regulator movement in, 3n; Antifederalists in, 7-8, 54-55, 107; sectional fears in, 7-8, 135, 285; and U.S. Constitution, 7-8, 17, 38, 54-55; political and social structure of, 17, 51-55, 57-59, 138, 184; trade with British West Indies, 17; and federal patronage, 24, 37-39; Federalists in, 25, 27-39, 45, 51-59, 100, 101-12, 115-18 *passim,* 134-38, 148-53 *passim,* 163-64, 170, 179-86, 229, 243, 248, 267-82, 284-85; House delegation of, 30, 148-52 *passim;* legislature of, 58-59, 104-105, 164, 185-86, 229, 236, 268, 277-78, 282, 300-301; Republicans in, 45-46, 102-103, 111, 116-17, 134-

South Carolina (*continued*):
38, 180, 184, 185, 230, 236, 248, 267-82 *passim;* social status of Federalists in, 51-59 *passim;* sectionalism within, 52, 56-59, 104-105, 117, 278-80, 281-82; Society of the Cincinnati in, 58, 170; slavery in, 58n, 163-64, 182, 194; Democratic-Republican Societies in, 59; attitudes toward Britain in, 105-12, 115-18; attitudes toward France in, 108-109, 163-64, 170, 180, 181; relations with federal government, 180; newspapers in, 183-84; and Kentucky Resolutions, 229, 301; Federalist press in, 253-54; and provisional army, 211, 300; mentioned, 6, 40, 48, 126
—Federalist strength in: sources of, 80, 185-86, 229, 281-82, 286n, 300-301, 303; decline of, 101-12, 137-38, 235, 273-82 *passim*, 288-90; revival of, 143, 165, 243-44
—in elections: of 1792, 35, 123; of 1796, 126, 134-38, 143, 274; of 1798, 172, 179-85; of 1800, 243, 248, 267-82, 285, 286n, 287, 303
—reaction to: Hamilton's financial policies, 15, 30-37 *passim;* Jay Treaty, 85, 112, 115-18, 134; XYZ mission, 170, 180, 186; Alien and Sedition Acts, 211, 212-13. *See also* Charleston, S. C.
South Carolina Gazette, 254
Spaight, Richard Dobbs, 175n
Spain, 16, 89, 96, 165, 171
Spartanburg, S. C., 185
Spartanburg district, S. C., 229
Spotsylvania County, Va., 156
Spotsylvania district, Va., 222
Stafford County, Va., 131
Stanly, John, 259
State Gazette of North Carolina, 130, 159, 173
Steele, John, 24-25, 34, 45, 79-80, 84, 113, 118, 175
Stephens, Edward, 12
Stevens, Daniel, 36-37

Stewart, John, 222
Stith, John, 171, 186-87
Stokes, Montfort, 80
Stone, David, 175, 178
Stuart, David, 10-11, 154-55
Sumter, Thomas, 30, 60n, 185, 213, 281

Taliaferro, Benjamin, 187
Tarboro, N. C., 79
Tattnall, Josiah, 64
Tazewell, Littleton W., 265
Telfair, Edward, 59, 61, 64, 69, 86-92 *passim*
Tennessee, 17n, 18, 23, 53, 61, 135, 158n, 170-71, 236
Thomas, Abishai, 14
Tidewater (Va.), 122, 129, 168, 191, 228
Timothy, Benjamin F., 254
Treaty of New York, 15, 16n, 32, 61, 64, 85, 89
Trenton, N. J., 221
Trumbull, Jonathan, 225
"Tub plot," 211-12n
Tucker, Thomas Tudor, 57, 111, 116, 286n
Twiggs, John, 86, 92

Vanderhorst, Colonel A., 104, 138n
Venable, Abraham, 149, 160
Vermont, 34
Virginia: political and social structure of, 5, 69-74 *passim;* and western territories, 6; and residence of national capital, 6; and U.S. Constitution, 7, 18-19, 72, 73n, 74; legislature of, 7n, 12, 120-22, 188, 190-91, 213-14, 217, 220, 221, 227, 236, 252, 293-97; Antifederalists in, 7n, 10, 69-70, 130; sectional fears in, 10-11; northern speculators in, 11; and Potomac River project, 18-19; and federal patronage, 24, 25, 39-45; Federalists in, 25, 39-45, 69-77, 100-101, 119-25 *passim,* 127-33 *passim,* 153-57, 168-69, 187-89, 190-93, 196, 205, 216-27, 230, 236,

Index / 325

Virginia (continued):
245-46, 248-53, 261-67, 284-85; Republicans in, 70-71, 72, 74-77 passim, 100-101, 122, 129, 132, 133, 188, 189-90, 191-92, 230, 236, 245, 287; Federalist press in, 80, 81n, 129-30, 131, 222-27, 229, 248-53, 264-65; British merchants in, 120, 129; attitudes toward Britain in, 120-21, 129; vote of censure against Washington, 121-22, 190-91, 193, 293-94; and Federalist petition campaign of 1796, 128-30 passim, 141; House delegation of, 147, 148, 152, 222; attitudes toward France in, 168-69; sectionalism within, 192-93; Indian massacres in, 195; and provisional army, 210, 214; political mobs in, 220-21; Republican press in, 224; and General Election Law of 1800, 227-28, 261-64, 265, 285, 287, 296-97; slavery in, 266; mentioned, 39n, 48, 136
—Federalist strength in: sources of, 80-81, 121-22, 190-93, 222, 227-28, 229, 285, 293-97; decline of, 100-101, 133, 236, 264-67 passim, 288, 289-90; revival of, 143, 165, 243-44
—in elections: of 1792, 123; of 1796, 130-33, 142-43, 192, 193; of 1797, 155-56; of 1799, 157, 187-89, 216-22 passim; of 1800, 245-46, 248-53, 261-67, 285, 287
—reaction to: Hamilton's financial policies, 10-12, 34, 35, 36-37, 39n, 42n, 43; Jay Treaty, 120-21, 128-30, 293-94; Alien and Sedition Acts, 154-55, 156-57, 211-12, 213-15, 294-95; XYZ mission, 168-69, 187, 188. See also Alexandria, Va.; Richmond, Va.

Virginia Argus, 260
Virginia Federalist, 222-27, 246, 248-53, 255, 264, 265
Virginia Gazette, 100-101, 129-30, 131, 254

Virginia Resolutions, 190-91, 193, 213, 214-15, 218-19, 221, 252
Wake County, N. C., 247, 260
Walton, George, 26n
Washington, Bushrod, 243, 279, 290n
Washington, George: reaction to Shay's rebellion, 4; fear of northern domination of the Union, 5-6; and Potomac River project, 5-6, 18-19; relations with Georgia, 15-16; and Society of the Cincinnati, 19-20; patronage policies of, 20-27, 28, 35, 36, 44-45, 50, 51, 53, 58n, 102-103, 125; southern tour of, 21, 27-28, 35; as symbol of national unity, 23; cabinet of, 23, 28, 86, 88, 89; Neutrality Proclamation of, 42n, 69, 74, 75, 93, 99; public service of, 70n; and Creek Indians, 86-89 passim, 96; and Jay Treaty, 114, 127, 128, 129, 141; vote of censure against in Virginia, 121-22, 190-91, 193, 293-94; and Henry, 125; and national elections, 127, 135, 188, 216; decision to retire, 130; and XYZ mission, 169; and provisional army, 173-74, 206-208, 209, 210, 215n, 235; develops conservative political philosophy, 202, 216-17; and high Federalists, 202n; and Alien and Sedition Acts, 215, 216, 217; death of, 235, 250-51, 272; Federalist idolatry of, 250-51, 266
Washington, William, 51, 138n, 185, 209, 211, 278, 280
Washington, D.C., 265, 266, 276
Washington, Ga., 170
Washington County, Ga., 89
Washington-Pinckney district, S. C., 281
Wayne, Anthony, 26, 27, 59, 60-68 passim, 93
Wereat, John, 92
Westmoreland County, Va., 168, 222, 285n

Whiskey Rebellion, 89, 90, 100, 119, 160
Wilkes County, Ga., 170
William and Mary College, students demonstrate at, 220
Williams, Robert, 236, 237
Williamsburg, Va., 76, 122, 129, 147, 215, 222
Williamson, Hugh, 13-14, 35n, 45
Willis, Francis, 34, 35
Wilmington, N. C., 177
Wilmington district, N. C., 261
Wilmington (N. C.) *Gazette*, 159, 161, 172
Winchester, Va., 119, 129, 148
Winchester district, Va., 142
Winn, Richard, 281

Wolfe, John Harold, 279
Wythe, George, 24, 75

XYZ mission: origins of, 150; membership of, 153; reaction to, 162, 167-72, 176-77, 180, 183, 186, 187, 188, 196, 200, 224-25, 297-98; and Congress, 197, 198; and Republicans, 198; and high Federalists. 199; mentioned, 146, 195, 196, 201, 213, 237. *See also* Franco-American relations

Yazoo sale: of 1789, 60n, 61-64; of 1795, 60n, 85, 90-99 *passim*, 118, 119, 133, 164, 186
York County, Va., 76, 147, 222

www.ingramcontent.com/pod-product-compliance
Lightning Source LLC
Chambersburg PA
CBHW020330240426
43665CB00043B/199